MURDOCH BOOKS

To Kylie

Very Best Wishes

Peter

ORGANUM
PETER GILMORE

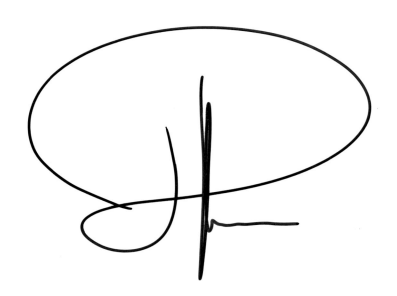

Organum refers to the idea that multiple harmonies can create a new sound. This term was originally applied to Gregorian chants in the ninth and tenth centuries when polyphonic sound was achieved. The same idea applies to barbershop singing, in which four voices can work together to create a new sound or fifth voice. This idea has resonated with me in the development of my cuisine. Multiple ingredients achieving harmony: flavours, textures, techniques, aroma, culture and innovation come together to create something new—a unique dish.

The principles of harmony in the coming together of many elements is the reason Organum is the word I have chosen to represent my cuisine.

Through my cuisine I search for the idea of Organum; for a sense of purity, which is the essence of something that is complete, where all the elements work together to create something new.

I believe that a cook must find a set of principles that they strongly believe in to bring focus to their cuisine: whether the principles are traditions that have stood the test of time; have a link to place and culture; or are a set of more universal foundations, truths and beliefs. You need this structure to work from in order to go forward. I urge my young cooks to take their time to develop, to find their own set of principles and beliefs about cooking and to allow this to evolve naturally from their own experiences. Ultimately, the cook you become and the dishes you create are a personal expression of your life experiences. Feeding people the food you love to cook and eat is a very personal gesture. This can be easily forgotten with the day-to-day pressure of running a restaurant and business, but this is something you must remind yourself of as it is at the heart of what you do.

My belief is that a dish must have, at its heart, harmony. It has to work on many levels but the ultimate goal is for the dish to be delicious. Texture, for me, has long been one of the most important qualities in creating my cuisine. Texture is our most fundamental connection to the food we eat. What's happening on the palate and the way the textures play off each other is the most sensual element of consuming a beautiful dish.

Getting the degree of flavour intensity right is a big part of creating a successful dish. Strength and intensity of flavour with balance is my aim. Combining flavours that will play off each other and enhance the whole experience is essential. I don't believe in throwing opposing, clashing and harsh flavours together. I feel there must be logic to the flow of flavours in a dish. Different notes working in some type of harmony is important to my cooking.

It can sometimes be a complex group of flavours but they are usually working to achieve a whole. At other times it can be great to work with a few limited flavours that are set at different pitches to intensify the whole. It may be the flavour of a raw mushroom set next to the flavour of a cooked or dried mushroom, then set next to the flavour of a fermented mushroom, which together enhance the natural flavour of beef, for example.

The way texture and flavours play off each other, the way they work together, is really the art of the cook and it is boundless with possibilities.

Nature's diversity—the sheer variety and complexity of the plant world—is quite astonishing. My appreciation for this increased dramatically when I started growing my own herbs and vegetables nine years ago. This deeply changed my approach to cooking. Experimenting with heirloom varieties of vegetables and realising just how much diversity is available has really pushed my cuisine forward.

I would like to dedicate this book to all the passionate farmers, producers
and suppliers who give me such incredible products to work with.
Without you, what I do would simply not be possible.
    It is my hope that this book will inspire the next generation of young
chefs to form meaningful, direct relationships with farmers and producers.
I believe this is the key to producing a cuisine of substance.
    I would also like to honour the memory of a very passionate young foodie,
Levi McCormack, whose spirit touched my heart.

DEDICATION

It all started with a pea blossom. I planted my first garden about nine years ago: for the first time I had a backyard with space for a garden. I started with herbs for use in the kitchen and the first vegetable I planted was the humble pea.

Planting the seed in the earth and watching it spring to life filled me with admiration for nature. This is something we all take for granted, but the cycle of life I observed in my garden is what sustains us and makes life possible. The sprout, coming to life from the earth; maturing into a larger plant that flowered, ready to be pollinated and, ultimately, to fruit; thus recreating the original pea that would start the cycle again. Observing this filled me with awe and connected me to the produce that I work with every day.

Understanding that I could use all the parts of the plant at all stages of its development was a revelation to me. I could use the shoots, the leaves, the fruit and, most unexpectedly, the blossoms. Back then, flowers were not fashionable for use in cooking.

It astonished me that the pea flower—so beautiful—actually tasted like peas, and gave me a new texture and ingredient to use in the creation of my dishes. The challenge then was to find a farmer who was willing to grow pea flowers for me. Most conventional farmers in my area simply wanted to plant a crop of peas and harvest them all at once when they were ready. The idea of going out each morning and hand picking the just-opened blossoms seemed absurd to them.

It took me a year to find a crazy couple willing to do this: an English photographer and his Finnish wife who had moved from Europe to the Blue Mountains, two hours west of Sydney, to start a new life. Richard and Nina Kalina decided they wanted to grow organic raspberries, gooseberries and currants. I could see their enthusiasm and passion for their berries and asked them if they would consider growing some heirloom vegetables for me. We spent the next six years working together, producing bespoke heirloom vegetables, herbs and flowers for Quay and ultimately for a number of other Sydney-based restaurants.

The process started in my garden at home. I would research vegetables I was interested in, order the seeds from far-flung corners of the world, grow them in my test garden to make sure they were something I wanted to incorporate into my cuisine. Then I would ask Richard and Nina to grow them on a larger scale for Quay. This was a huge learning curve for them as well as for me.

Richard and Nina have returned to Europe, where Richard works on The Eden Project in Cornwall; but over the years I have created a network of small independent growers from whom I source a lot of rare and unique ingredients. In the vegetable area, I now work very closely with Tim and Elizabeth Johnstone from Johnstone's Kitchen Gardens, only an hour west of Sydney.

My test garden now consists of four 10-metre-long raised beds in my backyard on the northern beaches of Sydney. It is here that I can grow and observe the life cycles of new plants: I never know what part of the plant I may be able to incorporate into my cuisine. I might find that a rare Japanese white radish has really delicious leaves, or that when a certain plant flowers and goes to seed an interesting seed pod is revealed: if it's juicy and tasty I'll use it.

Salty ice plant is a good example; I have discovered that it is at its most interesting when it is about to flower. The small flower nodules become blistered with salt-like crystals and are at their juiciest just before they flower. This plant is a succulent and has quite a pronounced salt flavour.

My garden remains a place of wonderment and imagination. It is where the origins of some of my favourite dishes have been created. It is a unique creative space where inspiration abounds.

01
CULTURED BUTTER WITH ESCHALLOTS & GARLIC
1 GARLIC CLOVE
2 SMALL GOLDEN ESCHALLOTS
150 G (5½ OZ) CULTURED BUTTER
   (SEE BASIC RECIPES)

Finely dice the garlic and eschallots and put them in a heavy-based saucepan with the cultured butter. Gently simmer for 2–3 minutes or until the garlic and eschallots are translucent. Set aside until required.

02
PEAS & PEA BLOSSOMS
2 KG (4 LB 8 OZ) BABY SPRING PEAS
   IN THE POD
80 PEA BLOSSOMS
16 CARROT BLOSSOM FLORETS
64 WHITE BEAN BLOSSOMS
24 AGRETTI SPRIGS

Shell the peapods to yield 800 g (1 lb 12 oz) peas. Set aside until required.

Trim the pea blossoms to the base of the blossom, leaving on just a couple of millimetres of green stem. Set half aside to be deep-fried, and reserve half to be used fresh.

Rinse the carrot and bean blossoms and the agretti in cold water, dry gently and set aside.

03
CRISP PEA BLOSSOM BATTER
100 G (3½ OZ) WHEAT STARCH FLOUR
50 G (1¾ OZ) CORNFLOUR (CORNSTARCH)
50 G (1¾ OZ) RICE FLOUR
100 ML (3½ FL OZ) SODA WATER

Mix all of the flours together in a bowl. Weigh out 50 g (1¾ oz) of the combined flour and whisk in the soda water to form a loose slurry. Set aside the remaining flour.

04
TO FINISH
2 LITRES (70 FL OZ) GRAPESEED OIL
SEA SALT

Bring 5 litres (175 fl oz) of water to the boil in a large saucepan.

In a large, heavy-based saucepan, heat the grapeseed oil to 180°C (350°F). Take the pea blossoms set aside for deep-frying and dip them individually into the batter then straight into the reserved dry combined flour, shaking off any excess. Put the battered flowers into the hot oil (without overcrowding the pan) and fry for 1 minute or until lightly golden. Drain on paper towel.

Add the peas to the boiling water and blanch for approximately 1–1½ minutes or until just tender. Drain the peas and immediately add the cultured butter mixture and season with fine sea salt to taste.

05
TO PLATE

Divide the hot buttered peas into 8 warmed serving bowls and garnish with fried pea blossoms, fresh bean, pea and carrot blossoms and agretti sprigs. Serve.

GARDEN PEAS, CULTURED BUTTER, SEA SALT, CRISP PEA BLOSSOMS

SERVES / 8

01

POMEGRANATE MOLASSES CRUMBS

200 ML (7 FL OZ) FRESH BEETROOT JUICE
   (ABOUT 4 MEDIUM-SIZE BEETROOT)
200 ML (7 FL OZ) POMEGRANATE MOLASSES
3 SLICES SOURDOUGH BREAD, 2 CM
   (¾ INCH) THICK, CRUSTS REMOVED
100 G (3½ OZ) CLARIFIED BUTTER, MELTED
   (SEE BASIC RECIPES)
100 ML (3½ FL OZ) GRAPESEED OIL

Combine the beetroot juice and pomegranate molasses in a small saucepan over medium heat and reduce by one quarter. Strain and allow to cool.

Thoroughly soak the sourdough slices in the beetroot mixture. Transfer to a wire rack and dehydrate approximately 2–3 hours in a 100°C (200°F/Gas ½) oven until the bread is thoroughly dry and brittle.

Break bread into small pieces and fry in a combination of clarified butter and grapeseed oil over medium heat until crunchy. Allow to cool. Store in an airtight container until required.

02

BEETS

32 BABY CHIOGGIA BEETROOT
8 BABY ALBINO BEETROOT
1 KG (2 LB 4 OZ) ROCK SALT

Trim the beetroot stems down so that just 5 mm (¼ inch) remains attached to the root. Wash well under cold running water and dry. Put the baby beets on a generous bed of rock salt on a large baking tray. Bake in a 180°C (350°F/Gas 4) oven for approximately 1 hour or until the skins are well blistered and the beetroot is very tender. Remove from the oven and cool slightly.

While still warm, wearing a pair of rubber gloves and using a paring knife, carefully peel the skin from the beets. Break the albino beets into two or three pieces with your hands. Do the same with just 8 of the Chioggia beets, leaving the rest whole. Put the peeled beets in a sealed container and refrigerate until required.

This salad utilises two rarer types of beetroot: Chioggia (candy-striped beetroot) and albino (pure white beetroot). The combination of the beets with truffle, sweet violets, pomegranate molasses crumbs, wild sour cherries, native currants and sheep's milk curd is an exotic but harmonious range of flavour and texture that play off each other. This salad builds in intensity on the palate. The flavours move from earthy mellowness to sour, bitter and sharp and the textures from soft, yielding and creamy to crisp and crunchy. It's a great dish to enliven the palate at the beginning of a meal.

03

BULL'S BLOOD LEAVES

20 G (¾ OZ) BABY BULL'S BLOOD BEET
  GREENS (APPROXIMATELY 2 PUNNETS)
300 ML (10½ FL OZ) GRAPESEED OIL

Trim the Bull's Blood leaves, blanch in boiling water then refresh in iced water. Dry thoroughly then lay the leaves out in a single layer on a baking tray lined with silicone paper. Place in a 100°C (200°F/Gas ½) oven for 2 hours or until dehydrated.

Heat the grapeseed oil to medium–high heat and deep-fry the leaves until crisp. Drain on paper towel.

04

DRESSING

50 ML (1¾ FL OZ) POMEGRANATE MOLASSES
50 ML (1¾ FL OZ) 10-YEAR-AGED
  BALSAMIC VINEGAR
50 ML (1¾ FL OZ) EXTRA VIRGIN OLIVE OIL
2 PINCHES OF SALT

Combine all the ingredients, whisk well and set aside until required.

05

TO FINISH

40 G (1½ OZ) AUSTRALIAN BLACK
  WINTER TRUFFLE
48 SWEET, EDIBLE VIOLETS

Use the tip of a small knife to cut 56 small pieces from the truffle. Rinse the violets in cold water and allow to dry.

06

TO PLATE

350 G (12 OZ) FRESH SHEEP'S MILK CURD
16 PRESERVED WILD ITALIAN SOUR
  CHERRIES, PITTED
160 AUSTRALIAN NATIVE CURRANTS

Generously dress the beets in the dressing and allow to sit for 2 minutes.

Place 4 half-tablespoon dollops of sheep's milk curd in the centre of each large serving plate. Arrange 3 whole and 2 broken pieces of the Chioggia beets and two pieces of the albino beets over the plate. Evenly scatter the cherries, truffle pieces, pomegranate molasses crumbs and native currants over the top. Garnish with fried Bull's Blood leaves and sweet violets.

SLOW-ROASTED CHIOGGIA & ALBINO BEETROOT, VIOLETS, TRUFFLES, NATIVE CURRANTS

SERVES / 8

01

BONE MARROW

8 VEAL MARROW BONES, 5 CM
   (2 INCHES) LONG
150 G (5½ OZ) MAPLE WOOD CHIPS

Soak marrow bones in cold, lightly salted water overnight in the refrigerator. Drain the water and place the marrow bones under cold running water for 1 hour to help flush the blood from the marrow. Push the marrow out of the bones using your thumb or a piece of dowel.

Soak the marrow a further 12 hours, in the refrigerator, in 3 changes of cold milk. Drain the marrow and place in a cold smoking apparatus. Lightly smoke for 1 hour using maple wood chips. Put the smoked bone marrow in an airtight container and refrigerate until required.

02

ROASTED ONE-YEAR ONION

4 JAPANESE ONE-YEAR ONIONS
   (SHIMONITA NEGI)
30 G (1 OZ) CLARIFIED BUTTER, MELTED
   (SEE BASIC RECIPES)
SEA SALT
ROCK SALT

Trim the one-year onions, reserving only the 10 cm (4 inch) long white base. Split each base in half lengthways and rinse the layers well under cold running water to remove any grit.

Place all the onion halves on a large sheet of silicone paper, drizzle with melted clarified butter, season with sea salt and wrap into a loose parcel. Bake the parcel on a tray with a bed of rock salt in a 180°C (350°F/Gas 4) oven for 10 minutes or until the onions are just soft. Keep warm until ready to plate.

03

TO FINISH

350 G (12 OZ) CLARIFIED BUTTER, MELTED
   (SEE BASIC RECIPES)
32 SMALL SPROUTS OF WHITE
   SPROUTING BROCCOLI
48 SEED STALKS OF MINUTINA
   (HERBA STELLA)
32 JAGALLO NERO TIPS
SEA SALT

Put a large saucepan of salted water on the stove and bring it to the boil. Put 300 g (10½ oz) of the clarified butter in a medium saucepan and bring to 50°C (120°F). Add the bone marrow pieces to the butter and cook for approximately 3–4 minutes until they are warmed through.

Blanch the white sprouting broccoli shoots for approximately 2 minutes, adding the jagallo nero tips and the minutina seed stalks for the last 30 seconds of cooking. Drain all of the vegetables, brush with the remaining clarified butter and season with sea salt.

04

TO PLATE

SEA SALT

In the centre of each warmed plate, place two halves of the one-year onion and an even mixture of all the other vegetables. Carefully break each piece of marrow in half and place on top of each mound of vegetables. Season the marrow with a little sea salt. Serve.

ROASTED ONE-YEAR ONION, WHITE SPROUTING BROCCOLI, JAGALLO NERO, MINUTINA, SMOKED BONE MARROW

SERVES / 8

TIM & ELIZABETH JOHNSTONE

ORGANIC KITCHEN GARDENERS
HAWKESBURY / NEW SOUTH WALES

The rewards of working with like-minded passionate people like Tim and Elizabeth are immeasurable. We inform, educate and inspire each other, which creates a relationship that is deeply satisfying and has enriched my life as a chef.

I started working with Tim and Elizabeth Johnstone in 2011 after my bespoke organic vegetable growers Richard and Nina Kalina returned to Europe. Tim read an article in *Organic Gardener* magazine on the produce I have grown for Quay, and asked whether he could supply some produce from his newly developed market garden. Tim and Elizabeth—along with Tim's brother Mark— leased a market garden site in the Hawkesbury region, an hour from Sydney, and had started producing their own vegetables to sell at farmers' markets.

Tim had completed a Bachelor of Systems Agriculture (Agribusiness) at the University of Western Sydney, Hawkesbury in 2003 and has continued to develop his passion and knowledge for permaculture and organic farming systems. We share a passion for heirloom vegetables and many of my regular visits to Johnstone's Kitchen Gardens are spent trawling through seed catalogues and deciding which vegetables to grow for upcoming seasons. Tim and Elizabeth are now Quay's major supplier of bespoke, grown-to-order organic vegetables.

Tim says, 'Over the years working with Pete we have tried quite a few different lines that haven't made it on to the plate. While this can be frustrating and sometimes costly, I really value the relationship that we have. It constantly pushes me to try new things and to think about what and how we grow and drives us to constantly innovate and improve. Sometimes our development process from concept to restaurant plate can literally be two years. A year for Peter to trial and for me to learn the new plant, perfect techniques and save seeds, and the second year to start commercial-scale production.'

I often find myself planning menus two or three seasons ahead. To work this closely with farmers like Tim and Elizabeth requires real trust and commitment from both parties. The rewards are beautiful, unique produce that enrich my dishes and provide my customers with a link to nature's incredible diversity.

Tim began with a 1000 square metre (quarter acre) garden. They are now cultivating almost 1.2 hectares (3 acres) on the original 1.6 hectare (4 acre) site and are soon to commence a long-term lease on a 4 hectare (10 acre) property, with plans to supply more Sydney-based restaurants with their unique organic produce.

A highlight of our working relationship was when Tim and Elizabeth hosted a 'Lunch in the Fields' event, at which René Redzepi (from Copenhagen's Noma restaurant) and I cooked for 60 people using Tim and Elizabeth's produce at the farm. This was an event that René and I had talked about doing for years and was a highlight of Sydney's Good Food Month in 2013.

The rewards of working with like-minded passionate people like Tim and Elizabeth Johnstone are immeasurable. We inform, educate and inspire each other, which creates a relationship that is deeply satisfying and has enriched my life as a chef.

ABOVE: Salty ice plant that has overwintered takes on a red–gold colour.

LEFT: White sprcuting broccoli.

01

AROMATIC CULTURED CREAM

15 ML (½ FL OZ) MILTON ANTIBACTERIAL
    STERILISING LIQUID, OR SIMILAR
1 LITRE (35 FL OZ) PURE JERSEY CREAM
½ TEASPOON CHEESE CULTURE (MM100)
½ TEASPOON ROASTED AND CRUSHED
    CELERY SEEDS
½ TEASPOON ROASTED AND CRUSHED
    FENNEL SEEDS
½ CUP INNER WHITE CELERY LEAVES
¼ CUP FENNEL FROND TIPS

Mix the sterilising solution in a clean sink
with cold water and sterilise a saucepan,
whisk, stainless steel spoons, a tray and a
1 litre (35 fl oz) plastic or glass container
with a lid in which to ferment the cream.
Drain the sterilised utensils on the sterilised
tray. Heat the cream in the saucepan to 90°C
(195°F) then cool to 25°C (77°F). Add the
cheese culture, seeds and herbs. Whisk to
combine well. Pour the cream mixture into
the sterilised container and cover with the lid.
Insulate the sides of the container with clean
kitchen towels. Put a lid on the styrofoam box.
Place the box in a corner of your kitchen
that doesn't get too hot or too cold, ideally
in a room around 20–22°C (68–72°F).
Leave the cream to ferment for 72 hours.
Check the cream at this time. It should smell
sweet but slightly sour. Refrigerate the
cream until required.

02

COLD SMOKED ANGASI OYSTERS

16 LARGE ANGASI (FLAT) OYSTERS
250 G (9 OZ) MAPLE WOOD CHIPS

Shuck the oysters and release them from
their shells, reserving all juices. Strain the
juices through a fine sieve. Place the shucked
oysters back into the shells with an equal
amount of the strained juice per oyster.

    Set the oysters on a bed of rock salt
on a tray so they are sitting flat. Put the
oysters into a cold smoking apparatus with
the maple wood chips and smoke gently for
1 hour. Set the oysters aside in a container
with the juices and reserve in the refrigerator
until required.

03

TO FINISH

250 G (9 OZ) AROMATIC CULTURED CREAM
JERSEY CREAM (OPTIONAL)
40 FLOWERING SALTY ICE PLANT BUDS
24 FRESH CHAMOMILE FLOWER BUDS
24 SWEET CICELY GREEN SEED PODS
16 SWEET CICELY FLOWERING TIPS
16 CARROT BLOSSOM FLORETS
16 YARROW BLOSSOMS
16 ELDERFLOWER BLOSSOMS
8 SPRIGS BRONZE FENNEL TIPS

Pass the aromatic cream through a fine sieve
to remove the seeds and herbs. Mix with a
spoon and add a little fresh jersey cream if
the consistency is too dry.

    Pick and gently wash all flowers and herbs
and dry on a clean tea towel (dish towel).

04

TO PLATE

Place a tablespoon of aromatic cultured cream
on the centre of each plate and spread it out
a little with the back of a spoon.

    Place 2 smoked oysters on each plate and
dress with a little of the reserved juices.

    Arrange aromatic herbs, flowers and salty
ice plant buds. Serve.

COLD SMOKED ANGASI OYSTERS, AROMATIC CULTURED CREAM, SALTY ICE BUDS

PREPARATION / 3 DAYS
SERVES / 8

01

AROMATIC OIL

30 G (1 OZ) DRIED MILD KOREAN CHILLIES,
 SEEDS REMOVED
50 G (1¾ OZ) MAPLE WOOD CHIPS
500 ML (17 FL OZ) EXTRA VIRGIN OLIVE OIL
30 G (1 OZ) GARLIC, FINELY SLICED
10 G (⅜ OZ) ESCHALLOTS, SLICED
10 G (⅜ OZ) TOASTED CORIANDER SEEDS,
 FRESHLY GROUND
4 THYME SPRIGS, STALKS REMOVED

Rehydrate the chilli flesh in 500 ml (17 fl oz) cold water and allow to soak for 2 hours.

Set up a cold smoking apparatus with the maple wood chips.

Remove the chillies from the water, place on a steamer tray and cold smoke over the maple wood chips for 1 hour. Put the olive oil in a small saucepan. Add the smoked chillies, garlic, eschallots, ground coriander seeds and thyme. Bring the oil and spices to simmering point and simmer on very low for 15 minutes. Turn off the heat and allow to infuse for 1 hour. Strain oil through a fine sieve and reserve. Makes about 400 ml (14 fl oz).

02

CLEAR TOMATO JUICE

3 KG (6 LB 12 OZ) VINE-RIPENED ROMA
 (PLUM) TOMATOES

In batches, blend the tomatoes in a blender or food processor on high. Line a fine sieve with 2 layers of fine muslin (cheesecloth) and place over a stainless steel bowl. Carefully pour the blended tomatoes into the lined sieve and put them in the refrigerator while you allow the mixture to slowly drip through the sieve. This could take up to 4 hours. You want the liquid to be clear so do not put any pressure on the tomatoes.

03

SEMI-DRIED TOMATOES

24 VINE-RIPENED ROMA (PLUM) TOMATOES
100 ML (3½ FL OZ) EXTRA VIRGIN OLIVE OIL
SEA SALT
CASTER (SUPERFINE) SUGAR

Cut the core from each tomato using the point of a sharp knife and place a small cross on the top of the tomato. Bring a large saucepan of water to the boil and have a large bowl of iced water at hand.

Blanch the tomatoes in 2–3 batches in the boiling water for approximately 30 seconds. Refresh immediately in the iced water. Peel the skin from the tomatoes and cut into quarters lengthways. Remove the seeds and inner flesh with a sharp knife, leaving the tomato quarters in the form of petals. Place the tomato petals onto 2 trays lined with silicone paper.

Brush with extra virgin olive oil. Lightly sprinkle with sea salt and caster sugar. Put the tomatoes in a 140°C (275°F/Gas 1) oven for approximately 1½–2 hours or until the tomatoes are semi-dried and lightly wrinkled, turning halfway through. Allow the tomatoes to cool. Store in an airtight container laid between sheets of silicone paper.

04

TO FINISH

50 ML (1¾ FL OZ) EXTRA VIRGIN OLIVE OIL
FINE SEA SALT

Place the tomato petals on a tray lined with silicone paper. Brush each petal with olive oil. Reheat in a moderate oven for 1–2 minutes.

Put the clear tomato juice into a saucepan and bring to the boil. You should have roughly 1 litre (35 fl oz) of juice. Add 200 ml (7 fl oz) of the aromatic oil to the tomato juice and return to the boil. Check the seasoning and add some sea salt if necessary.

05

TO PLATE

Depending on the size of the tomato petals, place 8–10 warmed petals in the base of each warmed, shallow serving bowl. Put the golden aromatic broth into a warmed teapot. Serve the tomatoes and pour the broth over them at the table.

SUMMER TOMATOES,
GOLDEN AROMATIC BROTH

SERVES / 8

01

PUMPKIN

1 YOUNG, FRESHLY PICKED KAKAI PUMPKIN, APPROXIMATELY 2 KG (4 LB 8 OZ)

Cut the kakai pumpkin in half and use a large spoon to carefully remove the inner soft flesh and seeds. Discard, or reserve for another use, the outer firm pumpkin flesh.

Pull apart the soft inner flesh and seeds into small, rough pieces approximately 2–3 cm (¾–1¼ inches) in diameter. Pull out the majority of the seeds and sort them into small and large seeds. Cover and reserve in the refrigerator until required.

02

BROWN BUTTER

250 G (9 OZ) UNSALTED BUTTER

Put the unsalted butter in a heavy-based high-sided saucepan. Melt over high heat until the butter starts to foam. Continue cooking until you notice the foam changing from white to a pale golden colour. Push aside the foam and check the colour of the butter: it should be just turning golden brown and you will smell a nutty aroma. At this point you need to arrest the cooking process. Do this by pouring all of the contents into a clean saucepan off the heat.

Carefully remove the foam with a ladle and discard. Pour the brown butter into a clean stainless steel or ceramic bowl, making sure you leave the browned sediment behind.

Repeat the decanting process by pouring the butter into another clean vessel, ensuring any last traces of sediment are left behind. Set aside until required.

03

TO FINISH

SEA SALT

Put 1 tablespoon of the brown butter in a large non-stick frying pan over medium heat. Add the soft kakai pumpkin flesh, lightly season with sea salt, toss gently to coat. Add the larger pumpkin seeds and 2 tablespoons of water. Cover the pan with a lid and allow the pumpkin and seeds to steam for 1½ minutes. Remove the lid, allow the majority of the liquid to evaporate then add the smaller seeds and warm through for a further 30 seconds.

04

TO PLATE

40 WHITE SOCIETY GARLIC FLOWERS

Divide the pumpkin flesh and seeds between 8 warmed plates. Drizzle half a tablespoon of brown butter over each plate. Garnish with society garlic flowers.

Sometimes when you have such beautiful produce you just want to present it in as natural a way as possible to really appreciate the essence of the ingredient. I grew these kakai pumpkins for the first time in the summer of 2013: they are more of a summer squash than a pumpkin. Picked young, the flesh and seeds are so delicious that a little brown butter and salt is enough adornment.

YOUNG KAKAI PUMPKIN, BROWN BUTTER

SERVES / 8

This dessert was inspired by a family trip to the Andalusian region of southern Spain, where I was struck by the perfume of citrus and the amazing array of almond-based biscuits, pastries and sweets. One of the most charming ways to acquire these delicacies is by tapping on the age-worn wooden door of a cloistered Catholic convent, where the nuns have been making these sweets for centuries. Money is slipped into a small hole in the door in exchange for an array of sweet almond delicacies. When I returned home the images of those almond pastries, citrus and flamenco were whirling around in my head. I started with a cake based on ground almonds, marzipan, sugar and eggwhite and the rest of the recipe fell into place. This dessert is topped with a stretched almond biscuit that resembles the twirl of a flamenco skirt. I love it when the memory of a place or experience inspires a new creation.

CITRUS & ALMONDS

PREPARATION / 2 DAYS
SERVES / 8

ORGANUM / THE PEA BLOSSOM

01
ALMOND ICE CREAM
450 G (1 LB) WHOLE RAW ALMOND KERNELS
1 LITRE (35 FL OZ) MILK
150 G (5½ OZ) EGG YOLK
375 G (13 OZ) CASTER (SUPERFINE) SUGAR

Roast the almonds whole on a tray in a 180°C (350°F/Gas 4) oven until deeply golden and aromatic. Put the roasted almonds in a food processor and roughly chop.

Meanwhile, place the milk in a medium saucepan and bring almost to the boil. Immediately add the almonds while they are still warm. Remove from heat, cool slightly then cover and allow the almonds to infuse the milk, in the refrigerator, overnight.

The next day, reheat the milk and almond mixture until it almost reaches boiling point. Strain through a fine sieve, discarding the solids.

Whisk the egg yolks and caster sugar together in a large bowl. Whisk in the hot almond milk. Put the mixture in a double boiler and cook, stirring constantly, until the mixture reaches 85°C (185°F) and has thickened slightly. Strain the mixture through muslin (cheesecloth) into a bowl and cool over ice.

Churn in an ice-cream machine until frozen, then transfer to a freezer until required.

02
ALMOND CAKE
300 G (10½ OZ) FLAKED ALMONDS, ROASTED
100 G (3½ OZ) MARZIPAN, FINELY DICED
1 VANILLA BEAN, SEEDS ONLY
100 G (3½ OZ) PLAIN (ALL-PURPOSE) FLOUR
5 EGGS
2 EGGWHITES, EXTRA
350 G (12 OZ) CASTER (SUPERFINE) SUGAR
CASTER SUGAR, EXTRA, TO SPRINKLE

Preheat oven to 190°C (375°F/Gas 5).

In a Robot Coupe or food processor blitz the almonds, marzipan, vanilla seeds and flour to a fine even consistency and set aside.

Put the eggs, extra eggwhites and sugar in an electric mixer and whisk on high speed until thick and pale. Fold the dry mixture through the egg mixture.

Line two 25 x 35 cm (10 x 14 inch) flat trays with silicone paper or baking paper, divide the combined mixture between them and spread it out to an even 1 cm (⅜ inch) thickness. Bake in the oven approximately 6–8 minutes until golden brown. Sprinkle with fine caster sugar. Transfer the cake, still on the paper, to a cooling rack and allow to cool completely. Put the cake in an airtight container until required.

03
LEMON CRÈME FRAÎCHE
250 G (9 OZ) CRÈME FRAÎCHE
50 ML (1¾ FL OZ) OF BASIC SUGAR SYRUP (SEE BASIC RECIPES)
5 G (³⁄₁₆ OZ) STRAINED LEMON JUICE
1 LITRE LIQUID NITROGEN

Whisk cold crème fraîche, cold sugar syrup and lemon juice together until small soft peaks form.

Wearing appropriate protective eyewear and gloves, pour the liquid nitrogen into an insulated bowl or a small styrofoam container (see glossary for more safety information).

Put the crème fraîche mixture in a piping bag and pipe the whole quantity into the liquid nitrogen. Allow to freeze for approximately 1 minute then scoop out with a slotted spoon and transfer to a clean bowl. Gently break into small irregular pieces. Store in a sealed container in the freezer until required.

04
LEMON CURD
3 EGGS
180 G (6¼ OZ) CASTER (SUPERFINE) SUGAR
90 G (3¼ OZ) UNSALTED BUTTER
125 ML (4 FL OZ) STRAINED LEMON JUICE

Whisk the eggs and sugar together in a medium bowl. Bring the butter and lemon juice to the boil, then, whisking constantly, pour the juice mixture onto the eggs and sugar. Constantly whisk over a double boiler until the mixture thickens. Cool over ice. Transfer to the refrigerator until required.

05
MERINGUE
50 G (1¾ OZ) EGGWHITE
50 G (1¾ OZ) CASTER (SUPERFINE) SUGAR
50 G (1¾ OZ) ICING (CONFECTIONERS')
   SUGAR

Whisk eggwhites to soft peaks. Gradually add the caster sugar as you continue whisking. Once all the sugar is combined and peaks are stiff and glossy, fold through the icing sugar until well combined.

Line a baking tray with silicone paper. Put the mixture into a piping bag fitted with a 5 mm (¼ inch) round nozzle and pipe dots onto the tray. Cook in the oven for approximately 15 minutes or until dry.

06
SUGAR CRYSTALS
150 G (5½ OZ) ISOMALT
45 G (1½ OZ) GLUCOSE
45 ML (1½ FL OZ) WATER

Line a baking tray with a silicone mat. Combine all ingredients in a small saucepan and stir over high heat until clear. Bring the mixture to 165°C (320°C) then remove from the heat. Spread the mixture onto the tray and allow to set.

Break the sugar into pieces, then blitz in a food processor to the texture of small crystals. Pass through a fine drum sieve. Line a baking tray with a silicone mat. Working in batches, spread the crystals out sparsely on the tray. Reheat in a 180°C (350°F/Gas 4) oven for approximately 3 minutes or until crystals melt and reform. Allow to cool then, using a large palette knife, scrape the crystals off the mat and store in an airtight container.

07
PULLED ALMOND TUILES
330 G (11¾ OZ) TRIMOLINE (INVERTED
   SUGAR SYRUP)
330 G (11¾ OZ) GLUCOSE
100 G (3½ OZ) FLAKED ALMONDS,
   ROASTED

In a medium saucepan, bring trimoline and glucose to the boil and cook until it reaches a medium caramel colour.

Line a baking tray with silicone paper or baking paper. Add almonds to the toffee, mix and pour onto the tray.

While the mixture is still warm, top with another sheet of silicone paper or baking paper and use a rolling pin to roll it out until 1 cm (⅜ inch) thick. Allow to cool completely.

Once the caramel is cool, blitz it in a food processor to a fine powder.

Line a clean baking tray with a silicone mat. Put the powder through a medium–fine sieve to sprinkle evenly over the tray and form a fine, even layer. Melt the powder in a 175°C (345°F/Gas 3–4) oven until it liquefies.

While the toffee is still warm, working quickly, use a large sharp knife to cut it into 10 x 15 cm (4 x 6 inch) strips. Lift the strips with a palette knife then, using your hands, pull the shorter edges of the strips apart gently until the toffee is very fine, thin and almost see-through. Twist the pulled toffee to form a shape like a twirling flamenco skirt. Use an electric fan to help cool the twists while you hold them in shape. When they hold their shape without assistance, carefully lay each tuile on a tray, allow to cool thoroughly and keep in an airtight container until required.

08
TO FINISH
MILK BISCUIT (SEE BASIC RECIPES)
NOUGAT (SEE BASIC RECIPES)
ICING SUGAR

Break a third of the almond cake into rough 2 cm (¾ inch) pieces with your hands. Put the cake pieces in a large mixing bowl and add a similar quantity of the meringue dots, crushed milk biscuit, chopped nougat and frozen lemon crème fraîche. Mix gently to combine. The mixture should contain an even amount of each ingredient.

Dust the tuiles with icing sugar.

09
TO PLATE
BERGAMOT JAM (SEE BASIC RECIPES)

Pipe 4 dots of lemon curd into the bottom of each serving bowl. Place a scoop of roasted almond ice cream on top of the curd. Top with 4 heaped tablespoons of the almond cake and meringue mixture. Pipe on 4 dots of bergamot jam. Sprinkle with sugar crystals. Carefully crown the centre of each dish with a tuile. Serve.

JEWEL SEA

AUSTRALIA IS SURROUNDED BY SEA. ITS UNIQUE AND DIVERSE MARINE LIFE PLAYS A MAJOR PART IN IDENTIFYING WHAT AUSTRALIAN CUISINE IS ALL ABOUT.

TASMANIAN GALAXY SQUID / ENOPLOTEUTHIS GALAXIAS
HARVEST / WINTER

I love a sunburnt country,
A land of sweeping plains,
Of ragged mountain ranges,
Of droughts and flooding rains.
I love her far horizons,
I love her jewel-sea,
Her beauty and her terror —
The wide brown land for me!

DOROTHEA MACKELLAR, 'My Country'

Australia is surrounded by sea. Its unique and diverse marine life plays a major part in identifying what Australian cuisine is all about. The words 'girt by sea' appear in our national anthem; and 'our land abounds in nature's gifts of beauty rich and rare'.

When I was a child singing the national anthem at school, these words didn't really resonate with me, but I've come to realise our natural gifts are something to be treasured. Australia is known as the island continent and a lot of our seafood is unique: we are in a solid position of being able to manage this resource through sensible quotas and responsible fishing.

Whenever possible I try to buy seafood directly from the fisherman and support those who fish on a small scale, sustainably, by hand. Shellfish from crystal-clear Tasmanian waters—such as greenlip abalone, sea urchins, native Angasi oysters—as well as southern rocklobsters and beautiful line-caught Tasmanian trumpeter feature regularly on my menu. The colder southern waters produce particularly sweet shellfish.

Geographically, Australia's seafood is varied from the colder waters of Tasmania to the tropics of Queensland and the Northern Territory where I source hand-caught mud crabs and spanner crabs. We work with Craig Shephard, a free-diver working with Joto Fresh Fish, who collects tulip shell molluscs and sea urchins literally one kilometre off Sydney's coast, so that they are in our saltwater tanks within two hours of being pulled from the sea. It is such a privilege to be able to work with seafood this fresh.

We also source live wild king prawns, caught in waters just two hours north of Sydney. Our local waters also produce fantastic crayfish. From the pristine waters of Corner Inlet in Victoria we select line-caught sashimi-grade flathead and greenback flounder. From South Australia we acquire amazing octopus, squid and King George whiting. Australia's freshwater rivers produce some impressive seafood; such as the native Western Australian marron (freshwater crayfish); or Murray cod, which is predominantly farmed inland and is one of Australia's most highly prized freshwater fish.

Altogether Australia is blessed with the rich diversity of our seafood. The unique textures, flavours and quality of our marine resources play an integral part in defining our cuisine. The majority of Australia's population lives on the coast and our jewel sea plays a key role in our cultural identity.

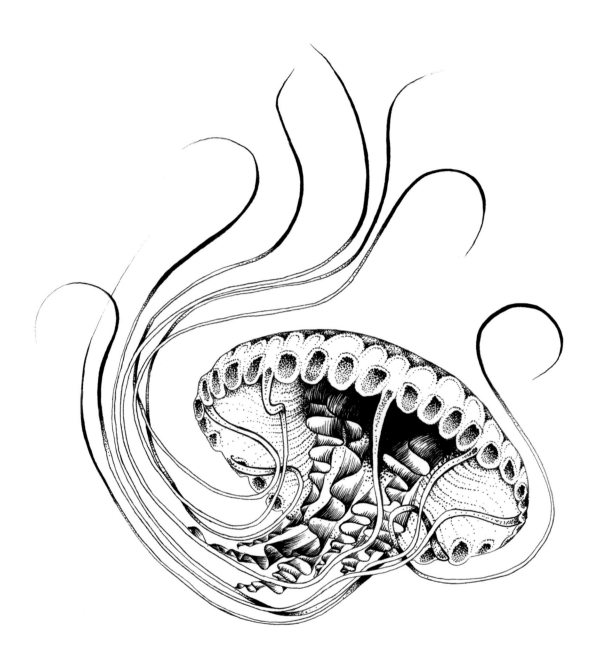

01

OCTOPUS

8 YOUNG COFFIN BAY OCTOPUSES,
    APPROXIMATELY 1 KG (2 LB 4 OZ)
    IN TOTAL
1 KG (2 LB 4 OZ) CLARIFIED BUTTER
    (SEE BASIC RECIPES)

Remove the tentacles of the young octopuses, reserving the heads for another use.

Heat the clarified butter in a saucepan until it reaches 70°C (165°F). Add the octopus tentacles to the clarified butter and stir to ensure even cooking. The tentacles should curl and take no more than 1½ minutes to cook. Remove from the butter, drain and keep warm.

02

TO FINISH

500 G (1 LB 2 OZ) TRIMMED AGRETTI
50 G (1¾ OZ) CLARIFIED BUTTER
    (SEE BASIC RECIPES), MELTED
SEA SALT
1 QUANTITY OF UMAMI CONSOMMÉ
    (SEE RECIPE ON PAGE 158)

Blanch the agretti in boiling salted water for 1 minute. Drain and dress with clarified butter and season to taste with sea salt.

Combine the octopus tentacles with the agretti, tossing well. Reheat the consommé.

03

TO PLATE

Place an even amount of octopus and agretti in each warmed serving bowl. Arrange the agretti to mirror the curl in the octopus tentacles. At the table, pour approximately 150 ml (5 fl oz) of hot umami consommé into each bowl. Serve.

The octopus I use are caught in the Coffin Bay area of South Australia, immediately ikijime spiked and then packed directly on ice. They are of sashimi-grade quality, which is rare for octopus of this size. Normally these small baby octopus are bycatch of trawled prawns and are not handled with such care. In this case they are deliberately caught using a specialised octopus trap that has been developed by Mark Eather.

SOUTH AUSTRALIAN OCTOPUS & AGRETTI

SERVES / 8

Squid is in its prime between September and November in Tasmanian waters. The squid I use is line caught and dispatched using the Japanese ikijime method, which instantly kills the squid by spiking its brain, reducing the stress and adrenaline pumping through its body.
It is then quickly placed into an ice slurry that immediately reduces its temperature. This process results in the squid being delivered in pristine condition. It is incomparable in quality, flavour and texture to squid that is fished by more conventional methods, where the animal slowly suffocates on the boat as part of the bycatch of net fishing.

IKIJIME TASMANIAN SQUID, SQUID INK CUSTARD, PINK TURNIPS, SOCIETY GARLIC FLOWERS

PREPARATION / 2 DAYS
SERVES / 8

01
SQUID RIBBONS
2 IKIJIME TASMANIAN SQUID,
 1.5 KG (3 LB 5 OZ) EACH

Clean and skin the squid. Cut the body flesh into two 10 cm (4 inch) squares, yielding 4 squares from the 2 squids. Lay the 4 squares on top of each other and wrap tightly in plastic wrap ensuring that the flesh remains flat. Sandwich the squid between two small baking trays and put it into a freezer, stacking the top tray with five or six dinner plates to add weight and compress the squid while freezing. Freeze for 24 hours.

Remove from the freezer, remove the plastic wrap and place the squid flat on a meat slicer. Slice on the thinnest possible setting, yielding at least twelve 10 cm (4 inch) squares.

Allow the squares to defrost and slice into 2 cm (¾ inch) wide ribbons. Refrigerate until required.

02
SQUID INK CUSTARD
400 ML (14 FL OZ) MILK
1 EGG
2 EGG YOLKS, EXTRA
1 TABLESPOON SQUID INK
SEA SALT

In a medium bowl, whisk all ingredients together. Fill eight 50 ml (1¾ fl oz) capacity round ramekins with the mixture. Cover each ramekin with plastic wrap and set aside in the refrigerator until required.

03
GARLIC CREAM
20 G (¾ OZ) UNSALTED BUTTER
3 GARLIC CLOVES, PEELED
500 ML (17 FL OZ) MILK
5 G (³⁄₁₆ OZ) AGAR AGAR
FINE SEA SALT

Melt the butter in a saucepan, add the garlic cloves and gently sweat them in the butter, being careful not to add any colour. Add the milk and bring it close to boiling point. Remove the pan from the heat and allow the garlic to infuse in the milk for 20 minutes. Pour the milk through a fine strainer into a clean saucepan and discard the solids. Return the pan to the heat and then whisk in the agar agar. Reheat the milk to 90°C (195°F), continuing to stir to activate the agar agar. Taste and season with sea salt. Refrigerate the milk and allow to set. Once set, put into a blender and process on high speed until a smooth paste is formed. The garlic cream should be the consistency of mayonnaise when reheated.

04
UMAMI CONSOMMÉ
1 QUANTITY OF UMAMI CONSOMMÉ
 (SEE RECIPE ON PAGE 158)

Put 500 ml (17 fl oz) consommé in a small saucepan and simmer until reduced to 100 ml (3½ fl oz).

05
TO FINISH
8 MEDIUM-SIZE PINK TURNIPS
550 G (1 LB 3 OZ) CLARIFIED BUTTER,
 MELTED (SEE BASIC RECIPES)
SEA SALT

Peel the pink turnips. Using a 3 cm (1¼ inch) round cutter, punch a cylinder out of each turnip. Cut each turnip cylinder into 8–10 thin discs.

Shake each ramekin of squid ink custard well to combine the mixture and steam at full steam, without removing the plastic wrap, for 8 minutes or until just set.

Heat 500 ml (17 fl oz) of the melted clarified butter in a wide saucepan until it reaches 70°C (160°F). Add the shaved squid ribbons and agitate with a pair of fine tongs to promote even cooking. The squid should only take 40–50 seconds to cook and should appear opaque. Remove immediately from the hot butter, lightly season with sea salt and drain the squid on a clean tea towel (dish towel).

Meanwhile, blanch the turnip discs in boiling water for 20 seconds, brush with remaining clarified butter and season.

06
TO PLATE
PINK SOCIETY GARLIC FLOWERS

In the centre of each warmed serving plate, add half a tablespoon of the garlic cream. Spread out a little with the back of the spoon. Using a round soup spoon, scoop out the hot squid ink custard and place in the middle of the garlic cream.

Reheat the reduced consommé and add half a tablespoon to each plate. Divide equal portions of both the shaved squid and the pink turnips over the top of each of the custards. Garnish with society garlic flowers. Serve.

DAVE ALLEN

FISHERMAN
ST HELENS / TASMANIA

It's hard to imagine a more inspired fisherman: Dave has incredible local knowledge and a real respect for the environment.

Dave Allen says his career started at the age of six, fishing recreationally from the family boat. His father was a stickler for looking after the catch—his philosophy was to always ice down promptly, never take more than you need and to return small fish to the water to catch another day.

At the age of 10, Dave had progressed to paddling his kayak to the middle of an island off the north coast of Tasmania to snorkel for abalone, which he cooked over a small open fire with garlic and butter. By the time he was 22, Dave was working as a deckhand, diving for abalone and scallops.

In 1995 he took a leap of faith and bought his own boat licence and a small, worn-out 5.5 metre (18 foot) aluminium fishing vessel. He decided to have a go at commercially diving for sea urchins but was fairly unsuccessful, so he then purchased a commercial diving licence for cockles (vongole): one of only three in the state of Tasmania. This proved to be a fruitful

enterprise until the market for his cockles fell over when his main buyer cancelled their contract. At that time, having acquired considerable debt, Dave decided to cold-call traders at the Sydney Fish Market. Fortuitously, his first phone call was to none other than one of Australia's best fishmongers, Wayne Hulme of Joto Fresh Fish, who immediately recognised the opportunity and agreed to take up his whole quota of cockles as long as he called them 'Bay of Fires Vongole': this was a great lesson for Dave in marketing.

From that point onwards he developed a strong working relationship with Wayne and his business partner Jules. Together they developed a range of highly regarded Bay of Fires seafood based on the ideals instilled by Dave's father at an early age; and expanded upon during visits to Japan where he observed the Japanese way of handling and processing fish and learnt the principles of ikijime.

In 2011, Dave felt the time was right to make the most of his updated skills and the

techniques for processing sea urchin that he'd acquired in Japan and give fishing for sea urchin another crack. It was not only plentiful but had been deemed an invasive marine pest by the Tasmanian state government. With this new and sustainable product, Dave's company, Seafoods Tasmania, was a medallist at the 2013 *delicious.* Produce Awards for Bay of Fires Uni (AAA Grade Sea Urchin Roe), which he now exports.

I've had the pleasure of visiting Dave and looking at his business first hand. It's hard to imagine a more inspired fisherman: he has incredible local knowledge and a real respect for the environment. I think the key to survival for small-scale fishermen is direct relationships with passionate providores and restaurants.

Dave says, 'It's a pleasure to be able to supply some of Tasmania's unique and beautiful seafood to a chef like Peter Gilmore, who really appreciates the effort that goes into ensuring the quality and freshness of my catch.'

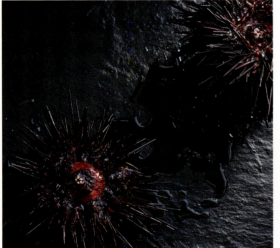

BELOW LEFT: Freshly caught uni (sea urchin).
BELOW: The Bay of Fires.

WAYNE HULME

FISHMONGER
BOTANY / NEW SOUTH WALES

'I was so excited to show it to Pete—a beautiful, live hand-harvested scallop from Western Australia—only to stare in shock because Peter was more interested in the frilly bits around the white flesh; bits that I would have thrown in the bin.'

Wayne Hulme is the most passionate person I know when it comes to seafood. His enthusiasm for everything that comes from the sea is infectious. A keen fisherman himself, Wayne heads up Joto Fresh Fish, along with owner Jules Crocker. Jules set up Joto more than 15 years ago, starting with one refrigerated van and a small rented premises in Clovelly, New South Wales. Wayne joined Jules at Joto in 2010. Joto Fresh Fish has grown to be recognised as one of Sydney's premier seafood suppliers and now has a purpose-built factory in Botany, ten delivery trucks and 29 staff. I deal directly with Wayne for about 80 per cent of my seafood requirements, for two main reasons:

his passion and commitment to quality and the personal relationships he has developed with small-scale sustainable fishermen.

Wayne believes that gaining an understanding of a species of fish—what they eat, how and where they move and live—is vital, before even thinking about fishing for them. Being able to bring that knowledge about a species to a passionate chef and, in turn, learning about the techniques a chef applies to bring out the best flavour and texture from the fish, is really what drives Wayne.

In Wayne's own words about our working relationship, he cites one classic example that sums up what we do. He recalls the day he brought me a Rottnest Island

scallop to look at: 'I was so excited to show it to Pete—a beautiful, live hand-harvested scallop from Western Australia—only to stare in shock because Peter was more interested in the frilly bits around the white flesh; bits that I would have thrown in the bin. He dehydrated them then grilled them and included me in the tasting. Lo and behold, the texture was completely unexpected, delicious and a perfect accompaniment to the meat inside. Lesson learnt, Wayne! Since that day I have put everything from a hermit crab to a bar cod tongue in front of Pete without feeling stupid.'

CRAYFISH CONSOMMÉ

Make a quantity of umami consommé using the recipe on page 158, replacing 500 g (1 lb 2 oz) squid trimmings with 1 kg (2 lb 4 oz) crayfish legs and head shells, crushed. When making the raft, replace 150 g (5½ oz) dried chestnut mushrooms, 20 g (¾ oz) dried kombu and 20 g (¾ oz) dried wakame with 50 g (1¾ oz) ginger, thinly sliced and 100 g (3½ oz) spring onions, thinly sliced, adding the ginger and spring onions to the chicken in the food processor. Cool the consommé and refrigerate until required.

02

TO FINISH
2 KG (4 LB 8 OZ) CRAYFISH
40 JUST-PICKED DAY LILIES
SEA SALT
2 TEASPOONS XANTANA (FERMENTED
   CORNSTARCH)

Submerge the crayfish into a deep water bath with plenty of ice, for half an hour to help humanely dispatch the crayfish.

Bring a large stockpot of salted water to the boil. Blanch the crayfish for 3 minutes and immediately return to the iced water. Once the crayfish is chilled, remove the tail section.

Cut along both sides of the underside of the tail with a sharp pair of scissors and lever out the meat with your fingers. Remove the legs and crack the shells with the back of a heavy knife. Carefully pick out all of the leg meat. Refrigerate. Use a sharp knife to cut the tail meat in half lengthways and slice each half into 2 mm (1⁄16 inch) thick medallions. Refrigerate until required.

Carefully separate the day lily petals from the stems. Set aside until required.

Bring the crayfish consommé to the boil and reduce until you only have 1 litre (35 fl oz) remaining. Check the seasoning at this point and add more salt if required.

Transfer 100 ml (3½ fl oz) of the consommé into a small bowl. Sprinkle the xantana over the top and whisk well until smooth. Pour this back into the hot consommé, whisking over heat until well combined. Simmer for 2 minutes on medium heat, whisking constantly until you get a light syrupy consistency. Keep warm.

03

TO PLATE
50 G (1¾ OZ) UNSALTED BUTTER
SEA SALT

Heat 500 ml (17 fl oz) of the thickened consommé in each of two large woks or wide-based saucepans until they both reach a gentle simmer. Put the crayfish medallions and leg meat with the butter into one wok and the day lily petals into the other wok. Stir the crayfish through the simmering liquid for approximately 1½ minutes until it turns opaque. Stir the day lilies for approximately the same amount of time. Check the seasoning on the crayfish and season lightly with the sea salt if required. Use a slotted spoon to layer an even amount of crayfish flesh and day lilies into each warmed serving bowl. Serve.

TASMANIAN CRAYFISH, WILTED DAY LILIES

SERVES / 8

This is a new ingredient that Wayne Hulme and I have been working on recently. Deep-sea hermit crabs are incredibly delicious. The tail meat of a hermit crab has a flavour and texture somewhere between lobster and crab and is similar in size to a langoustine or king prawn. The hermit crabs you can find on the beach are far too small to consider using, but these deep-sea hermit crabs are quite large. They are bycatch in crayfish pots and are normally thrown back into the sea, as there is currently no official market for them. The challenge is convincing crayfishermen to go to the trouble of processing these hermit crabs when they can get such high prices for crayfish. Wayne and I are working with a couple of crayfishermen to look at catching these hermit crabs in their off season. Some work also needs to be done on establishing the available stocks of hermit crabs but anecdotal evidence suggests they are plentiful.

HERMIT CRAB, FERMENTED CHILLI & BEAN BLOSSOMS

SERVES / 8

01

GARLIC OIL

100 ML (3½ FL OZ) GRAPESEED OIL
2 GARLIC CLOVES, THINLY SLICED

Warm the oil to 50°C (120°F) in a small stainless steel saucepan. Add the garlic then remove the pan from the heat and allow to infuse for 2 hours at room temperature. Strain, discarding the solids, and refrigerate the oil until required.

02

FERMENTED CHILLI PASTE

100 G (3½ OZ) MILD KOREAN FERMENTED
   RED CHILLI PASTE
50 G (1¾ OZ) KOREAN FERMENTED WHOLE
   YELLOW BEAN MISO
15 ML (½ FL OZ) GARLIC OIL (SEE ABOVE)
10 ML (⅜ FL OZ) VIRGIN BLACK SESAME OIL

Combine all of the ingredients, whisking well. Pass through a fine drum sieve. Cover and refrigerate until required.

03

TO FINISH

100 G (3½ OZ) CLARIFIED BUTTER
   (SEE BASIC RECIPES)
24 HERMIT CRAB TAILS
FINE SEA SALT
50 G (1¾ OZ) BEAN SPROUTS, TOPPED
   AND TAILED
50 G (1¾ OZ) UNSALTED BUTTER, MELTED
120 BEAN BLOSSOMS

Put the clarified butter in a large non-stick frying pan over high heat. Season the hermit crab tail meat with fine sea salt and pan-fry for 1 minute on each side. Drain the hermit crab meat on paper towel and keep warm until ready to plate.

Blanch the bean sprouts in boiling salted water for 30 seconds. Dress with half of the melted unsalted butter. Season with sea salt and drain on paper towel.

Blanch the bean blossoms in boiling salted water for 5 seconds, remove with a slotted spoon, drain on paper towel then dress with the remaining melted butter and season with sea salt.

04

TO PLATE

Place half a tablespoon of fermented chilli paste in the centre of each warmed serving plate and spread it out with the back of a spoon. Lay 3 pan-fried hermit crab tails over the paste, top with a small bundle of the blanched bean sprouts, garnish with blanched bean blossoms and serve.

01

FERMENTED WHITE LENTIL LEAVES

150 G (5½ OZ) WHITE LENTILS
  (URAD DAL, SKINNED AND SPLIT)
300 ML (10½ FL OZ) STILL MINERAL WATER
30 G (1 OZ) SEA SALT

Wash the white lentils under plenty of cold running water and drain well. In a sterilised jar with a screw-top lid, put the still mineral water and the salt and mix well. Add the lentils and leave to ferment at room temperature for 3 days.

After 3 days drain the lentils: they should have a slightly sour flavour. Place the drained lentils in a medium saucepan and cover with cold water. Bring to the boil over medium heat, then reduce the heat to low and simmer for approximately 20 minutes or until tender. Drain well.

While the lentils are still warm, place 2 tablespoons of lentils at a time between two sheets of silicone paper and roll out with a heavy rolling pin until 1 mm (1/32 inch) in thickness. The lentils should crush and stick together. Repeat this process until all the lentils are rolled out.

Place the silicone sheets of lentils onto baking trays and heat in a 180°C (350°F/Gas 4) oven for 10 minutes or until the lentils are golden brown. Remove the top silicone sheets and carefully lift off the lentil leaves. Break into small pieces and transfer to an airtight container until required.

02

SALTED MULLET ROE

250 G (9 OZ) FRESH GREY MULLET ROE SAC
1 LITRE (35 FL OZ) STILL MINERAL WATER
40 G (1½ OZ) SEA SALT

Freeze the grey mullet roe sacs overnight to ensure that any parasites are killed. Defrost.

Divide the water and salt equally between two bowls. Place the roe sac in the first bowl. Using a pair of sharp scissors cut the skin of the roe sac to expose the roe. Gently remove the roe from each sac, using a blunt knife to gently scrape it out. Discard the skin.

Using a whisk, gently agitate the roe to help separate the eggs.

Allow the roe to sit in the brine for 10 minutes. Carefully pour through a fine drum sieve, discarding the brine.

Using a pair of tweezers, remove any veins or blood vessels from the roe. Carefully transfer the roe with a palette knife or plastic pastry scraper to the fresh bowl of brine. Gently agitate the eggs again using a whisk. Allow to sit for a further 10 minutes before once more pouring the roe through a fine drum sieve. Remove any veins you may have missed the first time. Allow the eggs to drain completely.

Transfer the roe to an airtight container, seal and refrigerate until required.

Trumpeter is a thick, fine white-fleshed fish caught off the east coast of Tasmania. I poach the fish in crème fraîche; the lactic acid in the crème fraîche helps to tenderise the fish and imparts a beautiful flavour. Warm salted mullet roe adds a briny sea intensity to the dish, contrasted with the sweet earthy potato cream. The fermentation of the urad dal (lentils) helps to create crispness and depth of flavour in the resulting textural leaves.

POACHED TRUMPETER

3 KG (6 LB 12 OZ) WHOLE TRUMPETER
100 G (3½ OZ) CRÈME FRAÎCHE
150 ML (5 FL OZ) PURE CREAM (35% FAT)
SEA SALT

Fillet the trumpeter and remove the skin. Cut eight 150 g (5½ oz) portions. Combine the creams and season with sea salt to taste. Place each portion of trumpeter into a small cryovac bag with 30 ml (1 fl oz) of the cream mixture. Seal and refrigerate until required. Do not prepare the fish more than 3 hours in advance of serving.

04

POTATO PURÉE

500 G (1 LB 2 OZ) ANDEAN GOLD OR DUTCH CREAM POTATOES
100 ML (3½ FL OZ) PURE CREAM (35% FAT)
100 G (3½ OZ) CRÈME FRAÎCHE
100 G (3½ OZ) BUTTER
SEA SALT

Wash the potatoes well and put them into a large saucepan of cold water with a little sea salt. Bring to the boil, reduce to a simmer and cook until the potatoes are tender when tested with a knife point. Drain the potatoes. Wearing rubber gloves, peel the potatoes while they are still warm. Process the potatoes through a mouli grater, add the cream, crème fraîche and butter and mix well. Season to taste. Pass the mixture through a fine drum sieve. Cover and refrigerate until required.

05

TO FINISH

500 ML (17 FL OZ) PURE CREAM (35% FAT)
100 G (3½ OZ) UNSALTED BUTTER
24 YOUNG BULBED SPRING ONIONS, PEELED AND HALVED
100 G (3½ OZ) PICKED AND WASHED GOLDEN ORACH (MOUNTAIN SPINACH) LEAVES
50 ML (1¾ FL OZ) MELTED UNSALTED BUTTER, EXTRA
SEA SALT

For the potato cream, measure 300 g (10½ oz) of the potato purée and heat in a small saucepan while gradually whisking in 400 ml (14 fl oz) of the cream. Taste and adjust seasoning. Allow this mixture to cool slightly. Fill an espuma gun (cream syphon) about half full with the potato, screw on the lid then add two gas charges. Shake the container well between charges. Leave the espuma gun in a warm spot in the kitchen until required.

Prepare a water circulator to 55°C (130°F). Add the bags of fish and cook for approximately 12 minutes, depending on the thickness of the fish fillets.

Reheat the remaining potato purée with the remaining 100 ml (3½ fl oz) cream. Check and adjust seasoning.

Melt 100 g (3½ oz) unsalted butter in a small saucepan, and add the drained salted mullet roe. Place the saucepan over gentle heat and mix well until just warm.

Blanch spring onions in boiling salted water for about 2 minutes until tender. In the last 10 seconds of cooking add the orach. Drain the orach and onions well. Brush with the extra melted butter and season to taste.

06

TO PLATE

1 TABLESPOON GAI LAN (CHINESE BROCCOLI) FLOWER PETALS
1 TABLESPOON OF YELLOW CHOY SUM (CHINESE FLOWERING CABBAGE) PETALS
1 TABLESPOON WHOLE WHITE EDIBLE LINARIA FLOWERS

Place a tablespoon of the potato purée in the centre of each warmed serving bowl. Top the purée with a portion of the poached fish that has been lightly broken apart. Top the fish with a tablespoon of the warmed salted mullet roe. Top with spring onions and orach.

Top the dish with 2 tablespoons of the potato cream from the espuma gun. Sprinkle over the fermented white lentil leaves and garnish with the petals and flowers. Serve.

POACHED TRUMPETER, POTATO CREAM, SALTED MULLET ROE, FERMENTED WHITE LENTIL LEAVES

PREPARATION / 3 DAYS
SERVES / 8

01

ABALONE

8 BABY GREENLIP ABALONE, 120 G
   (4¼ OZ) EACH
250 ML (9 FL OZ) CHICKEN STOCK
   (SEE BASIC RECIPES)

Put the live abalone into a large bowl of iced water for 1 hour to humanely dispatch them. Shuck the abalone with a large kitchen spoon.

Use a sharp knife to remove all the intestines and digestive tracts, leaving only the meat of the abalone intact. Cover the abalone and refrigerate for 24 hours. This process helps tenderise the abalone by allowing it to go through the rigor mortis process.

Put the abalone in a large cryovac bag with the chicken stock, seal and steam at 85°C (185°F) for 10 hours. Remove from the steamer and place the bag in an ice water bath to rapidly chill the abalone. Store, in the bag, in the refrigerator until required.

02

LIGHT SHIITAKE, WAKAME & ANCHOVY BROTH

200 G (7 OZ) UNSALTED BUTTER
250 G (9 OZ) FRESH SHIITAKE MUSHROOM
   TRIMMINGS, OR SLICED SHIITAKE
   MUSHROOMS
1 KG (2 LB 4 OZ) CHICKEN WINGS, CHOPPED
500 G (1 LB 2 OZ) SQUID TRIMMINGS,
   OR SLICED SQUID
500 G (1 LB 2 OZ) SCALLOP TRIMMINGS,
   OR SLICED SCALLOPS
10 ESCHALLOTS, THINLY SLICED
100 ML (3½ FL OZ) BROWN RICE VINEGAR
200 ML (7 FL OZ) OLOROSO SHERRY
5 LITRES (175 FL OZ) CHICKEN STOCK
   (SEE BASIC RECIPES)
10 G (⅜ OZ) DRIED WAKAME PIECES
3 INNER WHITE CELERY STALKS,
   THINLY SLICED
1 TEASPOON XANTANA (FERMENTED
   CORNSTARCH)
FERMENTED ANCHOVY JUICE, TO SEASON

RAFT

500 G (1 LB 2 OZ) SKINLESS CHICKEN
   BREAST, CHOPPED
100 G (3½ OZ) DRIED CHESTNUT
   MUSHROOMS
10 CM (4 INCH) SQUARE OF DRIED KOMBU
12 EGGWHITES

Put the butter, shiitake mushrooms, chicken wings, squid, scallop and eschallot in a large stockpot over medium–high heat, moving the ingredients around regularly with a wooden spoon until lightly golden. Deglaze with the brown rice vinegar and oloroso sherry. Bring to a boil over high heat and allow most of the liquid to evaporate. Add the chicken stock, wakame and celery, bring almost to a boil then reduce to a simmer, without skimming at all, and continue to simmer for 2 hours.

Remove from the heat and allow the flavours to infuse for 1 hour. Strain into a clean stockpot, discarding the solids. Skim all the fat from the top of the stock. Allow the stock to cool completely.

To make the raft, put the chicken breast, chestnut mushrooms and roughly torn kombu into a food processor and process until well combined. Lightly whisk the eggwhites and fold through the processed mixture. Whisk this raft well into the cooled stock then put it over medium heat. Once the stock has reached simmering point, use a wooden spoon to check that there are no raft solids stuck on the bottom of the pot. Do not disturb the raft again after this point. Keep the pot on the barest simmer for 1 hour. Remove from the heat and allow the raft to slowly sink into the stock, leaving it infused for a period of 1 hour. Carefully ladle the stock through a fine sieve lined with muslin (cheesecloth) into a clean saucepan. You should have 2 litres (70 fl oz) of stock left. If you have more, reduce over medium heat until you have just 2 litres left.

Transfer 100 ml (3½ fl oz) of the stock into a small bowl. Sprinkle the xantana over the top and whisk well until smooth. Pour this back into the hot stock, whisking over heat until well combined. Season to taste with anchovy juice. You will have more broth than is required for this recipe: you can easily freeze the remainder for another use.

ROASTED GREENLIP ABALONE, HEIRLOOM CUCUMBERS, BARLETTA ONIONS, SEAWEED

PREPARATION / 2 DAYS
SERVES / 8

03
VEGETABLES

40 BABY WHITE HEIRLOOM CUCUMBERS
  (SEE GLOSSARY)
40 BABY BARLETTA ONIONS
30 G (1 OZ) GOLDEN ORACH
  (MOUNTAIN SPINACH)
32 AGRETTI SPRIGS
40 BEAN BLOSSOMS
3 SHEETS OF HIGH-QUALITY KOREAN
  TOASTED NORI

Lightly peel the baby cucumbers and cut in half lengthways. Store in a container of cold water in the refrigerator. Trim and peel a couple of layers from the baby onions to ensure they are roughly the size of a small marble. Remove any stems from the orach, wash and dry. Pick and wash the agretti sprigs. Wash and dry the bean blossoms. Tear the toasted nori into roughly 5 cm (2 inch) squares.

04
TO FINISH

50 G (1¾ OZ) CLARIFIED BUTTER
  (SEE BASIC RECIPES)
100 G (3½ OZ) UNSALTED BUTTER
100 ML (3½ FL OZ) CHICKEN STOCK
  (SEE BASIC RECIPES)
FINE SEA SALT
50 G (1¾ OZ) UNSALTED BUTTER,
  EXTRA, MELTED

Put a large saucepan of salted water over high heat and bring to the boil.

Open the cryovac bag and remove the abalone, discarding the stock. Cut each abalone into 8 pieces. Melt the clarified butter in a large non-stick frying pan over high heat. Pan roast the abalone pieces until golden brown. Remove from the heat, place on a tray lined with silicone paper and keep warm.

Reheat 800 ml (28 fl oz) of the reserved light shiitake, wakame and anchovy broth.

Put 50 g (1¾ oz) of the unsalted butter with the chicken stock in a large saucepan over high heat. Add the cucumber halves and sauté for about 1 minute. Turn off the heat, season with sea salt and keep warm.

Blanch the baby onions in the boiling salted water for 2 minutes. Meanwhile, reheat the pan-roasted abalone in a 200°C (400°F/Gas 6) oven for 1 minute. Quickly heat a medium saucepan containing the remaining unsalted butter, add the golden orach and sauté for 30 seconds, then add the torn nori. Toss together for 10 seconds. Season with sea salt and drain on a clean tea towel (dish towel).

In the last 5 seconds of the onion cooking time, add the bean blossoms and agretti sprigs then drain the vegetables and agretti on a clean tea towel and brush with the extra melted unsalted butter. Lightly season with sea salt.

05
TO PLATE

Place 4 pieces of the roasted abalone in the centre of each warmed serving bowl. Add an equal quantity of sautéed baby cucumbers to each bowl. Divide half the golden orach and nori mixture between the bowls. Place another 4 pieces of pan-roasted abalone on top. Add the rest of the golden orach and nori mixture. Garnish with an equal amount of baby onions, agretti sprigs and bean blossoms.

Put the boiling broth into a cast-iron teapot or similar vessel and serve the abalone to your guests. Pour approximately 100 ml (3½ fl oz) of the broth over each dish, at the table.

Greenlip abalone are sourced by divers in the southern waters of Australia. The secret to their tenderness in this recipe is to allow them to go through rigor mortis for 24 hours in the refrigerator before steaming them for 10 hours. They are then briefly roasted in clarified butter until they turn golden brown.

The idea for this dish came from a trip to the Great Barrier Reef a few years ago. Snorkelling over the reef and observing the complexity of the coral gardens with so many varied shapes, textures and colours, I decided to create a dish with these elements in mind. Nature's sheer diversity provides endless inspiration.

THE REEF

SERVES / 8

01

DORY ROE WITH LEMON ZEST

200 G (7 OZ) FRESH SILVER DORY ROE SACS
1 LITRE (35 FL OZ) STILL MINERAL WATER
50 G (1¾ OZ) SEA SALT
½ LEMON
50 ML (1¾ FL OZ) EXTRA VIRGIN OLIVE OIL

Freeze the silver dory roe sacs overnight to ensure that any parasites are killed. Defrost.

Divide the water and salt equally between two bowls. Place the roe sac in the first bowl. Using a pair of sharp scissors cut the skin of the roe sac to expose the roe. Gently remove the roe from each sac, using a blunt knife to gently scrape it out. Discard the skin.

Using a whisk, gently agitate the roe to help separate the eggs.

Allow the roe to sit in the brine for 10 minutes. Carefully pour through a fine drum sieve, discarding the brine.

Using a pair of tweezers, remove any veins or blood vessels from the roe. Carefully transfer the roe with a palette knife or plastic pastry scraper to the fresh bowl of brine. Gently agitate the roe again using a whisk. Allow to sit for a further 10 minutes before once more pouring the roe through a fine drum sieve. Remove any veins you may have missed the first time. Allow the roe to drain completely.

Put the roe into a small bowl. Use a fine microplane to zest the half lemon over the roe and stir in the olive oil. Transfer the roe to an airtight container, seal and refrigerate until required.

02

EGGWHITE & SMOKED EEL PEARL FLOWER

70 G (2½ OZ) BONELESS, SKINLESS SMOKED
    EEL MEAT
200 ML (7 FL OZ) MILK
70 G (2½ OZ) WHITE-FLESHED FISH,
    SUCH AS BLUE-EYE TREVALLA,
    SNAPPER OR COD
60 G (2¼ OZ) UNSALTED BUTTER,
    SOFTENED
40 ML (1¼ FL OZ) EXTRA VIRGIN OLIVE OIL
½ LEMON, JUICE
60 G (2¼ OZ) MASHED POTATO
FINE SEA SALT
30 G (1 OZ) CRÈME FRAÎCHE
500 ML (17 FL OZ) GRAPESEED OIL
100 ML (3½ FL OZ) STRAINED EGGWHITE
8 GOLF-BALL-SIZE GREEN RADISHES

To make the smoked eel brandade, put the milk in a pan and bring to the boil, then remove the pan from the heat and add the smoked eel. Leave the eel to marinate in the warm milk for 10 minutes, then strain the eel and discard the milk. Steam the white fish until it flakes.

Put the eel and fish in a small bowl. Using a fork, mash them together with 30 g (1 oz) of softened butter. Drizzle over 20 ml (¾ fl oz) of olive oil and all of the lemon juice, mixing with the fork as you go. Add the mashed potato and mix well. Add the remaining butter and olive oil and mix well. Season to taste with sea salt. Allow the mixture to cool, then fold in the crème fraîche. Place the mixture in the refrigerator for at least 1 hour.

Take some of the mixture in the palm of your hand and roll into balls the size of a small marble. You will need 16 balls. You may have some mixture left over, which you can use elsewhere.

To make the eggwhite pearls, put the grapeseed oil in a small saucepan and heat to 70°C (165°F). Using an eye-dropper, drop the strained eggwhite into the oil, drop by drop, in rapid succession. When you have about 30 eggwhite droplets, stop and gently stir them around. They need about 1 minute in the oil to fully set. Carefully strain out the eggwhite pearls using a fine sieve and place the pearls on a flat metal tray. Repeat this process several times until you have a sufficient amount of eggwhite pearls to coat the balls of brandade.

To cover the brandade mixture with the eggwhite pearls, first line 16 demitasse cups with 12 cm (4½ inch) squares of plastic wrap. Put 1 teaspoon of eggwhite pearls in the middle of the square and spread them out so they form a single layer. Place a ball of brandade in the centre. Carefully lift up the four corners of the plastic wrap and twist them together to form a ball, then tie a knot in the plastic. The aim is to coat the brandade ball in the eggwhite pearls with the aid of the plastic wrap. When you have 16 perfectly covered balls, put them in the refrigerator until required.

Peel the radishes and cut into 3 cm (1¼ inch) thick slices. Using a 2 cm (¾ inch) round pastry cutter, cut out cylinders from the radish. Use a mandolin to slice the cylinders into 1 mm (1/32 inch) thin discs. You will need 96 discs (six discs per flower, for a total of 16 flowers). Blanch the radish discs in boiling water for 10 seconds and refresh in iced water. Dry the discs thoroughly.

Lay 15 cm (6 inch) squares of plastic wrap over 16 demitasse cups, leaving a slight dip in the middle of the plastic. Place six overlapping discs of radish in the centre of the plastic wrap to form a small circle. Place an eggwhite and smoked eel pearl in the centre and pull each corner of the plastic wrap together so the slices of radish come up the sides of the pearl. With your fingers, pinch the base so the radish petals stick to the pearl. Refrigerate in the demitasse cups for 1 hour.

03

TAPIOCA COOKED IN EEL STOCK

1 INNER WHITE CELERY STALK
½ FENNEL BULB
1 LITRE (35 FL OZ) CHICKEN STOCK
   (SEE BASIC RECIPES)
50 ML (1¾ FL OZ) WHITE SOY SAUCE
100 G (3½ OZ) SMOKED EEL, FINELY SLICED
½ GARLIC CLOVE
10 G (⅜ OZ) BONITO FLAKES
5 CM (2 INCH) SQUARE OF KOMBU
100 G (3½ OZ) TAPIOCA

Roughly chop the vegetables and put them in a large saucepan with the remaining ingredients except the kombu and tapioca. Bring close to boiling point and then reduce to a gentle simmer for 30 minutes. Remove from heat, add the kombu and allow to infuse for 30 minutes. Strain, discarding the solids.

   Return the liquid to a clean saucepan and add the tapioca. Bring to the boil, stirring regularly. Reduce to a rapid simmer and cook, stirring regularly to prevent the tapioca from catching, for 10 minutes or until you notice only a small dot of starch in the middle of the tapioca: the outside will be translucent. Pour the tapioca into a sieve and briefly drain then pour the tapioca out onto a flat tray to cool. Refrigerate in an airtight container until required.

04

SASHIMI SEAFOOD PREPARATION

200 G (7 OZ) FLATHEAD FILLETS,
   SKIN REMOVED
200 G (7 OZ) GARFISH FILLETS,
   SKIN REMOVED
200 G (7 OZ) TRUMPETER FILLETS,
   SKIN REMOVED
2 TENTACLES FROM A 2 KG (4 LB 8 OZ)
   OCTOPUS
1 WHOLE SQUID, 1.5 KG (3 LB 5 OZ)
4 SEA SCALLOPS, FRESHLY SHUCKED
8 ANGASI (FLAT) OYSTERS

Cut the flesh of the flathead, garfish and trumpeter fillets into 5 mm (¼ inch) thick sashimi-style slices. Cut off the octopus suckers with a sharp knife and reserve the tentacles for another use. Remove the squid tentacles and leave them whole. Split the squid body in half, clean it and remove the skin. Open out flat. Slice the squid body horizontally into 2 mm (1⁄16 inch) thick sheets. Then cut it into 1 cm (⅜ inch) wide ribbons. Slice the scallops horizontally into 2 mm (1⁄16 inch) thick discs. Shuck the Angasi oysters and remove the frill from each. Reserve the frill in the natural oyster juices in an airtight container. Reserve the rest of the oyster meat for another use, such as the oyster cream recipe (see Basic Recipes) used for plating this dish. Refrigerate all the prepared seafood until required.

05

TO FINISH

500 ML (17 FL OZ) GRAPESEED OIL
250 ML (9 FL OZ) WHITE SOY SAUCE
1 PUNNET WHITE FUNGUS
8 AGRETTI SPRIGS
8 ICE PLANT SPRIGS
SEA SALT

Warm the grapeseed oil to 70°C (160°F) in a small saucepan. Briefly poach the octopus suckers for 1 minute, remove and drain. Briefly poach the squid tentacles for 1½ minutes, remove and drain. Briefly poach the squid ribbons for 1 minute, remove and drain.

   Put the white soy sauce into a bowl. Keeping the three types of fish sashimi separate, put each type into the white soy sauce for 10 seconds then remove and drain. Put the sashimi scallops into the white soy sauce for 10 seconds, remove and drain. Put the oyster frills into the white soy sauce for 5 seconds, remove and drain.

   Wash the agretti and ice plant in cold water and dry. Break the white fungus into 16 small pieces.

06

TO PLATE

OYSTER CREAM (SEE BASIC RECIPES)
16 SALTED DAIKON TWISTS
   (SEE BASIC RECIPES)

In the centre of each serving plate, place half a tablespoon of oyster cream. Start building the reef by adding alternate layers of sashimi and poached seafood, interlaid with salted daikon twists and 3 half teaspoons each of dory roe and tapioca pearls. Finish with 2 eggwhite and smoked eel pearl flowers, white fungus, agretti and ice plant. Place one oyster frill near the front of the reef. Serve.

81

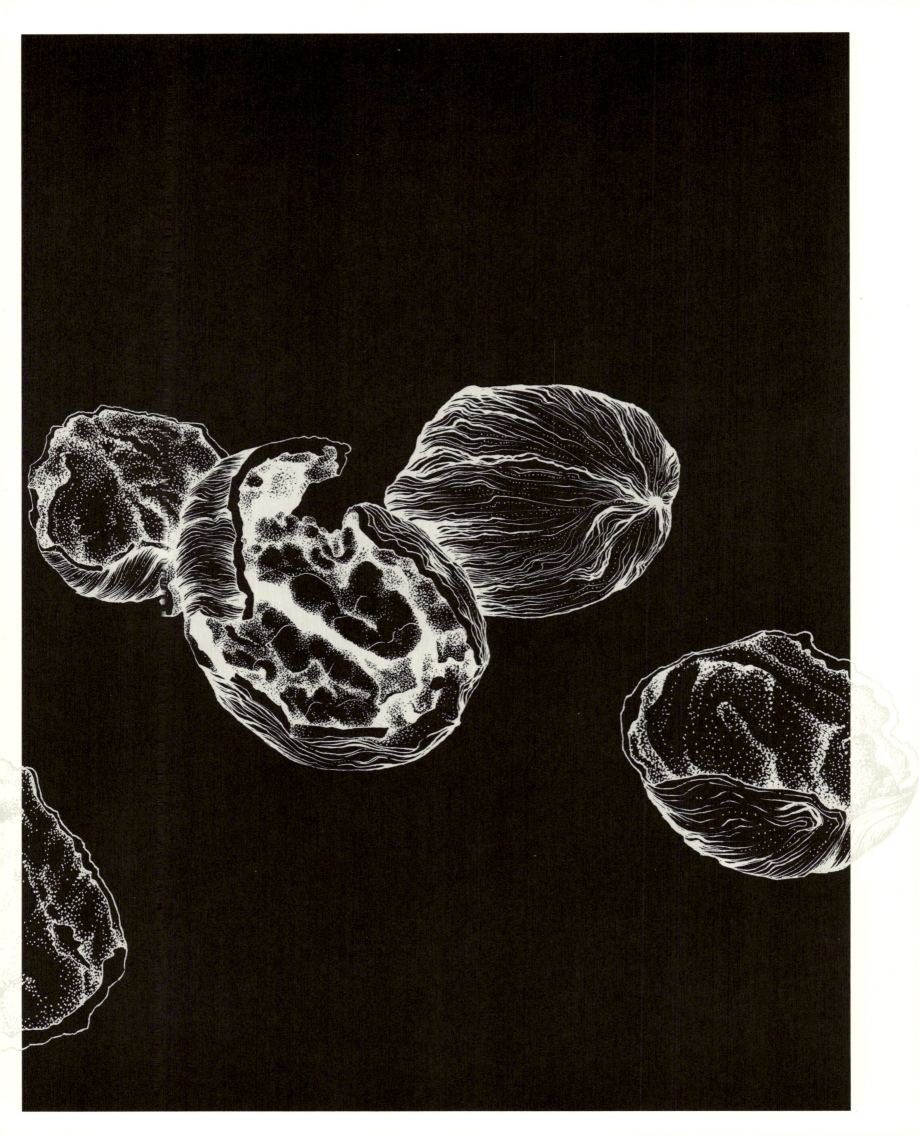

TEXTURE & SCULPTURE

THE THREE-DIMENSIONAL STRUCTURE OF THE ART THAT IS CUISINE LENDS ITSELF TO NUMEROUS POSSIBILITIES OF PRESENTATION.

WALNUTS / JUGLANS REGIA
HARVEST / AUTUMN

Texture has long played a major role in my cuisine. There are many elements that make a dish work—flavour marriages, temperature, visual structure, cultural influences and aroma—but of all of these the most direct and intimate part of the experience is texture.

When a single texture is wrong—rubbery eggs, overcooked pasta or a tough steak—you notice immediately and it can completely spoil the eating experience. When a texture is perfect, it is sublime. When textures are combined and play off and complement each other you really have something special; for example, the smoked and confit pig jowl, shiitake mushrooms, shaved scallops and Jerusalem artichoke leaves in this chapter is a dish that plays with texture on many different levels. The pig jowl itself is from a Berkshire pig with great intramuscular fat throughout the meat. The texture that is achieved by long slow cooking gives the pork an incredible mouth feel. Soft and yielding yet structurally sound, this—combined with silky, slippery shiitake mushrooms cut horizontally to maximise the external surface area of the mushroom, sautéed quickly in jamon, juniper and bay-infused butter—makes a great juxtaposition to the almost raw scallops. Both the scallops and the shiitake mushrooms mimic a different aspect of the fat from the pork. This dish is only completed by the texture of the crisp Jerusalem artichoke skins that play the role of the associated crackling that you enjoy when eating a roasted suckling pig.

Getting the combination of these textures in the right quantities at the right degree of contrast and pitch is a huge part of the process of creating a successful, texturally dynamic dish. This is why I feel texture is the most important element of a dish to get right.

Of course, everything else has to work on multiple levels for a dish to be truly exceptional. Another element that is of great interest to me is the sculptural nature of the food. Visual appeal is a very important aspect of creating a new dish. The three-dimensional structure of the art that is cuisine lends itself to numerous possibilities of presentation.

I feel there is huge scope for creating sculptural compositions by reflecting the ingredients in their natural state and environment. In my dish of walnut floss, bitter chocolate black pudding and fungi I wanted to create an organic structure that presents the various forms of fungi, including field mushroom gills, dried shiitake powder and shaved white truffles. The rapid reaction of the ammonium bicarbonate in the black pudding dumpling brings forth random attractive organic shapes, representing the intricate details found in nature.

The idea for this dish was sparked while I was enjoying Sunday yum cha with my family. One of my favourite dumplings, wu gok—which I have been eating in Chinese restaurants since I was a child—is a yam pastry with an external latticework of layered crispness encasing a mixture of moist savoury pork and seafood. I wanted to recreate the textural sensation of this dumpling: my first job was to find out how. I discovered that this traditional recipe relies on the combination of a small amount of ammonium bicarbonate and the natural starch of the yam. When fried at high temperature, the yam dough puffs and crisps giving a lacy effect. I decided to apply this technique to steamed walnuts and chestnuts instead of the traditional yam. I filled the dumpling with bitter chocolate black pudding then applied various shavings of fungi to enhance the organic nature and visual intricacies of the structure.

WALNUT FLOSS, BITTER CHOCOLATE BLACK PUDDING, FUNGI

SERVES / 8

BITTER CHOCOLATE
BLACK PUDDING

500 ML (17 FL OZ) PIG'S BLOOD (FRESH OR
   POWDERED AND RECONSTITUTED)
25 ML (1 FL OZ) SHERRY VINEGAR
50 ML (1¾ FL OZ) OLOROSO SHERRY
200 G (7 OZ) PORK BACK FAT, FINELY DICED
8 SMALL ESCHALLOTS, FINELY DICED
1 GARLIC CLOVE, FINELY DICED
80 G (2¾ OZ) DOUBLE CREAM (45–50% FAT)
100 G (3½ OZ) SOURDOUGH CRUMBS
10 G (⅜ OZ) FINE SEA SALT
100 G (3½ OZ) BITTERSWEET CHOCOLATE
   (72%), FINELY GRATED

Put the pig's blood in a bowl and add the
vinegar and sherry, then set aside. Take half
the diced pork back fat and render it by gently
heating it in a saucepan. Strain and discard
any solids. Put the rendered fat into a pan and
sauté the shallots and garlic until translucent.
Remove the pan from the heat and cool
slightly, then add the remaining fat and double
cream and mix well. Add this to the pig's blood
mixture in the bowl, then add the sourdough
crumbs, salt and chocolate.

You can make a traditional blood sausage
by filling fresh pig or lamb intestine skins and
poaching the sausages in water for about
25 minutes at 75°C (165°F) or, as we do in the
restaurant, you could place the blood sausage
mixture in a cryovac bag to a thickness of
3 cm (1¼ inches) and steam in a temperature-
controlled combi-oven at 75°C (165°F) for
25 minutes, carefully turning the bag halfway
through the cooking process to ensure even
cooking. Alternatively, you could cook it in the
cryovac bag by creating a water bath using a
large deep baking tray on the stovetop and
using a thermometer, carefully turning the
bag halfway through.

Allow the black pudding to cool, then
carefully remove it from the bag and cut it into
pieces as directed in the recipe. You can store
the black pudding in the refrigerator for up
to 4 days.

02

SHIITAKE MUSHROOM POWDER

24 MEDIUM TO LARGE FRESH SHIITAKE
   MUSHROOMS

Carefully peel the mushrooms, discarding the
skin. Slice the shiitake horizontally across the
mushrooms, from the top, making the slices
as thin as possible. Leave behind the gills.
Dehydrate the slices in a 100°C (200°F/Gas ½)
oven for 2–3 hours or until completely dry.

Process the dried mushroom flesh in a
spice grinder to a fine powder and store it in
an airtight container until required.

FIELD MUSHROOM GILLS

4 LARGE FIELD MUSHROOMS

Use a sharp paring knife to carefully scrape
the gills from the underside of the mushroom
cap, making sure they are completely
separated from the mushroom flesh: there
should be no white flesh attached. Reserve
the mushroom flesh for use in the roasted
chestnut and mushroom cream recipe on
the next page.

Put the gills in an airtight container,
covered with a damp cloth, and refrigerate
until required.

04

ROASTED CHESTNUT & MUSHROOM CREAM

400 G (14 OZ) WHOLE FRESH CHESTNUTS
RESERVED FIELD MUSHROOM FLESH
    (FROM FIELD MUSHROOM GILLS RECIPE)
2 SMALL GARLIC CLOVES, FINELY DICED
4 ESCHALLOTS, FINELY DICED
1 INNER WHITE CELERY STALK,
    FINELY DICED
150 G (5½ OZ) UNSALTED BUTTER
1.5 LITRES (52 FL OZ) CHICKEN STOCK
    (SEE BASIC RECIPES)
SEA SALT FLAKES
100 ML (3½ FL OZ) CREAM, LIGHTLY
    WHIPPED

Cut a small cross in the top of each chestnut and roast in a 180°C (350°F/Gas 4) oven for 30 minutes or until tender. Allow to cool slightly, then peel, removing the outer shell and inner skin.

Thinly slice the reserved field mushroom flesh and place in a medium saucepan with the garlic, eschallots, celery and 50 g (1¾ oz) of the butter. Sauté the vegetables over medium heat for 5 minutes or until softened. Add the chestnuts and chicken stock and reduce until virtually all of the stock has been absorbed into the chestnuts.

Put the mixture in a blender with the remaining unsalted butter, season with sea salt and blend on high until smooth. Pass through a fine drum sieve and set aside until required. Just before serving, gently reheat the chestnut cream then remove from the heat and fold through the whipped cream.

05

WALNUT FLOSS DUMPLINGS

100 G (3½ OZ) WHOLE FRESH CHESTNUTS
60 G (2¼ OZ) WALNUT KERNELS
200 ML (7 FL OZ) MILK
25 G (1 OZ) UNSALTED BUTTER
½ LEVEL TEASPOON AMMONIUM
    BICARBONATE
30 G (1 OZ) FINE GLUTINOUS RICE FLOUR
20 ML (¾ FL OZ) BOILING WATER
8 HEAPED TEASPOONS BITTER CHOCOLATE
    BLACK PUDDING
1 LITRE (35 FL OZ) GRAPESEED OIL

Cut a small cross in the top of each chestnut and roast in a 180°C (350°F/Gas 4) oven for 30 minutes or until tender. Allow to cool slightly, then peel, removing the outer shell and inner skin. Reserve and keep warm.

Place the walnut kernels and milk in a small saucepan and simmer for 15 minutes. Drain, discard the milk and use a small paring knife to peel the skin from the walnuts. Cover with a tea towel (dish towel) to keep the flesh warm.

While the chestnut flesh and walnut flesh are still warm, put them in a mouli grater fitted with the smallest attachment, add the butter and process. Sprinkle the ammonium bicarbonate over the chestnut mixture and mix through. Put the glutinous rice flour in a separate bowl, pour the boiling water over it and mix vigorously with a wooden spoon until it forms a ball. Using your hands, mix the chestnut and rice flour mixtures together until well combined. Cover with plastic wrap and set aside.

Scoop a tablespoonful of the mixture into the palm of your hand and use your other hand to flatten it to a disc 8 cm (3¼ inches) in diameter, approximately 4 mm (⅛ inch) thick. Place a teaspoon of the black pudding in the centre of the disc and fold the disc in half, pressing the sides together to form a half-moon-shaped dumpling. Repeat until you have 8 dumplings.

Heat the grapeseed oil to 190°C (375°F) in a deep heavy-based saucepan. Fry the dumplings in two batches in the hot oil for approximately 1–1½ minutes or until golden brown and puffed. Keep the dumplings warm.

06

TO FINISH

1 FRESH ALBA WHITE TRUFFLE,
    APPROXIMATELY 40 G (1½ OZ)

Reheat the roasted chestnut and mushroom cream. Finely shave the truffle.

07

TO PLATE

Dust the walnut floss dumplings with the shiitake powder. Top with shaved truffle and mushroom gills. Place half a tablespoon of roasted chestnut and mushroom cream in the centre of each warmed serving plate. Place a garnished walnut floss dumpling on top of the purée. Serve.

Sometimes a dish's simplicity can belie its complexity. To start with, this dish utilises David Blackmore's incredible 100 per cent pure Wagyu beef. The tenderness and complexity of flavour from the beef is a great starting point. The beef is cold smoked with a combination of hickory and maple wood chips. The gentle, mysterious flavour of the smoke permeates the beef. The umami richness of the 10-year-aged Korean soy sauce that dresses the beef adds another layer of savoury complexity. The addition of fresh salted dory roe enhanced with lemon zest gives a textural, salty and aromatic counterpoint to the beef. These textures are married together with the heat and lusciousness of the horseradish juice soured cream. The ethereal nature of the dried milk skin adds one more element of texture and visual appeal.

RAW SMOKED BLACKMORE WAGYU, FRESH DORY ROE, HORSERADISH JUICE SOURED CREAM, MILK SKIN

SERVES / 8

01

FRESH DORY ROE

400 G (14 OZ) FRESH SILVER DORY
  ROE SACS
2 LITRES (70 FL OZ) STILL MINERAL WATER
100 G (3½ OZ) SEA SALT

Freeze the silver dory roe sacs overnight to
ensure that any parasites are killed. Defrost.

Divide the water and salt equally between
two bowls. Place the roe sac in the first bowl.
Using a pair of sharp scissors cut the skin of
the roe sac to expose the roe. Gently remove
the roe from each sac, using a blunt knife to
gently scrape it out. Discard the skin.

Using a whisk, gently agitate the roe to
help separate the eggs.

Allow the roe to sit in the brine for
10 minutes. Carefully pour through a fine
drum sieve, discarding the brine.

Using a pair of tweezers, remove any
veins or blood vessels from the roe. Carefully
transfer the roe with a palette knife or plastic
pastry scraper to the fresh bowl of brine.
Gently agitate the eggs again using a whisk.
Allow to sit for a further 10 minutes before
once more pouring the roe through a fine
drum sieve. Remove any veins you may
have missed the first time. Allow the eggs
to drain completely.

Transfer the roe to an airtight container,
seal and refrigerate until required.

02

RAW SMOKED BLACKMORE WAGYU

800 G (1 LB 12 OZ) CENTRE-CUT BLACKMORE
  WAGYU RUMP
150 G (5½ OZ) MIXTURE OF HICKORY
  AND MAPLE WOOD CHIPS

Cut the Wagyu into 4 equal portions.

In a cold smoking apparatus smoke the
Wagyu over the wood chips for 1½ hours
being careful to keep the Wagyu at
a consistent 4°C (39°F).

03

**HORSERADISH JUICE
SOURED CREAM**

200 G (7 OZ) HORSERADISH ROOT
200 G (7 OZ) CRÈME FRAÎCHE
100 ML (3½ FL OZ) PURE CREAM (35% FAT)
SEA SALT

Peel the horseradish root and put it through
a juicer: this should yield about 25 ml (1 fl oz)
of juice. In a bowl, combine the crème fraîche
and cream with a pinch of salt. Mix in the
horseradish juice. If your horseradish is not
particularly strong, you can gradually mix in
more juice to taste. The cream should have
a strong flavour but not be too overpowering.

04

TO FINISH

80 ML (2½ FL OZ) 10-YEAR-AGED
  TRADITIONAL KOREAN SOY SAUCE
160 ML (5¼ FL OZ) EXTRA VIRGIN OLIVE OIL
1 LEMON, ZEST FINELY MICROPLANED

Cut the beef into 1 cm (⅜ inch) cubes. Dress
with aged soy sauce and 80 ml (2½ fl oz)
of the olive oil. Add the remaining olive oil
and the lemon zest to the fresh dory roe and
gently mix through.

05

TO PLATE

MILK SKIN (SEE BASIC RECIPES)

Place 100 g (3½ oz) of the dressed beef in
the centre of each plate. Spread out so that
the beef is roughly in a single layer. Top with
4–5 teaspoons of the dory roe. Drizzle the
dory roe and beef with the horseradish juice
soured cream and top with finely broken up
milk skin. Serve.

For me this dish truly represents my approach to cooking. The processes the ingredients go through make the dish far greater than the sum of its parts. The pork jowl is initially steamed in salted chicken stock for eight hours. It is then cold smoked over maple wood chips and finally confit in an infused jamon, bay and juniper butter. The fresh shiitake are peeled and shaved by hand across the mushroom.

The shiitake are sautéed in infused butter to re-emphasise the fragrance of the juniper and bay. The shiitake gain an intense umami dimension and a silky, slippery texture. This is then re-emphasised with the shaved almost-sashimi scallops that also mimic and build on the texture of the fat surrounding the jowl. These textures are all contrasted against the crisp Jerusalem artichoke leaves. The leaves themselves represent the crisp crackling associated with pork but have an earthy dimension to their flavour.

This dish builds intensity of flavour and texture through every process, ultimately creating what I consider to be the perfect dish.

SMOKED & CONFIT PIG JOWL, SHIITAKE, SHAVED SEA SCALLOP, JERUSALEM ARTICHOKE LEAVES, JUNIPER, BAY

SERVES / 8

01
PIG JOWL
2 WHOLE BERKSHIRE PIG JOWLS
500 ML (17 FL OZ) LIGHTLY SALTED
   CHICKEN STOCK (SEE BASIC RECIPES)
150 G (5½ OZ) MAPLE WOOD CHIPS

Blanch the two pig jowls in a large saucepan of boiling salted water for 1 minute, then remove and allow to cool. Place the jowls in a large cryovac bag and add the salted chicken stock. Seal the bag with a gentle amount of vacuum. Steam the jowls at 90°C (195°F) for 8 hours. Alternatively you could simmer the jowls in chicken stock in a casserole dish in the oven at 90°C for 8 hours; however, you will need to top up the stock occasionally so the cheeks remain submerged in liquid.

Remove the cryovac bags from the steamer and submerge in a bath of iced water to rapidly cool. Once completely cold, remove from the cryovac bag. Cut away all the skin and fat around the central piece of meat, leaving just 5 mm (¼ inch) of fat on top of the meat. Cut each jowl into 4 pieces, 3 cm (1¼ inches) wide by 5 cm (2 inches) long. Now set up a cold smoking apparatus and smoke the jowl pieces for 1 hour, until they are lightly perfumed with smoke. Cover and refrigerate the jowl until required.

02
BAY & JUNIPER INFUSED BUTTER
600 G (1 LB 5 OZ) CLARIFIED BUTTER
   (SEE BASIC RECIPES)
3 FRESH BAY LEAVES
10 JUNIPER BERRIES
10 SLICES JAMON

Put the clarified butter in a small saucepan and heat to 70°C (160°F). Bruise the bay leaves and juniper berries and add them to the butter with the jamon. Remove from the heat and allow to infuse for 30 minutes. Strain the butter, discarding the solids, and reserve until required.

03
JERUSALEM ARTICHOKE LEAVES
16 JERUSALEM ARTICHOKES
300 ML (10½ FL OZ) GRAPESEED OIL
300 G (10½ OZ) CLARIFIED BUTTER
   (SEE BASIC RECIPES)

Wash the Jerusalem artichokes in plenty of cold water, removing any dirt from the skins. Steam the Jerusalem artichokes until well cooked. While still warm, cut the Jerusalem artichokes in half lengthways. Remove the skin with a small paring knife, keeping the skin as intact as possible. Scrape the inside of the skin gently to remove any flesh that is still attached and set the flesh aside for another use. Allow the skins to dry at room temperature for an hour or so and then pat dry with a clean cloth. Heat the grapeseed oil and clarified butter together in a medium saucepan to 160°C (315°F). In batches, fry the artichoke skins gently until crisp and golden. Drain on paper towel and reserve.

04
WHITE SOY & SEAWEED DRESSING
150 ML (5 FL OZ) WHITE SOY SAUCE
1 TEASPOON DRIED WAKAME

Warm the soy sauce in a small saucepan to simmering point. Add the wakame. Remove from the heat and allow to steep for 10 minutes. Strain and discard wakame, then reserve the soy sauce until required.

05
TO FINISH
250 G (9 OZ) FRESH SHIITAKE MUSHROOMS, PEELED AND SLICED ACROSS THE MUSHROOM INTO 1 MM (1⁄32 INCH) THICK DISCS
8 LARGE SEA SCALLOPS, SLICED INTO 1 MM (1⁄32 INCH) THICK DISCS

Place 500 ml (17 fl oz) of the bay and juniper infused butter into a medium saucepan or in a bain-marie over a water circulator. Bring the butter to 70°C (160°F). Cut each piece of jowl in half lengthways, yielding 16 pieces. Heat the jowl in the butter for approximately 7 minutes until the jowl is completely heated through and almost falling apart.

Meanwhile, in a medium frying pan heat the remaining 100 ml (3½ fl oz) of the infused butter over high heat. Add the shaved shiitake mushrooms and sauté until lightly golden brown. Drain on a tray lined with a clean tea towel (dish towel). Line a baking tray with silicone paper, lay the sliced scallop discs out on the tray and lightly dress them with the white soy and seaweed dressing. Place the tray in the oven for 10 seconds to just warm the scallops.

Remove the jowl from the infused butter and drain briefly on a tray lined with silicone paper.

06
TO PLATE
40 WHITE SOCIETY GARLIC FLOWERS

Place 2 pieces of jowl in the centre of each warmed serving plate. Pile an even quantity of sautéed shiitake mushrooms onto each jowl portion. Place an even portion of warm dressed scallops on top of each mushroom pile. Garnish with the crisp Jerusalem artichoke leaves and white society garlic flowers. Serve.

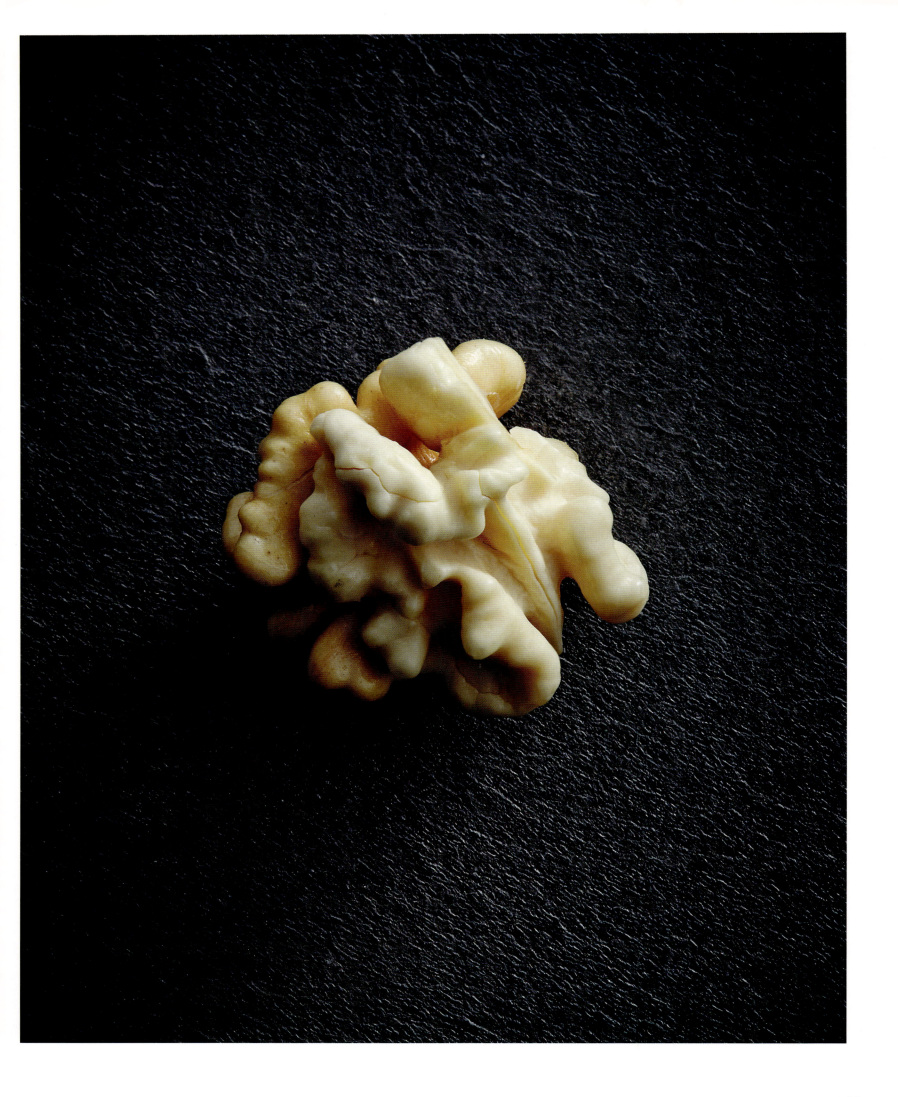

This dish is inspired by the classic pairing of chicken, cream and vin jaune. The chicken is poached on the bone in salted brine and then finished in cream. It is accompanied by the textural elements of fresh green walnuts and steamed brioche. Green walnuts are a seasonal treat available in early autumn: they have a milky crispness similar to green almonds and are skinned by hand to remove the bitter outer layer. The dish is finished with a reduced intense vin jaune emulsion and gai lan flowers.

CHICKEN COOKED IN CREAM, STEAMED BRIOCHE, GREEN WALNUTS, VIN JAUNE EMULSION

SERVES / 8

01

VIN JAUNE EMULSION

100 ML (3½ FL OZ) VIN JAUNE
20 G (¾ OZ) UNSALTED BUTTER
3 GARLIC CLOVES, PEELED
500 ML (17 FL OZ) FULL-CREAM MILK
5 G (³⁄₁₆ OZ) AGAR AGAR
FINE SEA SALT

Reduce the vin jaune over a low heat until only 30 ml (1 fl oz) remains. Set aside.

Melt the butter in a saucepan, add the garlic cloves and gently sweat them in the butter, being careful not to let them colour. Add the milk and bring it close to boiling point. Remove the pan from the heat and allow the garlic to infuse in the milk for 20 minutes. Pour the milk through a fine sieve into a clean saucepan, and discard the solids. Return the pan to the heat and then whisk in the agar agar. Reheat the milk to 90°C (195°F), continuing to whisk to activate the agar agar. Taste and season with sea salt. Refrigerate the milk and allow to set. Once set, put into a blender, add the reduced vin jaune and blend on high until a smooth paste is formed. The garlic cream should be the consistency of mayonnaise when reheated.

02

CHICKEN POACHED IN CULTURED CREAM

2 LITRES (70 FL OZ) CHICKEN STOCK
  (SEE BASIC RECIPES)
80 G (2¾ OZ) SALT
1.8 KG (4 LB) FREE-RANGE CHICKEN
200 ML (7 FL OZ) CULTURED CREAM
  (SEE BASIC RECIPES) OR CRÈME FRAÎCHE

Put the chicken stock and salt into a medium stockpot, just large enough to fit the chicken and stock, with a tight-fitting lid. Bring the stock to the boil and submerge the whole chicken in the stock, put the lid on and immediately turn off the heat. Remove from the stove and allow to stand on a bench for 1½ hours. Do not remove the lid.

Put the whole stockpot in the refrigerator or coolroom until the chicken and brine are completely cold. It is fine to do this the night before you plan to serve this dish.

Remove the chicken from the brine. Put the chicken on a chopping board and carefully remove the breasts with a sharp knife, keeping the skin on the breasts. Place each chicken breast in an individual cryovac bag with 100 ml (3½ fl oz) of cultured cream in each bag. Seal with a gentle pressure. Reserve in the refrigerator until ready to finish the dish.

03

WALNUTS

16 WHOLE GREEN WALNUTS
  IN THE SHELL
300 ML (10½ FL OZ) FULL-CREAM MILK

Working with one nut at a time, wrap the walnut in a tea towel (dish towel) and use a mallet to crack the shell. Remove the walnut halves or broken quarter pieces and peel the outer skin off the walnut with a small sharp paring knife. Immediately put each walnut into the milk to avoid oxidisation. Continue until all the walnuts are processed.

04

STEAMED BRIOCHE

1 EGG
150 ML (5 FL OZ) FULL-CREAM MILK
FINE SEA SALT
½ BRIOCHE LOAF, CRUST REMOVED
  (SEE BASIC RECIPES)
1 QUANTITY OF MILK SKIN (SEE
  BASIC RECIPES)

Combine the egg and milk together and season with a pinch of salt. Tear the brioche into 32 small marble-sized pieces. Soak the brioche pieces in the egg and milk mixture for around 30 seconds so that the brioche just absorbs a little of the liquid. Place the pieces in a single layer on a tray lined with silicone paper and put them in a steamer on high for 5 minutes or until just set. In the meantime, crush the milk skin into fine pieces and spread them in the base of a flat 20 x 30 cm (8 x 10 inch) container. As soon as the brioche pieces come out of the steamer, roll them in the crushed milk skin to coat. Place the coated brioche pieces onto a clean tray lined with silicone paper. Set aside until required.

05

TO FINISH

Preheat a water circulator to 68°C (154°F). Put the cryovac-packed chicken breasts into the water circulator and heat for approximately 15 minutes or until the internal temperature reaches 64°C (147°F). In the meantime, reheat the vin jaune emulsion.

06

TO PLATE

40 GAI LAN (CHINESE BROCCOLI) BLOSSOMS

Place half a teaspoon of vin jaune emulsion in the centre of each warmed serving plate and use the back of a spoon to spread it out into a 10 cm (4 inch) long thin strip. Remove the chicken from the cryovac bags and cut each breast into 4 even slices. Check that the chicken is at the point of being just cooked through: if you feel it needs further cooking, flash in a medium–hot oven. As the chicken was cooked in a brine it should not need further seasoning. Meanwhile, drain the walnut pieces from the milk, put them on a tray lined with silicone paper and gently warm for 1 minute in a moderate oven. Quickly reheat the steamed brioche at full steam for 1 minute. Place 1 slice of chicken along the strip of vin jaune emulsion on each plate, then place small dots of the emulsion all over the top and sides of each chicken slice. You could use a small plastic squeeze bottle for this step. Alternate walnut pieces, steamed brioche pieces and gai lan flowers all over the top and sides of the chicken. Serve.

BRAISED QUAIL

8 LARGE QUAIL
3.5 LITRES (122 FL OZ) CHICKEN STOCK
  (SEE BASIC RECIPES)
100 G (3½ OZ) SEA SALT
30 G (1 OZ) CLARIFIED BUTTER
  (SEE BASIC RECIPES)
1 ESCHALLOT, CHOPPED
1 INNER WHITE CELERY STALK, CHOPPED
1 GARLIC CLOVE, CHOPPED

Remove the quail breasts, still on the crown (breast bone), from the carcass. Reserve the legs, wings and trimmings. Combine 2 litres (70 fl oz) of the chicken stock with the sea salt to form a brine and heat to 60°C (140°F). Poach the quail crowns, maintaining the heat at 60°C for 20 minutes. Remove the quail from the liquid and allow to cool completely.

In the meantime, put the quail legs, wings and trimmings with the clarified butter in a frying pan and brown them over medium heat until golden. Transfer the bones to a clean saucepan and add the eschallot, celery and garlic and the remaining chicken stock. Simmer gently for 2 hours, skimming the top for any impurities. Strain, place in a clean pan and simmer for about 30 minutes or until reduced to about 200 ml (7 fl oz) of thin glaze.

ROASTED CHESTNUT CREAM

400 G (14 OZ) WHOLE FRESH CHESTNUTS
2 SMALL GARLIC CLOVES, FINELY DICED
4 ESCHALLOTS, FINELY DICED
1 INNER WHITE CELERY STALK,
  FINELY DICED
150 G (5½ OZ) UNSALTED BUTTER
1.5 LITRES (52 FL OZ) CHICKEN STOCK
  (SEE BASIC RECIPES)
SEA SALT FLAKES
100 ML (3½ FL OZ) CREAM, LIGHTLY
  WHIPPED

Cut a small cross in the top of each chestnut and roast in a 180°C (350°F/Gas 4) oven for 30 minutes or until tender. Allow to cool slightly, then peel, removing the outer shell and inner skin.

Place the garlic, eschallots, celery and 50 g (1¾ oz) of the butter in a medium saucepan and sauté over medium heat until translucent. Add the chestnuts and chicken stock and reduce until virtually all of the stock has been absorbed into the chestnuts.

Place the mixture into a blender with the remaining unsalted butter, season with sea salt and blend on high until smooth. Pass through a fine drum sieve and set aside until required. Just before serving, gently reheat the chestnut cream then remove from the heat and fold through the whipped cream.

BRAISED QUAIL, BRIOCHE PORRIDGE, ROASTED CHESTNUT CREAM, TRUFFLE, CHESTNUT FLOSS

SERVES / 8

03

BRIOCHE PORRIDGE

70 G (2½ OZ) UNSALTED BUTTER
10 G (⅜ OZ) AUSTRALIAN BLACK WINTER
   TRUFFLE (OR PÉRIGORD)
1 ESCHALLOT, FINELY DICED
½ GARLIC CLOVE, FINELY DICED
40 G (1½ OZ) DAY-OLD BRIOCHE CRUMBS
   (SEE BASIC RECIPES)
300 ML (10½ FL OZ) CHICKEN STOCK
   (SEE BASIC RECIPES)
2 TABLESPOONS CRÈME FRAÎCHE

Soften 20 g (¾ oz) of the unsalted butter and put it in a bowl. Use a microplane to grate the truffle over the butter. Add a pinch of salt, mix well and refrigerate until needed.

Heat the remaining unsalted butter in a medium saucepan and sweat the eschallot and garlic until translucent. Add the brioche crumbs and mix well. Sweat for a further minute. Add the chicken stock, mix well and gently simmer until most of the liquid has been absorbed. Whisk in the crème fraîche and reserved truffle butter. Gently simmer for 5–10 minutes, as you would for a porridge. Season to taste.

04

CHESTNUT FLOSS

200 G (7 OZ) STEAMED FRESH CHESTNUT
   FLESH (ABOUT 15 CHESTNUTS)
50 G (1¾ OZ) UNSALTED BUTTER
1 LEVEL TEASPOON AMMONIUM
   BICARBONATE
60 G (2¼ OZ) FINE GLUTINOUS RICE FLOUR
40 ML (1¼ FL OZ) BOILING WATER
1 LITRE (35 FL OZ) GRAPESEED OIL

While the chestnut flesh is still warm, place in a mouli grater with the butter and process. Sprinkle the ammonium bicarbonate over the chestnut mixture and mix through. Put the glutinous rice flour in a separate bowl, pour on the boiling water and mix vigorously with a wooden spoon until it forms a ball. Mix the chestnut and rice flour mixtures together until well combined. Cover with plastic wrap and set aside.

Heat the grapeseed oil to 190–200°C (375–400°F) in a deep heavy-based saucepan. Take a level tablespoon of the chestnut mixture in the palm of your hand and flatten until you have a 10 cm (4 inch) wide disc, 2 mm (1⁄16 inch) thick.

Fry the disc in the hot oil. The disc will appear to dissolve then crisp chestnut floss will appear on the top of the oil. Fry until golden brown, approximately 1–1½ minutes. Carefully remove the floss with a slotted spoon and drain well on paper towel. Repeat with the remaining mixture, straining the oil between each batch of floss. Once cooled, store the floss in an airtight container.

05

TO FINISH

30 G (1 OZ) AUSTRALIAN BLACK WINTER
   TRUFFLE (OR PÉRIGORD)
20 G (¾ OZ) UNSALTED BUTTER

Roughly grate the truffle.

Remove the skin from the poached quail breasts and carve the breast off the bone. Carve each breast into 8 even slices about 5 mm (¼ inch) thick.

Reheat the glaze over medium heat, adding the unsalted butter. Reduce heat to low, put the quail flesh into the glaze and reheat gently.

Gently reheat both the porridge and the roasted chestnut cream.

06

TO PLATE

Place 1 tablespoon of the chestnut cream in the centre of each warmed serving bowl. Top with 2 tablespoons of the brioche porridge. Place an even portion of braised quail on top of the porridge. Generously scatter the chestnut floss over the quail. Finish with grated truffle. Serve.

JOSEF GRETSCHMANN

ORGANIC DAIRY FARMER
DELORAINE / TASMANIA

Joe and Antonia firmly believe that organic farming principles not only take care of the environment but also produce healthier and tastier food.

Joe was born into a family of dairy farmers in a Bavarian village where every farmer made their own cheese. Joe studied agriculture then, in 1986, his sense of adventure led him to move to Australia with his wife Antonia. Soon afterwards, the Gretschmanns bought Elgaar Farm near Deloraine in northern Tasmania. They immediately set about converting the farm to a completely organic system. Joe planted herbs such as shepherd's purse, selfheal, chicory and Persian clover among the farm's grasses and installed a mixed herd of Jersey and Guernsey cows to produce the tastiest milk possible. The farm received official organic certification in 1991.

Joe and Antonia firmly believe that organic farming principles not only take care of the environment but also produce healthier and tastier food. Every one of their valued cows is given a name; they graze on lush organic meadows and in the pastures trees have been planted to provide shade from the sun and shelter from the weather. Josef prides himself on the fact that in the past 10 years he has only needed to call in a vet once and that was to help with a difficult birth. The Gretschmanns' cows are treated with respect and dignity. Any illness is treated with natural remedies: no antibiotics or hormones are used.

The Gretschmanns produce a great range of handmade cheeses, and old-fashioned non-homogenised milk and cream.

After visiting Joe and Antonia's farm a couple of years ago I made the decision to swap all my milk and cream requirements in the kitchen to Elgaar Farm. Once I had seen their dedication and tasted the quality of their milk I felt I could not use a lesser standard in terms of ethics and flavour. All of their milk and cream is delivered in glass bottles, which we return to them for recycling.

Josef and Antonia—along with other passionate farmers I have connected with—have convinced me that not only is growing organically and really looking after the land and soil vital to our environmental future, but that love and nurture of the land translates into real flavour.

RIGHT: A Jersey cow stands among a herd of Guernseys.

BELOW: Processing the fresh Jersey milk.

This textural dessert has an elegant simplicity to its form. The milk and sugar crumbs—made from dried milk skin, caramelised starch sheets and pulled butter toffee—present what appears to be a crystalline structure. At the core of the dish is a delicate just-set Jersey cream enriched with soft salted caramel. The textural interplay results in an exciting contrast on the palate. The sweetness is offset by the sharp astringency of the natural prune juice extraction.

JERSEY CREAM, PRUNE, SALTED CARAMEL, MILK & SUGAR CRYSTALS

PREPARATION / 2 DAYS
SERVES / 8

01

PRUNE JUICE SYRUP

1 KG (2 LB 4 OZ) UNPITTED PRUNES
200 ML (7 FL OZ) PEDRO XIMENEZ SHERRY

Put the prunes in a bowl and pour over enough warm water to just cover. Cover and soak overnight at room temperature.

Strain the prunes, reserving the soaking liquid. Slip the stones from the prunes and discard.

Put the prune flesh, soaking juices and sherry into a pressure cooker. Cook for 2 hours on full pressure. Remove from the heat, allow the pressure to subside, then pass the mixture through a fine sieve, pushing down with the back of a spoon to extract as much liquid as possible. Strain the prune juice syrup again through a fine sieve. Chill until required.

02

CUSTARD CREAM MIXTURE

75 G (2¾ OZ) EGG YOLK
1 EGG
100 G (3½ OZ) CASTER (SUPERFINE) SUGAR
450 ML (16 FL OZ) PURE CREAM (35% FAT)
2 VANILLA BEANS, SEEDS ONLY
150 G (5½ OZ) DOUBLE CREAM (45–50% FAT)

Whisk the egg yolks, egg and sugar together until pale and creamy. Bring the pure cream and vanilla to the boil and pour over egg mixture while continuously whisking.

Pass the mixture through a fine sieve, place in a cryovac bag and seal.

Steam the bag at 85°C (185°F) for 10 minutes then put it into an ice bath to stop the cooking process.

Measure 150 g (5½ oz) of the cooled custard and add the double cream, whisking them together until soft peaks form. Cover and refrigerate until required.

03

PULLED BUTTER TOFFEE

100 G (3½ OZ) TRIMOLINE (INVERTED SUGAR SYRUP)
100 G (3½ OZ) LIQUID GLUCOSE
60 G (2¼ OZ) UNSALTED BUTTER, SOFTENED
¼ TEASPOON SALT
½ VANILLA BEAN, SEEDS ONLY
20 ML (¾ FL OZ) WATER

Put all ingredients in a large heavy-based saucepan over high heat and whisk well to combine. Continue to whisk periodically, while you bring the temperature to 150°C (300°F): when it reaches this point it should be a nice golden colour.

Lay silicone paper on a heatproof bench and carefully pour the mixture onto the paper. Place another sheet of silicone paper on top of the mixture and use a rolling pin to roll out to about a 5 mm (¼ inch) thickness. Be careful, as the mixture is extremely hot. Allow the toffee to cool. Once cooled break into roughly 5 cm (2 inch) square pieces.

Put a couple of pieces at a time on a baking tray lined with a silicone baking mat. Place in a 170°C (325°F/Gas 3) oven for 2–3 minutes. Remove from the oven. When just cool enough to handle but still quite warm, use your hands to pull the edges of the toffee apart. You need to pull it until it is almost see-through. Cut the thick edges off with a pair of scissors. Repeat this process with the remaining pieces. Store the toffee shards in an airtight container with silica gel until required.

04

JERSEY MILK BAVAROIS

2 SHEETS OF TITANIUM-STRENGTH
   GELATINE
500 ML (17 FL OZ) FRESH JERSEY MILK
75 G (2¾ OZ) CASTER (SUPERFINE) SUGAR
250 ML (9 FL OZ) PURE JERSEY CREAM
   (35–40% FAT), WHIPPED TO SOFT PEAKS

Soak the gelatine leaves in cold water for
5 minutes.

Put the jersey milk and sugar in a
saucepan over high heat, stir until the sugar
has dissolved and bring to the boil. Remove
from the heat. Squeeze out excess water from
the gelatine leaves and add to the hot mixture.
Whisk well and pour through a fine sieve.
Cool over ice until the mixture reaches
around 14°C (57°F); that is, just before it
is about to set. Fold the whipped cream
through the chilled milk mixture.

Line 8 Asian rice bowls with plastic wrap.
Three-quarter fill the bowls with the jersey
cream mixture. Gently tap to make sure the
cream fills the bowl and there are no air
bubbles. Refrigerate for a minimum of 4 hours.

05

CARAMELISED STARCH SHEETS

500 G (1 LB 2 OZ) CASTER (SUPERFINE)
   SUGAR
500 ML (17 FL OZ) WATER
CANOLA OIL SPRAY
32 POTATO STARCH SHEETS, 8 CM
   (3¼ INCHES) SQUARE

Combine the sugar and water in a saucepan,
stir over high heat until the sugar has
dissolved then bring to the boil. Remove
from the heat and allow to cool completely.

Line a large baking tray with a silicone
baking mat and spray with canola oil.
Dip each starch sheet into the cooled sugar
syrup, holding the corners, and carefully lay
onto the silicone baking mat, leaving a small
space between each starch sheet. Put the
tray in a 180°C (350°F/Gas 4) oven until the
sheets become a deep golden colour, roughly
10 minutes. You may need to do this in
batches. Allow to cool and store in an airtight
container, with silicone paper in between
each starch sheet.

06

SALTED CARAMEL WHIP

250 G (9 OZ) CASTER (SUPERFINE) SUGAR
125 ML (4 FL OZ) WATER
175 ML (5½ FL OZ) PURE CREAM (35% FAT)
50 G (1¾ OZ) UNSALTED BUTTER, SOFTENED
10 G (⅜ OZ) FINE SEA SALT

Combine the sugar and water in a
heavy-based saucepan over high heat.
Stir just until the sugar dissolves, then bring
to the boil and cook without stirring until it
becomes a dark caramel. Remove from the
heat and carefully pour on the cream, very
slowly, as it will bubble up quite violently.
Return to the heat and stir until well combined
and smooth.

Remove from the heat and allow the
caramel to cool to 40°C (105°F). Put the
caramel in the bowl of an electric mixer with
a whisk attachment and whisk on medium
speed, gradually adding the softened butter
and salt until combined. Then whisk on high
speed until lightly aerated. Allow to cool at
room temperature. If not using straight away,
refrigerate until required, but bring it back to
room temperature before use.

07

TO FINISH

MILK SKIN (SEE BASIC RECIPES)

Remove the jersey milk bavarois in the rice
bowls from the refrigerator. Using a round
spoon, scoop a neat hole from the centre to
about half the depth of the bavarois in each
bowl. Rewhisk the custard cream mixture until
light peaks form. Spoon the custard mixture
into the hole in the bavarois and smooth over
so it is level with the surface of the bavarois.

In a large bowl, put equal amounts of the
milk skin, caramelised starch sheets and pulled
butter toffee and use your hands to break
them up into small pieces. Mix well.

08

TO PLATE

Place a tablespoon of the caramel whip into
the centre of each serving bowl. Spread out
with the back of a soup spoon until it makes
a circle just a little narrower than the diameter
of your bavarois. Make a small well in the
centre of the caramel whip. Pour 2 teaspoons
of the prune juice syrup into the well.

Carefully invert the jersey milk bavarois
with custard cream onto the caramel whip and
prune juice syrup and peel off the plastic wrap.

Take a generous handful of the combined
milk skin, caramelised starch sheets and
pulled butter toffee shards and place it on
top of each bavarois. Allow to form a natural
dome over the jersey cream. Drizzle around
the edges with an extra 1–2 teaspoons of the
prune juice syrup. Serve.

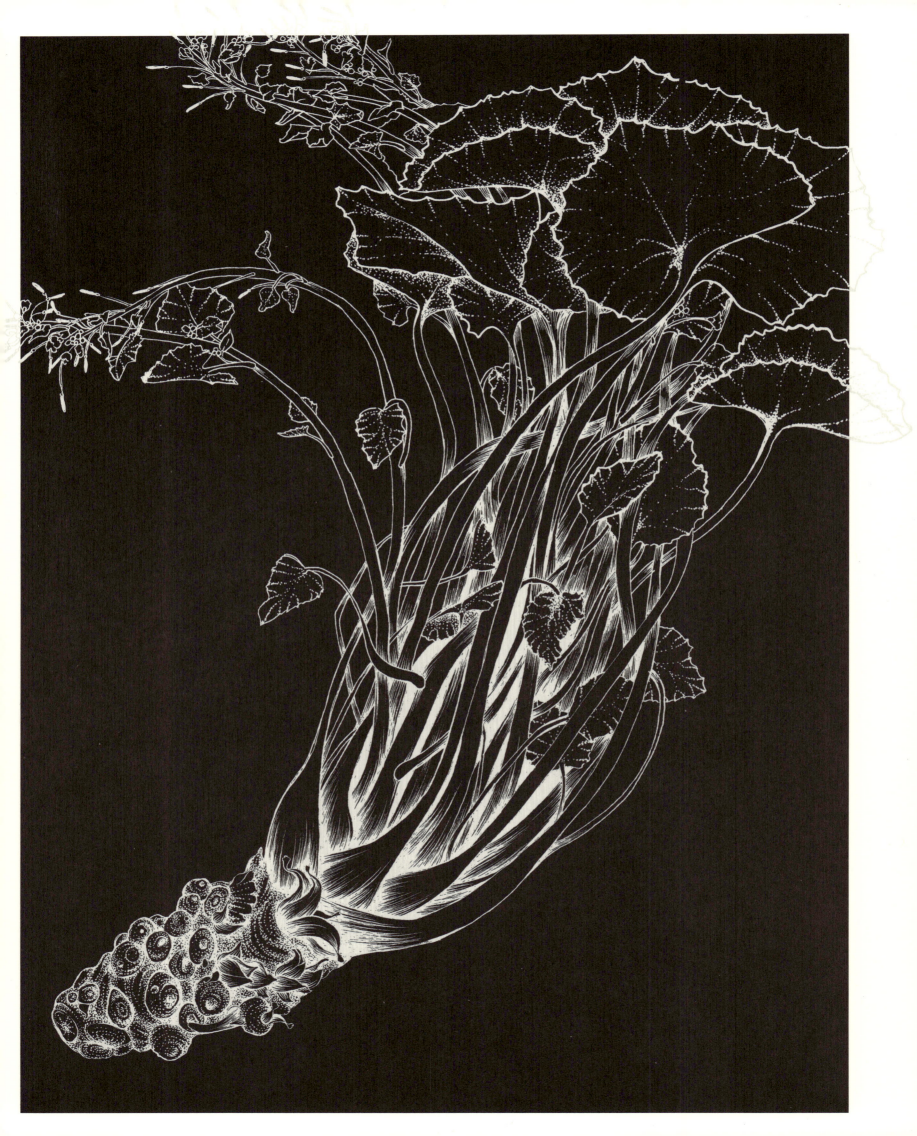

CULTURAL OSMOSIS

WHAT IS AUSTRALIAN CUISINE AND HOW IS IT UNIQUE? THIS IS THE QUESTION I AM ASKED MOST OFTEN BY INTERNATIONAL JOURNALISTS.

WASABI / WASABIA JAPONICA
HARVEST / AUTUMN

Because of our diverse immigration, the demand for authentic fresh ingredients from many cuisines has meant modern Australian chefs have a large palette of ingredients to work with.

Today's Australian cuisine is the result of exposure to a great variety of cultures, which have had a profound influence on the way we eat. I grew up being exposed to Italian, French, Chinese, Thai, British, Indian and Japanese cuisines. It was not unusual for my parents to take us to restaurants that served these traditional cuisines.

My mother learnt to cook Italian, French and Chinese food from friends and had a great interest in experimenting with many other national specialities. I would say that many Australians growing up in the 1970s would have had similar experiences. Australian palates today are very open to a wide range of flavours and without a traditional national cuisine our modern chefs have developed a freedom to explore without the restraints of cultural expectations of cuisine.

My culinary heritage is a multicultural one and this informs the way I think about food, the way I cook and the dishes I create.

Australia being a continent with a huge land mass has meant that it is possible to grow just about anything from anywhere in the world, somewhere in our country, whether it is the tropical north or the cool climates of the south. Because of our diverse immigration, the demand for authentic fresh ingredients from many cuisines has meant modern Australian chefs have a large palette of ingredients to work with.

The openness and influences of other cultures together with access to their particular cuisines' produce have formed the basis from which our country's modern cuisine has developed. It is not easy to define Australian cuisine, but the hallmarks are creativity and diversity with an understanding and respect for the traditions of many cuisines.

I have a real interest in Asian cuisines. Regional Chinese cuisines—with their emphasis on textural juxtapositions—and Japanese cuisine—with its respect for seasonality and emphasis on purity of flavour—really inspire and inform my food. This makes sense to me, as Australia is geographically close to Asia.

These influences are part of my story: they add their voice to my creative process and help me develop my version of a uniquely modern Australian cuisine.

01

GOOSE MASTERSTOCK

3.3 LITRES (115 FL OZ) CHICKEN STOCK
   (SEE BASIC RECIPES)
500 ML (17 FL OZ) NAMA SHOYU
   (UNPASTEURISED JAPANESE SOY SAUCE)
100 ML (3½ FL OZ) VIRGIN BLACK
   SESAME OIL
200 ML (7 FL OZ) FERMENTED PLUM JUICE
500 ML (17 FL OZ) OLOROSO SHERRY
1 LEVEL TABLESPOON LIQUID MALTOSE
60 G (2¼ OZ) GINGER, FINELY SLICED
100 G (3½ OZ) LONG GREEN SPRING ONION,
   WHITE PART ONLY
30 G (1 OZ) GARLIC, SLICED
15 G (½ OZ) CASSIA BARK
7 STAR ANISE
1 SMALL MANDARIN, PEEL
2 MUSCOVY GEESE, APPROXIMATELY 2.5 KG
   (5 LB 8 OZ) EACH

Combine all the masterstock ingredients
except for the geese and bring to a soft boil.
Reduce the heat to a low simmer and cook
for 1½ hours. Remove from the heat and allow
to cool completely. Strain the masterstock,
discarding the solids.

Put the masterstock into the pot of a
Gastrovac. Remove the legs and neck from
the goose.

Put the goose breasts, on the crown
(bone) into the masterstock, making sure both
are fully submerged. Place the pot onto the
Gastrovac and set it to 60°C (140°F) on full
vacuum for a period of 90 minutes.

Remove the pot from the Gastrovac and
immediately chill in the refrigerator, leaving
the goose in the masterstock until required.

02

FORBIDDEN RICE MIXTURE

20 ML (¾ FL OZ) GRAPESEED OIL
1 ESCHALLOT, FINELY DICED
1 GARLIC CLOVE, FINELY DICED
300 G (10½ OZ) KOREAN BLACK RICE,
   WASHED THREE TIMES IN COLD WATER
600 ML (21 FL OZ) CHICKEN STOCK
   (SEE BASIC RECIPES)
1.5 LITRES (52 FL OZ) GRAPESEED OIL,
   EXTRA, FOR DEEP-FRYING

Heat the grapeseed oil in a medium saucepan
and gently sweat the eschallot and garlic.
Add the rice and the chicken stock, bring to
the boil, then reduce the heat to low. Put a lid
on the saucepan and cook for 30 minutes until
most of the liquid has been absorbed and the
rice is tender.

Separate one third of the rice and set aside
to cool until required. While the remaining rice
is still warm, take 2 tablespoons at a time of
the warm rice and place between two pieces
of silicone paper. Use a heavy rolling pin to
press down and roll out the rice until the rice
grains flatten and clump together. Keep rolling
until you have formed a 1 mm (¹⁄₃₂ inch) thick
sheet of rice. Repeat this process until all of
the remaining rice has been processed. Dry the
rice sheets on the paper in a very low 100°C
(200°F/Gas ½) oven for about 30 minutes
or until stiff.

Heat the extra grapeseed oil in a deep
heavy-based saucepan to 180°C (350°F).
Fry the dried rice sheets in small batches until
puffed and crisp. Drain on absorbent paper.
Reserve the crisps and the cooled rice
until required.

---

*For this recipe I have developed an unusual masterstock based on oloroso sherry,
fermented ume (Japanese plum) liquid, raw Japanese soy sauce, Korean virgin black
sesame oil, liquid maltose, ginger, spring onions, star anise and cassia. With the use
of the Gastrovac, this intensely fragrant masterstock penetrates the goose flesh and
flavours and tenderises the meat. It also helps to break down the fat and skin of the goose
and the residual sugars penetrate the skin so that when the goose skin is later roasted
in a hot pan it will blacken and lightly caramelise without burning.*

03

BLACK MISO MIXTURE

1 TABLESPOON HIGH-GRADE, TRADITIONAL
    KOREAN BLACK MISO (SUBSTITUTE
    DOENJANG IF NOT AVAILABLE)
1 TABLESPOON CLARIFIED BUTTER
    (SEE BASIC RECIPES), AT ROOM
    TEMPERATURE
½ TEASPOON EXTRA VIRGIN BLACK
    SESAME OIL
2 TEASPOONS 10-YEAR-AGED KOREAN
    SOY SAUCE

Push the black miso through a fine sieve,
then combine with the rest of the ingredients
to form a smooth paste. Set aside.

04

HATSUKA RADISH

40 SMALL HATSUKA RADISHES

Peel the radishes and reserve in cold water
until required.

05

TO FINISH

250 G (9 OZ) SOY MILK CREAM
    (SEE BASIC RECIPES)
GRAPESEED OIL, FOR FRYING

Carve the goose breasts from the bone. In
a heavy-based ovenproof frying pan, heat
a drizzle of grapeseed oil on high heat and
place the goose breasts, skin side down,
in the pan. Transfer the pan to a 220°C
(425°F/Gas 7) oven and roast the breasts
skin side down for 5 minutes.

Measure out 8 tablespoons of the cooled
black rice and add 8 teaspoons of the black
miso mixture to this. Combine well. Put the
rice and miso paste mixture in a medium
non-stick frying pan, gently stir and heat.
Add 12 tablespoons of lightly crushed black
rice crisps. Combine well and heat through.
Keep the forbidden rice warm.

Blanch the hatsuka radish in a saucepan
of boiling water for 1 minute. Drain and
keep warm.

Remove the goose from the oven.
Cut each breast into two pieces and trim
to the desired shape.

06

TO PLATE

2 TEASPOONS VIRGIN BLACK SESAME OIL
2 TEASPOONS 10-YEAR-AGED KOREAN
    SOY SAUCE
WASABI FLOWERS

In the centre of each warm serving plate,
place a tablespoon of warm soy milk cream.

Place 2 tablespoons of forbidden rice
on the soy milk cream and place 5 hatsuka
radishes on top of the rice. Add a piece of
goose to each plate, drizzle with black sesame
oil and soy sauce and garnish with wasabi
flowers. Serve.

MY ROAST GOOSE, FORBIDDEN RICE, BLACK MISO, SOY MILK CREAM, HATSUKA RADISH, WASABI FLOWERS

SERVES / 8

This is a great example of cultural osmosis. For years, whenever the Quay staff had something to celebrate as a team we would end up in Chinatown. By far the most popular dish was live pipis from the tank steamed and served with XO sauce. XO sauce appears to have originated in Hong Kong in the 1970s, where the chefs all tried to outdo each other with the best version. It usually contains a good amount of dried chilli, and many umami-rich ingredients such as dried Chinese ham, dried scallops, dried prawns, mushrooms, ginger and garlic. About a year ago I decided to make my own version, inspired by the universal love for this sauce.

XO SEA

SERVES / 8

DRIED XO GARNISH

8 VERY THIN SLICES OF JAMON (SEE NOTE)
8 MEDIUM-SIZE FRESH SEA SCALLOPS
   WITHOUT ROE (SEE NOTE)
100 ML (3½ FL OZ) WHITE SOY SAUCE
8 MEDIUM-SIZE FRESH SHIITAKE
   MUSHROOMS (SEE NOTE)
150 G (5½ OZ) CLARIFIED BUTTER, MELTED
   (SEE BASIC RECIPES)
2 SEMI-DRIED MILD KOREAN RED CHILLIES,
   WHOLE
8 LIVE YABBIES

Lay the jamon slices on a baking tray lined with silicone paper and dehydrate under a heat lamp or in an 80°C (175°F/Gas ¼–½) oven until dry and crisp.

Slice the scallops into 1 mm (¹⁄₃₂ inch) discs. Brush the scallop slices with the white soy sauce and lay them out in a single layer on a baking tray lined with silicone paper. Dehdryate the scallops under a heat lamp or in an 80°C oven until dry and crisp.

Peel the skins from the shiitake mushrooms and brush the skins on both sides with clarified butter. Reserve the mushroom caps for another use. Place the skins on a baking tray lined with silicone paper and dehydrate under a heat lamp or in an 80°C oven until dry and crisp. If you are drying extra mushrooms for the stock you can dehydrate them at the same time.

Dehydration time for each ingredient will vary so you will need to use your own judgement. Note that all the dried ingredients need to be made on the day of serving this dish and need to be stored in an airtight container until service.

Soak the chillies in cold water for 5 minutes. Split in half and remove seeds. Scrape the flesh from the skin then gently cut the skins into 1 cm (⅜ inch) squares. Allow the chilli skins to dry naturally on a sheet of silicone paper at room temperature.

Place the live yabbies in a tub of iced water for 20 minutes to help humanely dispatch them. Blanch the yabbies in boiling water for 1 minute. Refresh in iced water. Peel the yabbies and discard the shells. With a sharp knife, remove the bright red skins from the yabbies and reserve. Refrigerate the yabby flesh until required.

Brush the yabby skins with clarified butter, lay them on a baking tray lined with silicone paper and dehydrate under a heat lamp or in an 80°C (175°F/Gas ¼–½) oven until dry and crisp.

NOTE / Ideally, while you are drying the ingredients for the garnish you should also dry some extra jamon, scallops and whole shiitake mushrooms for the XO sauce recipe; however, it is also acceptable to purchase the extra dried ingredients from an Asian grocery store.

02

XO SEA STOCK

100 ML (3½ FL OZ) GRAPESEED OIL
1 KG (2 LB 4 OZ) CHICKEN WINGS
1 SNAPPER HEAD
250 G (9 OZ) SQUID TRIMMINGS
1 SMALL BROWN ONION, CHOPPED
1 INNER WHITE CELERY STALK
½ CARROT, CHOPPED
250 ML (9 FL OZ) UNOAKED CHARDONNAY
2.5 LITRES (87 FL OZ) COLD WATER
250 G (9 OZ) CLAMS (VONGOLE)

Heat the grapeseed oil over medium–high heat in a stockpot or very large saucepan and add the chicken wings, snapper head and the squid trimmings. Turn occasionally until golden brown all over. Add the vegetables and continue to cook until the vegetables are lightly browned. Deglaze with the unoaked chardonnay. Once the wine has evaporated add the cold water. Bring to a simmer, skim and reduce heat to a low simmer. Cook for 2 hours.

Add the clams to the pot and bring back to the simmer. Simmer for a further 30 minutes. Strain through a fine sieve and discard all the solids.

Reserve the stock in the refrigerator until required.

03

XO SAUCE

200 ML (7 FL OZ) GRAPESEED OIL
75 G (2¾ OZ) GINGER, GRATED WITH
   A FINE MICROPLANE
75 G (2¾ OZ) GARLIC, GRATED WITH
   A FINE MICROPLANE
45 G (1½ OZ) MILD KOREAN RED
   CHILLI FLAKES
25 G (1 OZ) DRIED SCALLOPS (SEE NOTE)
50 G (1¾ OZ) DRIED SLICED JAMON
   (SEE NOTE)
50 G (1¾ OZ) DRIED WHOLE SHIITAKE
   MUSHROOMS (SEE NOTE)
150 ML (5 FL OZ) OLOROSO SHERRY
100 ML (3½ FL OZ) BROWN RICE VINEGAR
1.5 LITRES (52 FL OZ) XO SEA STOCK
500 ML (17 FL OZ) WATER
5 CM (2 INCH) SQUARE OF DRIED KOMBU
½ TEASPOON XANTANA (FERMENTED
   CORNSTARCH)
KOREAN FERMENTED ANCHOVY FISH
   SAUCE, TO TASTE

Heat the grapeseed oil in a stockpot or very large saucepan over medium heat. Add the ginger, garlic and chilli flakes and stir until well softened. Add the dried scallops, jamon and shiitake mushrooms. Sweat for a further 2 minutes. Deglaze with oloroso sherry and brown rice vinegar. Reduce on high heat until liquid has evaporated by half. Add the XO sea stock and water, and simmer very gently for 1 hour. Add the kombu square, remove from heat and allow to infuse for a further 1 hour. Strain the XO sauce through a medium sieve, allowing some but not all of the solids through. Lightly press on the solids in the sieve to extract the liquid. Put the XO sauce in a clean saucepan and bring it back to simmering point.

Transfer 100 ml (3½ fl oz) of the sauce into a small bowl. Sprinkle the xantana over the top and whisk well until smooth. Pour this back into the sauce, whisking over heat until smooth and slightly thickened.

Adjust the seasoning with Korean fermented anchovy fish sauce.

NOTE / See Dried XO garnish recipe, or purchase from an Asian grocery store.

04

SEAFOOD FOR POACHING

8 SEA SCALLOPS, ROE REMOVED
1 KG (2 LB 4 OZ) CLAMS (VONGOLE)
2 LIVE GREENLIP ABALONE,
   90 G (3¼ OZ) EACH

Slice the sea scallops into 2 mm (1/16 inch) thick discs and refrigerate until required. Steam open the clams and remove the gut sacs. Reserve the clam meat, refrigerating until required.

Meanwhile, place the live greenlip abalone in a large bowl of iced water for 1 hour to help humanely dispatch them. Use a large kitchen spoon to shuck the abalone from the shell. Trim away the viscera, leaving only the meat of the abalone. While the abalone is still in rigor, place it on a meat slicer and slice across the abalone to make 1 mm (1/32 inch) thick discs. Refrigerate until required.

05

TO FINISH

1 KG (2 LB 4 OZ) CLARIFIED BUTTER
   (SEE BASIC RECIPES)
RESERVED YABBY FLESH (SEE DRIED
   XO GARNISH RECIPE)
240 G (8¾ OZ) SQUID RIBBONS
   (SEE PAGE 54 FOR METHOD)

Heat 900 g (2 lb) of the clarified butter in a medium saucepan and bring to 70°C (160°F). Add the yabby flesh for 1 minute. Add the squid ribbons, sliced abalone, reserved clams and the sliced scallops. Stir to combine well and ensure even cooking. Cook for 1 minute further. All seafood should now be opaque in colour. Drain through a fine sieve.

Meanwhile, reheat the XO sauce to simmering point and heat the remaining clarified butter in a non-stick frying pan. Add all of the dehydrated XO garnish ingredients to the pan and cook over low heat to warm through.

06

TO PLATE

Place an even amount of the warm poached seafood in the base of each warmed serving bowl. Ladle over enough XO sauce to just cover the seafood. Garnish with an even quantity of dehydrated XO garnish ingredients. Serve.

STEPHEN WELSH

WASABI GROWER
LAUNCESTON / TASMANIA

'Our wasabi flowers have become one of our most important product lines, highly sought after by chefs all over the country. All thanks to that chance conversation with Peter and his enthusiasm and openness to try new things.'

Stephen and Karen Welsh, of Shima Wasabi, have been perfecting the art of growing Japanese wasabi in Tasmania for more than 12 years. This amazing plant is a semiaquatic herb, which evolved in the wild along the edges of high-altitude mountain streams in Japan. Its need for very specific cold-climate conditions makes it one of the world's most difficult crops to cultivate.

Stephen has developed a unique growing system utilising climate-controlled greenhouses and specifically designed hydroponics. The farm is located in the pristine environment of north-west Tasmania. Visiting Stephen's farm, it is apparent just how much time and investment in infrastructure the Welshes have devoted to produce their wasabi.

Thanks to their efforts, chefs all over Australia now have access to high-quality fresh wasabi.

Stephen has trialled several varieties of wasabi over the years and has asked me and other chefs for feedback to determine the best traits in each variety. This attention to detail has helped him to establish a reputation for producing the best wasabi in the southern hemisphere and to be able to supply chefs an exact, consistent product.

Regular communication with producers can yield unexpected results, and is the key to the evolution of products and ideas for dishes. Stephen says, 'I can still recall the telephone conversation I had with Peter several years ago when the idea of using fresh wasabi flowers came up. At the time we had never heard of anyone eating fresh wasabi flowers. I had mentioned the flowers in passing, noting that the wasabi plants were in bloom. Peter immediately asked what they looked and tasted like so we sent him samples. Much to our surprise he loved them and wanted more. As they say, the rest is history, and our wasabi flowers have become one of our most important product lines, highly sought after by chefs all over the country. All thanks to that chance conversation with Peter and his enthusiasm and openness to try new things.'

ABOVE: The wasabi roots take around two years before they are ready for harvesting.
LEFT: Wasabi plants in blossom.

KOJI

1 G (½₂ OZ) DEHYDRATED KOJI SPORES
(SEE GLOSSARY)
4 G (⅛ OZ) RICE FLOUR
1 KG (2 LB 4 OZ) JAPANESE KOSHIHIKARI
(SUSHI) RICE

Wash the rice in cold water several times to remove as much starch as possible.

Soak the rice in a couple of litres of cold water for 8 hours or overnight. Pour off all of the water and rewash the rice several times in changes of cold water to remove as much milky, starchy water as possible. This is an important step to ensure the rice does not stick together when steaming.

Wearing a face mask to avoid breathing in the spores, carefully mix the koji spores and rice flour. This process helps to spread the spores more evenly through the rice.

Line a steamer tray or basket with a double layer of muslin (cheesecloth). Put the washed and drained rice in the basket. Cover with muslin and steam on high for 1 hour. Once the rice has steamed, remove from steamer and open up the muslin. Allow the rice to cool slightly then break up the rice with your hands to separate all the grains. Using a digital thermometer, check the temperature of the rice.

Once it cools to 35°C (95°F), carefully sieve the koji spore and flour mixture over the rice. Mix thoroughly through the rice.

Take a clean double layer of muslin, wet it and wring it out. Place the koji rice in the centre of the cloth in a wide mound about 5 cm (2 inches) thick all over. Wrap the rice in the muslin and then wrap with two clean, dry tea towels (dish towels).

Now you can put the rice in a small styrofoam container with a lid or in an incubator set at 35°C (95°F). If using the styrofoam container, place it in a warm area of the kitchen with an outside temperature of 22–26°C (72–79°F). In colder climates you may need to place a 35°C water bottle inside the styrofoam container and replace it every 6 hours. The object, whether using the incubator or the styrofoam container, is to maintain the internal temperature of the rice, for the next 24 hours, at 32–38°C (90–100°F). This temperature range is critical for the mould to grow properly: too hot or too cold could kill the koji spores.

The koji rice will eventually start to generate its own heat. I would suggest checking the internal temperature of the rice with a temperature probe, every 4 hours. Monitor the rice closely, once it starts to generate its own heat you may need to decrease the temperature on the incubator or remove the water bottle or lid of the styrofoam box.

After 24 hours, unwrap the rice. You should see the beginning of the white mould forming around the grains of the rice. The koji rice should have a sweet bakery aroma. If the mould is any other colour than white discard the batch as you may have an inedible type of mould growing or it may indicate the koji rice has overheated and begun to spore. Start again from scratch.

If the mould is white and the smell is sweet, continue the incubation period for a further 24 hours; however, you should spread the rice into a thinner 2 cm (¾ inch) layer and rewrap in the muslin. This time do not wrap in the tea towels as the rice will now continue to generate its own heat. Return the rice to the incubator or styrofoam container and maintain the temperature at 32–38°C. After the second 24-hour period the koji rice should be ready. This time the rice should be coated in fluffy white mould and smell very sweet. At this point you can put the koji rice into airtight containers, cover and refrigerate for up to 4 days.

Alternatively, you can freeze the koji rice and store it for up to 3 months.

Koji is the starting point for Japanese staples such as miso, sake and shoyu. Aspergillus oryzae mould spores are grown on rice. Through fermentation, they convert hard-to-digest proteins, starches and fats into easily absorbed amino acids and simple sugars.

KOJI

PREPARATION / 3 DAYS
MAKES / 1 KG

01

SLOW-COOKED PORK BELLY
400 G (14 OZ) CULTURED CREAM
  (SEE BASIC RECIPES)
10 G (⅜ OZ) FINE SEA SALT
10 CM (4 INCH) SQUARE OF PORK BELLY

Churn the cultured cream into butter. Squeeze out any excess buttermilk, with your hands, under cold running water. This should yield 200 g (7 oz) of butter. Add salt to the butter and mix well.

Put the pork belly and butter into a cryovac bag and seal with light pressure. Steam in a water circulator at 90°C (195°F) for 10 hours.

Allow the belly to cool slightly and, while still in the bag, press it between two lightly weighted trays in the refrigerator, for a minimum of 4 hours.

02

SMOKED PORK RIB BROTH
100 G (3½ OZ) MAPLE WOOD CHIPS
2.5 KG (5 LB 8 OZ) PORK RIBS, CUT
  INTO PIECES
2 HAM HOCKS, SPLIT IN HALF
250 G (9 OZ) UNSALTED BUTTER
6 CHICKEN MARYLANDS
1½ BROWN ONIONS, CHOPPED
2 CARROTS, CHOPPED
250 ML (9 FL OZ) BROWN RICE VINEGAR
10 LITRES (350 FL OZ) COLD WATER

RAFT
15 G (½ OZ) DRIED JAMON, SLICED
50 G (1¾ OZ) DRIED CHESTNUT
  MUSHROOMS
1 CHICKEN BREAST
1 INNER WHITE CELERY STALK
½ ONION
½ CARROT
8 EGGWHITES

Set up a cold smoking apparatus with the maple wood chips. Cold smoke the pork ribs and ham hocks for 2 hours.

Melt the butter in a large stockpot and roast the pork ribs, ham hock, chicken marylands, brown onions and carrots until golden brown. Deglaze with the brown rice vinegar and reduce until most of the vinegar has evaporated. Add the water and simmer on low for 5 hours, skimming occasionally. After 5 hours, strain the stock and discard the solids.

Reduce the stock on a rapid simmer over medium–high heat for about 50 minutes or until you have 5 litres (175 fl oz) remaining.

Allow the stock to cool completely then remove any solidified fat from the surface. Make the raft by putting all of the ingredients except the eggwhites in a food processor. Process until well combined. In a separate bowl lightly whisk the eggwhites until soft peaks form and then mix them through the processed raft mixture until well incorporated. Put the cold stock on medium heat and immediately whisk in the raft. Continue whisking for 1–2 minutes and allow the stock to come to simmering point. Make sure the raft is not sticking to the bottom of the pot. Whisk one more time and then do not whisk again. Allow the stock and raft to very gently simmer for approximately 1 hour. The raft should be floating on top of the stock. Break a small hole in the raft and check that the stock beneath appears very clear. Remove the stockpot from the heat and allow it to sit for a further hour. Carefully ladle the stock from beneath the raft and pass it through a sieve lined with muslin (cheesecloth) to obtain a crystal-clear broth.

In this recipe I have decided to use koji-cultured rice as an ingredient instead of using it in its traditional fermentation role. The rice has a delicious sweetness and an aroma of freshly baked bread, which is enhanced by roasting. It is combined with sesame seeds and kombu, forming a textural layer on top of slow-cooked pork belly and ginger-infused milk curd; the dish is finished with a smoked pork rib broth.

03

INFUSED MILK FOR CURD

10 G (⅜ OZ) GARLIC, THINLY SLICED
8 G (¼ OZ) GINGER, THINLY SLICED
15 G (½ OZ) ESCHALLOT, THINLY SLICED
15 G (½ OZ) UNSALTED BUTTER
800 ML (28 FL OZ) MILK
SEA SALT

Gently sweat the garlic, ginger and eschallot with the butter in a saucepan over low heat. Be careful not to colour the vegetables. Add the milk and bring to 65°C (150°F). Remove from the heat and allow to infuse for 30 minutes. Strain the milk and discard the solids. Season to taste. Cover and refrigerate the infused milk until required.

04

ROASTED LAYERED KOMBU

50 ML (1¾ FL OZ) GRAPESEED OIL
3 SHEETS OF DRIED LAYERED KOREAN
   KOMBU

Put the grapeseed oil in a non-stick frying pan over medium–high heat and lightly pan-roast the kombu sheets until golden brown on both sides. Drain and allow to cool. Lightly crush. Store in an airtight container until required.

05

TO FINISH

250 G (9 OZ) CLARIFIED BUTTER
   (SEE BASIC RECIPES)
20 ML (¾ FL OZ) GRAPESEED OIL
150 G (5½ OZ) KOJI RICE (SEE PAGE 134)
50 G (1¾ OZ) WELL-ROASTED SESAME SEEDS
50 G (1¾ OZ) RICE LACE (SEE BASIC
   RECIPES), CRUSHED
25 ML (1 FL OZ) BROWN BUTTER
25 ML (1 FL OZ) VIRGIN BLACK SESAME OIL

Remove the pork belly from the cryovac bag and remove the skin with a sharp knife. Slice the pork belly into 4 mm (³⁄₁₆ inch) thick slices, then cut the slices into 3 cm (1¼ inch) pieces. You will need 8 pieces per portion. Melt the clarified butter in a saucepan to about 70°C (160°F). Add the pork belly slices and reheat for about 5 minutes, maintaining the temperature.

Meanwhile, put the grapeseed oil in a large non-stick frying pan over medium heat and fry the koji rice until golden brown. Remove from heat and add the sesame seeds, reserved crushed kombu and the crushed rice lace. Add the brown butter and sesame oil and reheat gently, combining well. Remove from heat and keep warm.

06

TO PLATE

8 ML (¼ FL OZ) LIQUID VEGETABLE RENNET
8 ML (¼ FL OZ) STILL MINERAL WATER
56 WASABI FLOWERS

Warm the infused milk to 30°C (86°F). Combine the vegetable rennet with the mineral water and add to the milk. Immediately pour an even amount of the milk into each bowl. This should set almost immediately. Remove the pork belly from the butter and drain on paper towel. Lay 8 slices of the pork belly over the set milk.

Bring the pork broth to the boil and pour 100 ml (3½ fl oz) of hot broth over the pork and milk curd. Spoon a generous tablespoon of the koji rice mixture on top. Garnish with wasabi flowers. Serve.

PORK BELLY, MILK CURD, ROASTED KOJI, SESAME, KOMBU, SMOKED PORK RIB BROTH

PREPARATION / 1 DAY
SERVES / 8

UMEBOSHI PURÉE

200 G (7 OZ) UMEBOSHI (FERMENTED
    JAPANESE PLUMS)
50 ML (1¾ FL OZ) SEMILLON VERJUS
    OR OTHER WHITE VERJUS
50 ML (1¾ FL OZ) KOREAN FERMENTED
    PLUM EXTRACT

Soak the umeboshi in 1 litre (35 fl oz) of cold water overnight. Drain and rinse well. Place the umeboshi, verjus and fermented plum extract in a small saucepan and cook gently over low heat until almost all of the liquid has evaporated.

Put the remaining contents of the saucepan in a drum sieve and push the flesh and juices through, discarding the seeds.

Cover and reserve the purée until required.

FRIED AMARANTH LEAF

SEA SALT
100 G (3½ OZ) BABY AMARANTH (CHINESE
    SPINACH) LEAVES
1 LITRE (35 FL OZ) GRAPESEED OIL

Bring a saucepan of water to the boil, season with sea salt and add the amaranth leaves. Blanch for 10 seconds then refresh in iced water. Squeeze the leaves to remove any excess water. Spread the leaves out on a silicone baking mat on a baking tray, place in a dehydrator or 100°C (200°F/Gas ½) oven for approximately 2 hours until the leaves are dry and brittle.

Heat the grapeseed oil in a large heavy-based saucepan to 180°C (350°F). Deep-fry the leaves in small batches until crisp. Drain well and set aside. Once cool, store in an airtight container until required. It's important to do this step on the day of serving.

DUCK POACHED IN GREEN PLUM MASTERSTOCK, UMEBOSHI, SPRING ALMONDS, AMARANTH

PREPARATION / 1 DAY
SERVES / 8

03
POACHED DUCK

2 WHOLE DUCKS, 2 KG (4 LB 8 OZ) EACH
1 QUANTITY OF GOOSE MASTERSTOCK
   (SEE MY ROAST GOOSE RECIPE,
   PAGE 122)
50 ML (1¾ FL OZ) GRAPESEED OIL
1 BROWN ONION, CHOPPED
1 CARROT, CHOPPED
1 LITRE (35 FL OZ) CHICKEN STOCK
   (SEE BASIC RECIPES)

Put the masterstock in the pot of a Gastrovac. Remove the legs and necks from the ducks and reserve.

Put the duck breasts, on the crown (bone) into the masterstock, making sure they are fully submerged. Place the pot onto the Gastrovac and set it to 60°C (140°F) on full vacuum for a period of 90 minutes. The Gastrovac method means that you can cook under a vacuum so that the liquid will boil and cook the protein at a lower temperature.

Remove the pot from the Gastrovac and immediately chill in the refrigerator, leaving the duck in the masterstock until required.

Once the duck has cooled in the refrigerator, cut the breasts from the bone and reserve the breasts in the refrigerator. Sauté the remaining carcasses, including the legs, in a heavy-based saucepan with the grapeseed oil, onion and carrot. Once golden brown, add the chicken stock and simmer for 2 hours on low heat. Strain, discarding the solids, and return the liquid to the boil and reduce to a thick glaze. Set aside until required.

04
SPRING ALMONDS

64 GREEN (SPRING) ALMONDS IN
   THE SHELL
MILK, TO COVER

Remove the outer green shell and the inner papery skin from the almond kernels. Split each almond in half along its natural seam. To avoid browning, store the split almond kernels in milk, in the refrigerator until required.

05
TO FINISH

30 G (1 OZ) UNSALTED BUTTER
SEA SALT

Remove the skin from the reserved duck breasts. Put the breasts and reduced glaze into a cryovac bag, seal and place in a water circulator at 55°C (130°F) for 10 minutes or until the duck breasts are warmed through.

Remove the duck from the bag and cut each breast in half on the diagonal to make 8 portions. Place the breast portions on a baking tray lined with silicone paper, spoon over the remaining glaze from the bag and flash in a 200°C (400°F/Gas 6) oven for 30 seconds.

Meanwhile, gently heat the umeboshi purée in a small saucepan. Remove the almonds from the milk and warm in a small saucepan with the butter and season with sea salt.

06
TO PLATE

Place 2 teaspoons of umeboshi purée in the centre of each warmed serving plate. Use the back of the spoon to spread it out a little.

Place a portion of hot duck breast on the purée. Garnish with fried amaranth leaves and spring almonds. Serve.

This recipe is a good example of the need to sometimes pare back overassertive flavours. Umeboshi has a wonderful flavour but it is intensely salty and sour. The umeboshi purée is tempered by soaking the heavily salted and fermented ume overnight in water and gently cooking in verjuice and fermented plum extract. If I were to use the umeboshi without this process it would completely dominate the flavour of the duck. This way the flavours are strong but in balance with each other.

PAUL LEE

ASIAN DRY GOODS SUPPLIER
MELBOURNE / VICTORIA

'Peter's vision and creative mind have taught us a great deal and have even made us search harder for new products, which we now include on our list.'

Paul and his wife Idylle Lee set up Table 181 in October 2011 with the view to introducing artisanal Korean ingredients and products into Australia. The couple felt strongly that the mass-produced products that were available at the time were not a great representation of what true Korean cuisine had to offer.

They made it their mission to search for traditionally made products that used long, slow labour-intensive processes like fermentation or sun-drying to achieve depth of flavour far superior to that of the mass-market, chemically assisted alternatives which had become a byproduct of Korea's fast-paced modern lifestyle. These traditional products are made in small quantities, by only a handful of dedicated artisans who utilise knowledge that has been passed down through the generations.

Paul is a supplier driven by passion, with an inherent understanding of great food. He is willing to search the length and breadth of his homeland to find exceptional products, in which flavour is the paramount concern. A great example of this was when I asked Paul to find the finest quality cold-pressed extra virgin white sesame oil, which he did; I then asked him whether anyone produced a virgin oil utilising black sesame seeds. Through growing sesame myself, I was aware that the seeds came in black, tan and white varieties, each with their own subtlety of flavour. It took Paul three months to find a small artisan producer who made virgin sesame oil using black seeds, as this is not common practice. The result is one of the most perfumed, intensely flavoured oils I've ever tried and is now a treasured ingredient that I've incorporated into quite a few of my recipes.

Says Paul, 'Chef Peter Gilmore was our first customer. Peter has an amazing palate and memory of taste and a great ability to connect raw ingredients with our products. We are constantly amazed at his creations and his ability to draw out the best from our products. His vision and creative mind have taught us a great deal and have even made us search harder for new products, which we now include on our list.'

This dish was inspired by the tradition in which rice is heated in a large stone pot so that the rice becomes crispy on the outside edge and soft in the centre. In my version I wanted to emphasise the textural contrasts of the ingredients. The slow-cooked lightly smoked pork cheek plays off against the crisp organic green rice; the silken tofu works beautifully against the roasted crisp seaweed, shiitake skins and rice lace. The flavours of aged soy and roasted virgin black sesame oil add depth and intrigue to the dish.

STONEPOT ORGANIC GREEN RICE & BUCKWHEAT, ROASTED SEAWEED, SHIITAKE SKIN, PIG CHEEK

SERVES / 8

01

SMOKY PORK CHEEK

1 KG (2 LB 4 OZ) SKINLESS, BONELESS
  PORK CHEEK
150 G (5½ OZ) MAPLE WOOD CHIPS
15 G (½ OZ) SEA SALT
300 G (10½ OZ) CLARIFIED BUTTER, MELTED
  (SEE BASIC RECIPES)

Put the pork cheek into a cold smoking
apparatus and smoke for 1 hour with the
maple wood chips.

Remove the pork from the smoker and
season liberally with the sea salt, rubbing it in
all over. Put the pork cheek in a cryovac bag
with the clarified butter. Seal and steam in a
water circulator or combi-oven at 85°C (185°F)
for 8 hours. Refresh in iced water. Store, in the
bag, in the refrigerator until required.

02

GREEN RICE

1 SMALL GARLIC CLOVE, FINELY DICED
1 ESCHALLOT, FINELY DICED
25 ML (1 FL OZ) GRAPESEED OIL
225 G (8 OZ) KOREAN GREEN RICE
250 ML (9 FL OZ) CHICKEN STOCK
  (SEE BASIC RECIPES)

Lightly sweat the garlic and eschallot in the
grapeseed oil. Add the green rice and stir well.
Add the chicken stock so that it just covers
the rice. Cover the rice with a cartouche.
Cook over low heat for approximately
20–25 minutes or until rice is just tender.
Alternatively, cook in a rice cooker. Store,
covered, in the refrigerator until required.

03

DRIED SHIITAKE SKINS

8 LARGE FRESH SHIITAKE MUSHROOMS
1 TABLESPOON CLARIFIED BUTTER, MELTED
  (SEE BASIC RECIPES)

Wipe the mushrooms with a clean, slightly
damp cloth, being careful not to tear the skin.
Using your hands, remove the skins from the
mushrooms. Reserve the mushroom flesh for
another use.

Put the shiitake skins on a baking tray
lined with silicone paper and brush with a
light coating of clarified butter on both sides.
Dry the shiitake skins under a heat lamp or in
a 100°C (200°F/Gas ½) oven for 45 minutes
or until dry and crisp. The butter lightly
caramelises the skins as they are drying.
Once dry and caramelised, remove the skins
from the tray and allow to cool on a fresh
sheet of silicone paper. Store in an airtight
container until required.

04

SEAWEED & SESAME SEED MIXTURE

GRAPESEED OIL, FOR FRYING
3 SHEETS OF COMPRESSED LAYERED
  DRIED KOREAN KOMBU
3 SHEETS OF SOY-SEASONED KOREAN
  TOASTED NORI
3 SHEETS OF RICE LACE (SEE BASIC
  RECIPES)
2 TABLESPOONS WHITE SESAME SEEDS,
  TOASTED
1 QUANTITY OF DRIED SHIITAKE SKINS

Put 2 teaspoons of grapeseed oil into a
non-stick frying pan over medium heat. When
hot, add 1 sheet of the layered kombu and fry
until lightly golden on both sides. Remove
and drain. Repeat with the remaining kombu
sheets, adding more oil as necessary. Allow to
cool completely.

In a mixing bowl, break the layered kombu
into small rough pieces, approximately 5 mm
(¼ inch) square. Repeat with the toasted
nori and rice lace. Add sesame seeds and the
shiitake skins and mix well. Store in an airtight
container until required.

05
ROASTED BUCKWHEAT
200 G (7 OZ) RAW BUCKWHEAT KERNELS
750 ML (26 FL OZ) GRAPESEED OIL

Put the buckwheat into a saucepan and cover well with cold water. Bring to the boil and cook for approximately 15 minutes or until tender.

Drain well and dry out under a heat lamp or in a 100°C (200°F/Gas ½) oven for approximately 1 hour until completely dehydrated and hard.

Heat the grapeseed oil in a deep saucepan to 190°C (375°F) and add the buckwheat in three separate batches. The buckwheat should slightly puff and become golden in colour. Drain on kitchen paper, cool and store in an airtight container.

06
TO FINISH
4 TABLESPOONS CLARIFIED BUTTER
  (SEE BASIC RECIPES)
250 G (9 OZ) SILKEN TOFU
4 GOLF-BALL-SIZED KABU (JAPANESE WHITE
  TURNIPS), PEELED AND THINLY SHAVED
150 G (5½ OZ) PICKED AND WASHED GOLDEN
  ORACH (MOUNTAIN SPINACH) LEAVES
8 ROUNDED SHEETS OF KOREAN ROCKWEED
1 TABLESPOON VIRGIN BLACK SESAME OIL
1 TABLESPOON 10-YEAR-AGED KOREAN
  SOY SAUCE
SEA SALT

Return the cryovac-packed pork cheek to a steamer or combi-oven at 85°C (185°F) and reheat for 15–20 minutes or until hot.

Put 1 tablespoon of the clarified butter in a large non-stick frying pan, add the cooked green rice and fry over high heat for approximately 3–4 minutes, turning the rice periodically. For the last minute, do not stir the rice: a golden crust will form on the base.

Meanwhile, cut the tofu into 8 equal pieces and steam gently until warmed through.

Blanch the shaved white turnips for 20 seconds. Remove and drain. Add the orach for 10 seconds, remove and drain. Brush the turnips and the orach generously with 1 tablespoon of melted clarified butter and season to taste.

Fry the rockweed sheets in 1 tablespoon of the clarified butter.

Once the rice has formed a golden crust add the roasted buckwheat and mix together with the rice. Add the sesame oil and soy sauce and combine well.

Remove the pork cheek from the cryovac bag and drain off the butter. Put the pork into a bowl and use a fork to break into rough shreds.

Reheat the seaweed and sesame mixture in a frying pan with the remaining tablespoon of clarified butter.

07
TO PLATE
SMOKED PORK RIB BROTH (SEE PAGE 136)
40 BEAN FLOWERS

Place a square of steamed tofu in the base of each serving bowl. Top with kabu and golden orach. Add 2 tablespoons of warm shredded pork cheek and 3 tablespoons of rice mixture. Add 3 tablespoons of smoked pork rib broth and 1 tablespoon of the seaweed and sesame mixture. Top with the rockweed. Garnish with 5 bean flowers per plate. Serve.

ELEMENTS OF INTENSITY

THE FLAVOUR INTENSITY OF A DISH IS A VITAL COMPONENT OF ITS SUCCESS, AND THE IMPACT CAN TRIGGER STRONG EMOTIONAL RESPONSES.

SHIITAKE MUSHROOMS / LENTINULA EDODES
HARVEST / WINTER

The overall impact of applying different techniques to a single ingredient is a stronger expression of the inherent flavour contained within that ingredient.

The flavour intensity of a dish is a vital component of its success, and the impact can trigger strong emotional responses, touching on memories of a time, place or situation ... and feelings of nurture and love.

Extracting clear and intense flavour is a very important process, but balancing the degree of intensity of that flavour is crucial for the overall harmony of the dish.

Intensity and complexity of flavour can be achieved in numerous ways: one of the most obvious being to concentrate flavour through slow reduction. Another way is through fermentation, in which flavours of a very complex nature can develop. The simple act of lightly salting a sliced mushroom, sealing it in a vacuum bag and allowing it to ferment at room temperature for 48 hours will produce an intensity that is far beyond the sum of its parts. Just simply sautéing these fermented mushrooms in butter and accompanying them with a piece of aged beef will raise the complexity of the flavour spectrum considerably.

For me, the act of salt-curing and sun-drying is akin to alchemy. Take mullet roe, for example: salt-curing it to extract the water content and then drying it slowly in the sun creates an intense, salty umami-enriched flavour with unique complexity. A similar level of intensity is achieved by dry-ageing meat.

Umami-rich foods are a great source of savoury intensity and the layering of these ingredients—as I demonstrate in the umami consommé—provides a deeply satisfying, rounded taste experience.

In my textural mushrooms, eggplants and miso dish, I demonstrate the complexity of flavour that can be achieved by manipulating a single ingredient, through a combination of techniques such as dehydrating, fermenting or even highlighting a less obvious part of an ingredient, such as the raw gills of a field mushroom. Even the way you slice an ingredient can influence the flavour by exposing more surface area. The overall impact of applying different techniques to a single ingredient is a stronger expression of the inherent flavour contained within it.

The sense of smell, strongly connected to memory, can play an integral role in the intensity of a dish. Perfume and aroma are powerful tools for stimulating the appetite and anticipating the experience to come.

A good example of this is found in my slow-cooked pig cheek, prunes, cauliflower cream, maltose crackling perfumed with prune kernel oil recipe. When the marzipan-scented prune kernel oil is drizzled onto the surface of the hot maltose crackling, it hits the diner's olfactories, inviting them into the dish containing intensely flavoured, slow-cooked prunes, and the overall eating experience is greatly enhanced.

When creating a new dish, careful consideration is given to texture, structure, ingredients and flavours. When it comes to flavour, intensity is the main consideration, and the way flavours work together, the way they stand alone, their strength or subtlety are all part of the process of creating impact.

The savoury complexity of this consommé is really the star of my squab and abalone dish. This consommé is an intricate layering of umami-rich ingredients starting with roasted fish heads, squid trimmings, scallop trimmings, chicken wings and stock vegetables. The stock is made and finished with a kilogram of fresh clams releasing their salty sea juices. It is then enriched and refined with a raft of dried shiitake and chestnut mushrooms, kombu and wakame seaweed, then finished with fermented anchovy brine. Umami is referred to as the fifth taste, the savoury element that is found in glutamate and ribonucleotide-rich foods such as fermented fish sauce, parmesan cheese, ripe tomatoes, kombu seaweed and shiitake mushrooms. This experience of savouriness is found in different combinations in most cuisines around the world, but it was first scientifically identified by Professor Kikunae Ikeda in 1908. One of his most important discoveries was that combining glutamate-rich foods—such as kombu seaweed—with foods that contain ribonucleotides—such as dried bonito flakes—makes the umami effect much greater, which explains the impact of the classic Japanese dashi stock.

UMAMI CONSOMMÉ

MAKES / 1.5–2 LITRES (52–70 FL OZ)

01

STOCK

2 SNAPPER HEADS, SPLIT IN HALF
   (ASK YOUR FISHMONGER TO DO THIS
   FOR YOU)
100 ML (3½ FL OZ) GRAPESEED OIL
2 KG (4 LB 8 OZ) CHICKEN WINGS, CHOPPED
500 G (1 LB 2 OZ) SQUID TRIMMINGS
500 G (1 LB 2 OZ) SEA SCALLOP TRIMMINGS
   OR SMALL SEA SCALLOPS
4 SMALL FENNEL BULBS, 3 DICED AND
   1 CHOPPED
4 INNER WHITE CELERY STALKS, DICED
½ BROWN ONION, DICED
250 G (9 OZ) UNSALTED BUTTER
2 GARLIC CLOVES, DICED
200 ML (7 FL OZ) GOOD-QUALITY
   APPLE VINEGAR
750 ML BOTTLE DRY UNOAKED
   CHARDONNAY
3 LITRES (105 FL OZ) CHICKEN STOCK
   (SEE BASIC RECIPES)
1 KG (2 LB 4 OZ) CLAMS (VONGOLE),
   SHELLS WELL SCRUBBED

Remove and discard the eyes and gills from the halved snapper heads, then wash thoroughly under running water to remove the excess blood. Pan-roast the snapper heads in a large saucepan with the grapeseed oil until lightly coloured. Add the chicken wings, squid and sea scallop trimmings and cook until the chicken wings and seafood are well coloured. Add the 3 diced fennel bulbs to the pan along with the celery, onion and butter. Continue to pan-roast the ingredients in the butter until everything is golden brown, stirring and scraping the base of the pan with a wooden spoon to make sure the ingredients are not sticking. Add the garlic and deglaze with the apple vinegar until almost all of the vinegar has evaporated. Stir and scrape well so that all of the brown bits on the bottom of the pan are dissolved. Add the wine and reduce until almost all of the wine has evaporated, then add the chicken stock and 2 litres (70 fl oz) of water and bring to simmering point.

Reduce the heat until the liquid is barely moving and cook over low heat for 2 hours. Do not remove the butter from the surface of the stock at this point, as the flavour of the butter will infuse with the stock. After 2 hours, add the clams to the stock, then add the chopped fennel.

Remove the pan from the heat and allow all the ingredients to infuse for 30 minutes. Carefully strain the stock through a fine sieve and discard the solids. Now you can remove any oil or butter from the surface of the stock with a small ladle. Strain the stock through a sieve lined with muslin (cheesecloth) into a clean stockpot or very large saucepan and allow to cool.

02

RAFT

2 SMALL CHICKEN BREASTS, SKIN REMOVED
150 G (5½ OZ) DRIED CHESTNUT
   MUSHROOMS
20 G (¾ OZ) DRIED KOMBU, BROKEN
   INTO SMALL PIECES
20 G (¾ OZ) DRIED WAKAME
10 EGGWHITES
FERMENTED ANCHOVY BRINE, TO SEASON

Meanwhile, to make a raft for the consommé, put the chicken breast, dried mushrooms, kombu and wakame into a food processor and chop finely. Lightly whisk the eggwhites by hand until soft peaks form and fold through the processed mixture.

Put the cooled stock in the stockpot over medium heat. Vigorously whisk the raft into the stock until well incorporated, stirring occasionally to make sure the raft is not sticking to the bottom of the pot. Allow the stock to come close to boiling point, then turn the heat down to the lowest possible setting; you want the stock to be barely simmering under the raft. Do not stir the raft again at this point.

Cook on very low heat for 30 minutes. Make a hole in the raft to check that it is fully cooked and that the stock is clear, then cook for a further 10 minutes. Remove the pot from the heat and set aside for 20 minutes. Carefully ladle the consommé from the pot into a sieve lined with a double layer of muslin (cheesecloth), making sure you don't break up the raft too much. You should have a crystal-clear, intensely flavoured consommé. Taste and adjust the seasoning with the anchovy brine. Keep the consommé in the refrigerator until required.

01

ABALONE

4 GREENLIP ABALONE, ABOUT 70 G
(2½ OZ) EACH
200 ML (7 FL OZ) CHICKEN STOCK
(SEE BASIC RECIPES)

Put the live abalone in a large bowl of iced water for 15 minutes to humanely dispatch them. Take a large tablespoon and shuck the abalone from the shell. Remove the intestines with a sharp knife and discard. Refrigerate the abalone for 24 hours.

Put the abalone in a small cryovac bag with the chicken stock, seal it and steam in a combi-oven at 85°C (185°F) for 8 hours. Allow to cool in the bag and refrigerate until required.

02

SQUAB

4 DRESSED SQUAB, ABOUT 450 G
(1 LB) EACH
100 G (3½ OZ) UNSALTED BUTTER
30 G (1 OZ) SEA SALT

Remove the squab breasts from the bone, leaving the skin on. Reserve the remaining squab parts for another use.

Soften the butter and add the sea salt. Put half a tablespoon of the salted butter onto each squab breast and place all the breasts in a cryovac bag in a single layer.

Heat a water circulator to 50°C (120°F). Poach the squab for 13 minutes, maintaining the 50°C (120°F) temperature. Remove the bag and put it into iced water. Once cold, transfer the bag to the refrigerator until required.

This dish combines two opposing textures of protein, the tender rare squab meat and the chewy resistance of the slow-cooked abalone, surrounded by rare herbs ranging in flavour from salty to grassy and peppery heat. The dish is mellowed by a soft spring garlic custard and balanced by the intense savoury flavour of the umami consommé.

03

SPRING GARLIC CUSTARD

2 SPRING GARLIC BULBS
20 ML (¾ FL OZ) GRAPESEED OIL
500 ML (17 FL OZ) MILK
SALT
1 EGG
3 EGG YOLKS, EXTRA

Finely slice the spring garlic bulbs and sweat them with the grapeseed oil in a saucepan over medium heat until translucent.

Add milk and bring to a gentle simmer. Cook for 2–3 minutes then remove from heat and allow the mixture to cool completely.

Strain and discard the solids.

Measure 400 ml (14 fl oz) of the spring garlic-infused milk and season to taste. Lightly beat the egg and egg yolks in a bowl and pour on the spring garlic milk. Pour the mixture through a fine sieve. Divide the mixture between eight round 50 ml (1¾ fl oz) capacity ramekins. Cover each ramekin tightly with plastic wrap and refrigerate until required.

04

TO FINISH

16 YARROW (MILFOIL) SPRIGS
16 SMALL ALEXANDERS LEAVES
16 PUNTARELLE (CATALONIAN
    CHICORY) TIPS
16 MINUTINA (HERBA STELLA) TIPS
16 AGRETTI TIPS
32 BABY PURPLE NASTURTIUM LEAVES
32 SALAD BURNET SPRIGS
16 ORACH (MOUNTAIN SPINACH) TIPS
32 SALTY ICE PLANT TIPS
16 WINTER PURSLANE SPRIGS
32 GAI LAN (CHINESE BROCCOLI) FLOWERS
100 G (3½ OZ) CLARIFIED BUTTER
    (SEE BASIC RECIPES), MELTED
1 LITRE (35 FL OZ) UMAMI CONSOMMÉ
    (SEE RECIPE ON PAGE 158)

Pick and wash all herbs in plenty of cold water. Pat dry and set aside.

Remove the abalone from the bag and slice into 5 mm (¼ inch) thick slices. Remove the squab breasts from the bag, remove the skin and slice into 5 mm (¼ inch) thick slices. On silicone paper, interlay 5 squab and 5 abalone slices. Brush with clarified butter and lightly season. Top with a second piece of silicone paper. Repeat until you have 8 portions completed.

Steam the spring garlic custards on full steam for approximately 8 minutes or until just set.

Reheat the consommé and check the seasoning.

Lay the squab and abalone between the sheets of silicone paper on a baking tray in a single layer and warm in a 180°C (350°F/Gas 4) oven for 1 minute.

05

TO PLATE

Using a round spoon, scoop out the hot spring garlic custard and place it in the centre of each serving bowl.

Using a palette knife, transfer the squab and abalone from the silicone paper to the top of the custards. Carefully arrange the herbs and flowers around the squab and abalone.

Put the hot consommé in a teapot. Serve, pouring the consommé from the teapot directly onto the dish, at the table.

SQUAB & ABALONE, SPRING GARLIC CUSTARD, RARE CULTIVATED HERBS, UMAMI CONSOMMÉ

PREPARATION / 2 DAYS
SERVES / 8

This dish emphasises the intensity of flavour that can be achieved by applying different techniques to a single ingredient: fermenting, dehydrating, frying, using the ingredient in its raw state and featuring unexpected parts of that ingredient, such as the dried shiitake skins. These different techniques, combined with a couple of complementary ingredients—miso and steamed grilled eggplant—all work together to create a powerful expression of the mushroom.

TEXTURAL MUSHROOMS, EGGPLANT, MISO

PREPARATION / 2 DAYS
SERVES / 8

01

FERMENTED SWISS BROWN MUSHROOMS

8 MEDIUM-SIZE SWISS BROWN MUSHROOMS
250 ML (9 FL OZ) STILL MINERAL WATER
8 G (¼ OZ) SEA SALT

Peel the mushrooms and cut the stems level with the base of the mushroom cap. Cut two 5 mm (¼ inch) thick slices off the mushroom from the base so that the cross-section of the mushroom includes both white mushroom flesh and brown gills. Place the 16 slices of mushroom in a cryovac bag in a single layer. Combine the mineral water and salt to form a brine then pour into the bag and seal it with a vacuum sealing machine. Allow the mushrooms to sit at room temperature, not above 25°C (77°F), for 2 days to ferment. After 2 days you can store the mushrooms, in the bag, in the refrigerator for up to 2 weeks.

02

MUSHROOM, MISO & EGGPLANT PASTE

2 MEDIUM-SIZE EGGPLANTS (AUBERGINES)
400 ML (14 FL OZ) GRAPESEED OIL
2 GARLIC CLOVES, FINELY SLICED
2 TEASPOONS LEMON JUICE
500 G (1 LB 2 OZ) FRESH SHIITAKE
   MUSHROOMS, STALKS REMOVED
300 G (10½ OZ) CLARIFIED BUTTER
   (SEE BASIC RECIPES)
2 TABLESPOONS KOREAN BLACK BEAN
   MISO (SUBSTITUTE DOENJANG IF
   NOT AVAILABLE)

Cut the eggplants in half lengthways. Cut 3 lengthways slits into the eggplant flesh. Put the eggplant halves into a cryovac bag with the grapeseed oil, garlic and lemon juice. Seal the bag and steam for 45 minutes or until tender but not falling apart.

Slice the shiitake mushrooms horizontally into thin discs, lay the slices in a single layer on two baking trays lined with silicone paper and dry out in the oven at 100°C (200°F/Gas ½), turning occasionally for 2–2½ hours or until completely dry.

Once the mushrooms are dehydrated, fry them with the clarified butter in a non-stick frying pan over low to medium heat for 1 minute or until golden brown. Drain and set aside.

Remove the eggplant flesh from the bag and separate the flesh from the skin with a knife. Squeeze out the flesh with your hands to remove as much oil as possible. Put the eggplant flesh in a food processor with the fried mushrooms and 1 tablespoon of black bean miso. Process on high until well incorporated. Push the purée through a fine drum sieve. Taste and check for salt level and, if needed, add a little more black bean miso. Set aside in the refrigerator.

03

STEAMED EGGPLANT

2 MEDIUM-SIZE EGGPLANTS (AUBERGINES)
300 ML (10½ FL OZ) GRAPESEED OIL
2 GARLIC CLOVES, FINELY SLICED
1½ TEASPOONS LEMON JUICE

Repeat the method in Step 02 for the steaming of the eggplant. Once steamed, remove the skin and cut the flesh into 2 cm (¾ inch) rough strips. Set aside until you are ready to finish the dish.

04

LARGE FIELD MUSHROOM GILLS, FRESH & POWDERED

4 LARGE JUST-PICKED FIELD MUSHROOMS, STALKS REMOVED

Peel the mushrooms, discarding the skin. With a sharp paring knife, remove the gills by gently scraping them from the underside of the caps. Ensure none of the mushroom flesh is attached to the dark gills. Place the gills in an airtight container lined with a clean, damp kitchen cloth. Cover and refrigerate until required.

To make the powder, remove the remaining dark mushroom flesh from under the caps with a sharp paring knife. Set aside. A small amount of white mushroom flesh may be left attached. Reserve the mushroom caps in an airtight container until required.

Take the dark mushroom flesh, place on a baking tray lined with silicone paper and bake in a 100°C (200°F/Gas ½) oven, turning occasionally, for 3 hours or until completely dry.

Grind the dehydrated mushroom flesh in a spice grinder until it forms a fine powder. Pass through a fine sieve and discard any coarse pieces. Set aside in an airtight container until required. Makes 2 tablespoons.

05

SHIITAKE MUSHROOM POWDER, DRIED SKINS, DRIED & FRIED FLESH

24 MEDIUM TO LARGE FRESH SHIITAKE
   MUSHROOMS, STALKS REMOVED
200 G (7 OZ) CLARIFIED BUTTER
   (SEE BASIC RECIPES)

Carefully wipe the shiitake mushrooms with a damp cloth to ensure there's no dirt left on the skins. Carefully peel the skins, aiming for as large and intact skin pieces as possible. Dehydrate the skins in a 100°C (200°F/Gas ½) oven for 2–3 hours or until crisp. When cool set aside in an airtight container.

Slice the remaining shiitake caps, cutting horizontally across the mushrooms from the top, making the slices as thin as possible and leaving behind the gills. Dehydrate the slices in a 100°C oven for 2–3 hours or until completely dry.

Half of the dried mushroom flesh should be processed into a powder in a spice grinder and put into an airtight container. Fry the remaining half in the clarified butter until golden brown. Drain the fried mushrooms and place in an airtight container when cool until ready to serve.

06

TO FINISH

FINE SEA SALT
200 G (7 OZ) UNSALTED BUTTER
100 G (3½ OZ) CLARIFIED BUTTER
   (SEE BASIC RECIPES)

Heat a chargrill or heavy-based frying pan until hot. Grill the steamed eggplant strips until golden brown. Lightly season with sea salt, set aside and keep warm.

Melt half the unsalted butter in a non-stick frying pan over low to medium heat.

Remove the fermented mushrooms from the brine and warm them gently in the melted butter. Set aside and keep warm.

Slice the reserved field mushroom caps on a Japanese mandolin to a 1 mm (1⁄32 inch) thickness. Melt the remaining butter in a large non-stick frying pan over low to medium heat and add 16 slices of the field mushroom flesh. Gently warm and set aside, keeping warm.

In a small saucepan, gently warm the mushroom, miso and eggplant paste.

Melt the clarified butter in a non-stick frying pan over low to medium heat. Add 24 pieces of the dried shiitake skins and warm through until translucent. Set aside.

07

TO PLATE

In the centre of each warmed large, flat white serving plate, place a tablespoon of the mushroom, miso and eggplant paste. Spread out with the back of the spoon.

Sprinkle over the dark gill powder and the white shiitake mushroom powder.

Place 2 slices of the fermented mushrooms on the paste, then place 3 strips of the chargrilled eggplant flesh on the paste. Slightly curl 2 pieces of the warmed white field mushroom flesh and place on the paste.

Finish the dish with shiitake skins, crisp dried and fried shiitake slices and the fresh field mushroom gills. Serve.

Of all the crustaceans that I use, wild sea prawns have the most robust flavour and are able to take strong, assertive accompaniments. In this dish, a delicious, intensely flavoured custard of sea urchin is complemented by the umami-rich salted egg yolk and cured mullet roe. These potent ingredients are balanced with fresh dory roe, lemon zest and crisp fried evening primrose flowers. The harmonious deep flavours and multiple textures work together to express the inherent taste of the sea in the wild prawns.

WILD SEA PRAWNS, CURED MULLET ROE, SALTED EGG YOLK, SEA URCHIN CUSTARD, DRIED EVENING PRIMROSE

PREPARATION / 4 DAYS
SERVES / 8

01

SALTED EGG YOLKS

500 G (1 LB 2 OZ) FINE SEA SALT
4 EGG YOLKS
500 ML (17 FL OZ) EXTRA VIRGIN OLIVE OIL

Put half the sea salt into a small, square stainless steel or glass container: the salt needs to be approximately 3 cm (1¼ inches) deep. Make 4 small round indents in the salt, roughly the same diameter as the egg yolks. Don't push down too hard: ensure there is at least 1 cm (⅜ inch) of salt between the base of the indent and the container bottom.

Working one at a time, gently place each yolk into one of the prepared salt bed indents.

Carefully and evenly spoon the remaining salt over the top of the yolks, ensuring they are completely covered. Wrap the container tightly in plastic wrap and leave in the refrigerator for a minimum of 48 hours and a maximum of 4 days.

Remove the egg yolks from the salt and carefully brush off as much salt as possible with your hands. Rinse off any remaining salt under cold running water. Allow the yolks to drain for a few minutes then put them on a plate. Working with two sheets of silicone paper, lightly brush the paper with some olive oil. Divide each egg yolk into 20 small rough pieces, using your fingers. Place each small piece of egg yolk between the oiled silicone paper and press down firmly with your thumb to flatten to about 1 cm (⅜ inch) diameter. Use a palette knife to remove the flattened pieces of egg yolk and put them in a container with the remaining extra virgin olive oil. Seal and store in the refrigerator until required. It is best to do this a couple of hours before serving.

02

DORY ROE WITH LEMON ZEST

200 G (7 OZ) FRESH SILVER DORY ROE SACS
1 LITRE (35 FL OZ) STILL MINERAL WATER
50 G (1¾ OZ) SEA SALT
½ LEMON
50 ML (1¾ FL OZ) EXTRA VIRGIN OLIVE OIL

Freeze the silver dory roe sacs overnight to ensure that any parasites are killed. Defrost.

Divide the mineral water and salt equally between two bowls. Place the roe sac in the first bowl. Using a pair of sharp scissors cut the skin of the roe sac to expose the roe. Gently remove the roe from each sac, using a blunt knife to gently scrape it out. Discard the skin.

Using a whisk, gently agitate the roe to help separate the eggs.

Allow the roe to sit in the brine for 10 minutes. Carefully pour through a fine drum sieve, discarding the brine.

Using a pair of tweezers, remove any veins or blood vessels from the roe. Carefully transfer the roe with a palette knife or plastic pastry scraper to the fresh bowl of brine. Gently agitate the roe again using a whisk. Allow to sit for a further 10 minutes before once more pouring the roe through a fine drum sieve. Remove any veins you may have missed the first time. Allow the roe to drain completely.

Put the roe into a small bowl. Use a fine microplane to zest the lemon over the roe and stir in the extra virgin olive oil. Transfer the roe to a plastic container, seal and refrigerate until required.

03

SEA URCHIN CUSTARD

500 ML (17 FL OZ) MILK
1 GARLIC CLOVE, THINLY SLICED
50 G (1¾ OZ) SEA URCHIN ROE,
    FRESHLY SHUCKED
1 EGG
2 EGG YOLKS
FINE SEA SALT

Warm the milk in a saucepan to simmering point and add the garlic. Remove from the heat and allow to infuse for 30 minutes. Strain the milk and discard the garlic. Put the roe, egg and egg yolks in a blender with the cooled infused milk and blend on high for 1 minute. Strain mixture through a fine sieve. Season with sea salt.

Line eight small Asian rice bowls with plastic wrap, making sure the plastic lines the bowls evenly without any gaps. Put approximately 60 ml (2 fl oz) of mixture into each bowl and cover tightly with more plastic wrap. Refrigerate until ready to steam.

04

DRIED EVENING PRIMROSE FLOWERS

80 FRESHLY PICKED EVENING
    PRIMROSE FLOWERS

Spread the flowers on a tray lined with silicone paper and dry in a dehydrator or 80°C (175°F/Gas ¼–½) oven for approximately 2 hours until brittle.

Allow to cool and store the flowers in an airtight container until required.

05

TO FINISH

40 MEDIUM-SIZE FRESH GREEN WILD
    SEA PRAWNS IN THE SHELL
FINE SEA SALT
100 G (3½ OZ) CLARIFIED BUTTER
    (SEE BASIC RECIPES)
70 G (2½ OZ) BOTTARGA (DRIED
    SALT-CURED MULLET ROE)
20 ML (¾ FL OZ) GRAPESEED OIL

Set a steamer on high. Remove the sea urchin custard bowls from the refrigerator and shake to recombine. Steam on high for approximately 10 minutes or until just set. Remove the custards from the steamer and keep warm.

Steam the prawns for approximately 1 minute. Remove from the steamer and allow to cool slightly. Wearing a pair of plastic gloves, peel the prawns while still warm. Remove the digestive tract. Split the prawns in half lengthways with a sharp knife. Put the prawns in a bowl and sprinkle with a small amount of fine sea salt.

Melt the clarified butter in a small saucepan until it reaches 60°C (140°F). Add the dory roe with lemon zest and stir. Grate half the bottarga into the butter mixture, stir to combine well and pour the mixture over the prawns. Mix to dress the prawns well in the butter mixture. Quickly heat the grapeseed oil in a non-stick frying pan until it is hot. Briefly fry the dried evening primrose flowers for approximately 30 seconds until they become crisp. Drain on paper towel.

06

TO PLATE

Remove the top layer of plastic wrap from the custards. Invert each custard onto the centre of a warmed serving bowl and peel away the bottom layer of plastic wrap. Place 10 prawn halves on top of each custard, with an even amount of dressing and roe. Shave the remaining bottarga directly over the prawns. Use tweezers to remove the salted egg yolk pieces from the oil and place 10 pieces on top of each dish and garnish with the fried evening primrose flowers. Serve.

DAVID BLACKMORE

WAGYU BREEDER
MELBOURNE / VICTORIA

I admire David's strong ethical standards and commitment to animal welfare, which ensure that Blackmore Wagyu cattle are raised in a sustainable environment without growth hormones, antibiotics or genetically modified food.

David Blackmore, a fifth-generation farmer born in South Australia, is a recognised pioneer and leader in Wagyu beef production. During the past 25 years, through an incomparable understanding of Wagyu bloodlines and genetics and by adhering to a controlled, innovative breeding program, David has established a world-class herd of breeding cattle that today produces 100 per cent full-blood Wagyu beef sought after by leading chefs around the globe.

David's involvement with Wagyu began in 1988 when, through his research, he discovered a small number of Wagyu cattle that had been exported from Japan to America for research. These were the first known Wagyu outside of Japan. Knowing that crossing Wagyu with other breeds increases meat quality and value, David secured exclusive rights to import embryos and semen into Australia. From 1992 to 2004, David imported more than 80 per cent of the available genetic stock.

With a strong respect for Japanese feeding and farming methods, David was able to develop a relationship with the breeders; as a result he is one of the few Westerners privileged to be invited to Japanese bull studs, agricultural research centres, universities, prominent breeder farms, feed facilities and abattoirs.

I admire David's strong ethical standards and commitment to animal welfare, which ensure that Blackmore Wagyu cattle are raised in a sustainable environment without growth hormones, antibiotics or genetically modified food.

It is such a pleasure to be able to work with this exceptional quality beef: its texture is unparalleled, and when Blackmore Wagyu is aged, by Anthony Puharich at Vic's Premium Quality Meat, the umami richness is intensified and just one taste is something that you will never forget.

ANTHONY PUHARICH

BUTCHER
MASCOT / NEW SOUTH WALES

'Peter's love and passion for what he does and the industry as a whole is infectious; his appreciation and respect for ingredients and for the people who produce them is second to none.'

I have worked closely with Anthony Puharich since I began at Quay in 2001. Anthony had established a great reputation within the industry in a relatively short period of time after opening Vic's Premium Quality Meat with his father Victor in 1996. Victor is a fourth-generation butcher from Croatia, and together they have built one of Australia's leading meat wholesaling businesses. Through their commitment to quality and their relationships with farmers and chefs they now supply more than 80 per cent of Australia's top restaurants.

Finding suppliers and producers of extraordinary quality and exacting standards is important for me as a chef. To know that I can rely 100 per cent on my supplier and that their standards are as high as my own is crucial.

Anthony and Vic's commitment to sourcing, butchering and the artisanal skills of curing and dry-ageing meat is exceptional. Their passion for butchery has been exemplified in the creation of one of the world's finest retail butcher stores. Victor Churchill, which opened in 2009 and is located on Queen Street in Woollahra, Sydney. Victor Churchill won the New York-based *Interior Design* Best of Year 2010 award for best in retail: it was competing against international retail giants, such as Hermès and Louis Vuitton, yet walked away with the top gong. Victor Churchill has become a destination for international foodies.

What has impressed me most about Anthony is his honesty and direct accountability for his products and his commitment to working with excellent producers like David Blackmore.

In Anthony's own words: 'I have been working closely with Peter Gilmore for 13 years now, from the very first week he took over as chef at Quay.

'I have enjoyed watching Quay go from strength to strength over the years, but more importantly I have enjoyed seeing Peter achieve so much on a personal level, reaching the rare and lofty heights of being recognised as a world-renowned chef. Peter's love and passion for what he does and the industry as a whole is infectious; his appreciation and respect for ingredients and for the people who produce them is second to none.

'Knowing and dealing with Peter Gilmore has made me a better butcher and supplier.'

In Australia we produce ethically raised, pasture-fed veal: male calves are sourced from dairy cattle, raised on their mother's milk and eat fresh grass in the field. In this recipe I have gently poached the veal in rendered smoked bone marrow, which imparts a beautiful flavour. The veal is served with black pudding, morel cream, wild grey ghost mushrooms and crisp umami-rich shiitake skins.

PASTURE-RAISED VEAL, RENDERED SMOKED BONE MARROW, BITTER CHOCOLATE BLACK PUDDING, GREY GHOST MUSHROOMS

PREPARATION / 1 DAY
SERVES / 8

01

RENDERED SMOKED BONE MARROW

500 G (1 LB 2 OZ) BEEF BONE MARROW
2 LITRES (70 FL OZ) COLD MILK
50 G (1¾ OZ) MAPLE WOOD CHIPS
125 ML (4 FL OZ) COLD WATER

Constantly run cold water over the bone marrow for 1 hour to help flush out any residual blood. Soak the bone marrow in the milk in a refrigerator overnight.

Remove the bone marrow from the milk and rinse well in cold water.

Set up a cold smoking apparatus with the maple wood chips and cold smoke the bone marrow for 1 hour.

Put the bone marrow in a heavy-based saucepan with the cold water and slowly and gently render over low heat until it is completely dissolved in the water. Strain and refrigerate until required.

02

DRIED SHIITAKE SKINS

32 MEDIUM-SIZE FRESH SHIITAKE
    MUSHROOMS
1 TABLESPOON CLARIFIED BUTTER
    (SEE BASIC RECIPES), MELTED

Wipe mushrooms with a clean, slightly damp cloth, being careful not to tear the skin. Using your hands, remove the skins from the mushrooms. Reserve the rest of the mushrooms for another use.

Put the shiitake skins on a baking tray lined with silicone paper and brush with a light coating of clarified butter on both sides. Dry the shiitake skins under a heat lamp or in a 100°C (200°F/Gas ½) oven for 45 minutes or until dry and crisp. The butter lightly caramelises the skins as they are drying. Once dry and caramelised, remove the skins from the tray and allow to cool on a fresh sheet of silicone paper. Store in an airtight container until required.

03

BLACK PUDDING & MOREL CREAM

50 G (1¾ OZ) UNSALTED BUTTER
2 ESCHALLOTS, FINELY DICED
1 GARLIC CLOVE, FINELY DICED
50 G (1¾ OZ) SWISS BROWN MUSHROOMS,
    FINELY DICED
25 G (1 OZ) DRIED MOREL MUSHROOMS,
    SOAKED IN SEVERAL CHANGES OF
    COLD WATER UNTIL ALL GRIT HAS
    BEEN REMOVED
200 ML (7 FL OZ) CHICKEN STOCK (SEE
    BASIC RECIPES)
150 G (5½ OZ) BITTER CHOCOLATE BLACK
    PUDDING (SEE PAGE 88)
50 ML (1¾ FL OZ) PURE CREAM (35% FAT)

Melt half the butter in a small saucepan with the eschallots and garlic and sweat gently over low heat until translucent. Add the swiss brown mushrooms and morels and sweat for a further 5 minutes. Add the chicken stock and simmer on medium heat for 20 minutes until the mushrooms are soft and most of the liquid has evaporated. Transfer the mixture to a blender. Add the black pudding, remaining butter and cream and blend on high for 2–3 minutes. Pass the mixture through a fine drum sieve. Reserve in an airtight container in the refrigerator until required.

04

TO FINISH

1 KG (2 LB 4 OZ) PASTURE-RAISED,
    GRASS-FED VEAL FILLET
1 QUANTITY BITTER CHOCOLATE BLACK
    PUDDING (SEE PAGE 88)
40 WILD GREY GHOST MUSHROOMS OR
    SMALL SWISS BROWN MUSHROOMS
50 ML (1¾ FL OZ) GRAPESEED OIL
50 G (1¾ OZ) UNSALTED BUTTER

Trim the veal fillet of all the fat and sinew. Cut the fillet into 32 slices, 1 cm (½ inch) thick and refrigerate until required. Cut the black pudding into 32 squares, 3 cm (1¼ inches) wide and approximately 2 cm (¾ inch) thick and refrigerate until required.

Brush and wipe the grey ghost mushrooms and set aside.

Warm the smoked rendered bone marrow in a large heavy-based frying pan until it reaches 70°C (160°F). Meanwhile, in a clean saucepan, reheat the black pudding and morel cream.

Put the grapeseed oil into a shallow non-stick frying pan and heat on high heat. Shallow-fry the black pudding squares for 1 minute on each side. Put the fried squares onto a tray lined with silicone paper and keep warm.

Meanwhile, add the slices of veal fillet to the warm rendered bone marrow and poach for approximately 2 minutes or until the veal slightly changes colour to opaque. Drain the veal, lay it on a tray lined with silicone paper and keep warm.

Put the unsalted butter in a clean non-stick frying pan over medium heat. Briefly sauté the grey ghost mushrooms on both sides.

Put the reserved shiitake skins on a tray lined with silicone paper in a medium oven to gently reheat for 1 minute.

05

TO PLATE

In the centre of each large warmed serving plate, place 4 slices of the veal. Cover with 4 random dots of the black pudding and morel cream and 4 pieces of the fried bitter chocolate black pudding. Top with an even amount of grey ghost mushrooms and dried shiitake skins. Serve.

LACTIC ACID FERMENTED SCORZONERA

50 G (1¾ OZ) SEA SALT

1 LITRE (35 FL OZ) STILL MINERAL WATER

400 G (14 OZ) SCORZONERA
(BLACK SALSIFY)

Sterilise a 1 litre (35 fl oz) capacity preserving jar and a plastic dariole mould.

Dissolve the salt in the mineral water and put the liquid into the sterilised preserving jar. Have a large bowl of iced water at the ready with plenty of ice in it.

Peel the scorzonera one at a time and quickly submerge in the iced water to ensure it doesn't oxidise and discolour. Remove one root at a time and, using a vegetable peeler, peel into long strips and immediately resubmerge them in the ice. Once all the scorzonera is peeled into strips, drain briefly on a clean kitchen cloth and put it into the salt water solution in the jar.

Place a sterilised plastic dariole mould in the top of the jar and close the lid. This ensures the strips remain submerged in the liquid. Close the lid tightly. Store at room temperature in your store cupboard or pantry. A minimum of 2 weeks is required for a good flavour to develop but this will store for months, unopened.

Refrigerate when opened. Ensure no mould growth is present on the scorzonera.

Lactic acid bacteria fermentation is a transformative, almost alchemic, process that can be applied to most vegetables. If vegetables are submerged in water and deprived of oxygen, the bacteria on the vegetables initiate fermentation; adding a small percentage of salt helps draw out additional water from the vegetables and creates a natural brine. Salt also produces a selective environment that narrows the range of other bacteria, giving the salt-tolerant lactic acid bacteria the advantage. This helps keep the vegetables crisp and inhibits surface moulds. Sliced or shaved vegetables plus salt, plus an oxygen-deprived environment, plus time, equals preservation but—more importantly for my uses—it also creates depth of flavour.

LACTIC ACID FERMENTED SCORZONERA

PREPARATION / 2 WEEKS

SERVES / 8

David Blackmore's highly marbled, intensely flavoured Wagyu beef needs equally strong, assertive accompaniments. The idea of serving beef with salty caramelised oysters is a slightly unusual one but has its roots in the 1970s Australian classic 'carpetbag steak'. The salty sweet flavour of oysters in this recipe is not far removed from stir-fried beef and oyster sauce. In fact, the roasted whole-bean miso I use in this recipe is a hybrid of the ancient traditions of fermented black soybeans and Japanese whole-bean miso. The flavours of fermentation in both the miso and the scorzonera create strong umami-rich flavours to complement the beef. To complete the circle, scorzonera is often referred to as oyster plant, because its flavour is reminiscent of oysters.

POACHED BLACKMORE WAGYU, ROASTED WHOLE-BEAN MISO, CARAMELISED ANGASI OYSTERS, LACTIC ACID FERMENTED SCORZONERA

PREPARATION / 3 WEEKS
SERVES / 8

WHOLE-BEAN MISO

200 G (7 OZ) MIXED WHOLE DRIED BEANS,
   SUCH AS CANNELLINI, YIN YANG,
   BORLOTTI
2 G (¹⁄₁₆ OZ) DEHYDRATED KOJI SPORES
   (SEE GLOSSARY)
5 G (³⁄₁₆ OZ) RICE FLOUR
250 G (9 OZ) STILL MINERAL WATER
15 G (½ OZ) SEA SALT

Soak your chosen beans in plenty of cold water overnight. Drain the beans and put them in a combi-oven or steamer on full steam for approximately 1 hour or until the beans are soft to the touch.

Remove the beans from the steamer and place them on a sheet of clean, damp muslin (cheesecloth) in a single layer. Allow the beans to cool to approximately 35°C (95°F), checking with a temperature probe. Working quickly and wearing a face mask so as not to inhale any koji spores, mix the spores and rice flour together and then use a fine sieve to sift the mixture evenly over the still-warm beans. Mix the beans thoroughly, ensuring they are evenly coated with the spores and flour mixture. Bundle the beans into the centre of the muslin and fold over the cloth to form a snug wrapping around the beans. Wet a clean tea towel (dish towel) and wring it out well. Wrap the bean parcel in the damp tea towel then wrap a clean dry tea towel around the outside.

Put the parcel into an incubator set at 35°C (95°F) for 24 hours. Alternatively, you can put the parcel into a styrofoam container with a tight-fitting lid. Put a water bottle filled with 35°C (95°F) water next to the beans. Secure the lid and place the box in a warm part of the kitchen. If using the water bottle method, you will need to keep a check on the temperature and replace the water bottle 3–4 times over the 24-hour period.

After 24 hours, remove the beans from the incubator or styrofoam container and open up the package. You should start to see a whitish, fragrant sweet-smelling mould developing on the beans. If so, you are on the right track. If not, discard the beans and start the recipe again.

Spread the beans out in a single layer onto a tray lined with clean damp muslin. Cover with another layer of clean damp muslin and return the beans to a 35°C (95°F) incubator or styrofoam box with a water bottle for a further 24 hours. After this period, the beans should be covered in a fine whitish mould and the smell should be sweet, fragrant and slightly yeasty, like freshly baked bread. The smell and colour is the best indicator that you have successfully grown the correct mould. If the smell is not sweet and the mould has other coloured hues in it I would recommend discarding the batch and starting again.

The white koji mould, if incubated for longer than 48 hours, can start to form greenish–yellow patches that indicate sporulation of the mould. Although it's not necessarily dangerous for use in this particular recipe, it would be preferable to start the batch again. If the mould is white and smelling sweet, proceed to the next step.

Dry out the koji-inoculated beans in a dehydrator or low oven set at 80°C (175°F/Gas ¼–½) for approximately 1 hour or until the beans start to shrivel a little. Make a brine by combining the filtered water and salt, then mix until dissolved. Place the beans into a cryovac bag and pour in the cold brine. Vacuum seal the bag on medium pressure. Put the bagged beans in the pantry and leave them at room temperature—approximately 23°C (73°F)—for 1 week. Transfer the beans to a cool dark place, such as a cellar, at about 15°C (59°F). If this is not possible, place in the refrigerator. The beans will have enough flavour to use after a 3-week waiting period; however, as long as they are kept in the sealed bag with the brine in the refrigerator they can be stored for up to 6 months.

02

POACHED BEEF

1 KG (2 LB 4 OZ) TRIMMED BLACKMORE
   PURE-BRED WAGYU FILLET
150 G (5½ OZ) UNSALTED BUTTER, MELTED
50 ML (1¾ FL OZ) 10-YEAR-AGED KOREAN
   SOY SAUCE

Put the beef fillet, butter and soy sauce into
a large cryovac bag and vacuum seal at
medium pressure. Set a water circulator at
55°C (130°F). Submerge the beef in the water
bath and cook for approximately 45 minutes
or until the beef's internal temperature is
53°C (127°F). Transfer the beef, still in the bag,
into an ice water bath to rapidly chill, then
refrigerate until required.

03

MALTOSE POWDER

150 G (5½ OZ) LIQUID MALTOSE

Place the liquid maltose on a tray lined with a
silicone mat and bake in a 220°C (425°F/Gas 7)
oven until the maltose is vigorously bubbling.
Remove the tray from the oven and allow the
maltose to cool and set completely. Once set,
break it up and put it in an upright blender.
Blend until a fine powder is formed. Sieve
through a medium–fine sieve and store the
powder in an airtight container until required.

04

TO FINISH

16 ANGASI (FLAT) OYSTERS
200 G (7 OZ) LACTIC ACID FERMENTED
   SCORZONERA (SEE PAGE 184)
100 G (3½ OZ) CLARIFIED BUTTER
   (SEE BASIC RECIPES)
50 G (1¾ OZ) UNSALTED BUTTER
20 G (¾ OZ) CLARIFIED BUTTER,
   EXTRA, MELTED

Shuck the oysters, place them on a tray and
refrigerate until required. Drain the scorzonera
and squeeze out any excess juice. Refrigerate
until required.

Reheat the Wagyu beef in a 50°C (120°F)
water circulator: this will take approximately
15 minutes.

Drain the fermented beans from the brine
and set aside 48 whole beans: choose the
nicest looking as these are for the garnish.
Finely chop the rest of the beans by hand.
Melt 80 g (2¾ oz) of the clarified butter in
a non-stick frying pan, add the chopped beans
and lightly fry them until golden brown.
Set aside and keep warm. In a small saucepan,
melt a further 20 g (¾ oz) clarified butter,
add the whole beans and lightly sauté to
warm through, then set aside and keep warm.

Melt the unsalted butter in a small
saucepan and add the drained scorzonera.
Toss the scorzonera until it is warmed through
but do not allow it to colour. Set aside and
keep warm.

Sift the maltose powder over the top
of the oysters. Heat a non-stick frying pan
until very hot. Brush the pan with the melted
clarified butter and sear the oysters, maltose
powder side down. Allow the oysters to
caramelise for a good 30 seconds. Briefly turn
the oysters and allow them to cook on the
other side for 10 seconds. Remove the oysters,
place on a tray and keep warm.

05

TO PLATE

100 ML (3½ FL OZ) WARMED VEAL GLAZE
   (SEE BASIC RECIPES)
SEA SALT

Remove the beef from the cryovac bag and
slice it into 8 even portions. Brush the beef
with the warmed veal glaze, put the beef
pieces on a flat tray and flash in a 200°C
(400°F/Gas 6) oven for 30 seconds. Place
the beef in the centre of each warmed serving
plate. Spoon a tablespoon of the browned,
chopped bean miso on top of the beef.
Garnish with the whole warmed beans.
Place the caramelised oysters on top and
a bundle of the warmed scorzonera next
to the beef. Serve.

This dish is all about texture. It has been with me for quite a few years now. I have refined it over the years to essentially just four main components: the soft melting pig cheek, the crisp maltose crackling, the tart prune and the luscious cauliflower cream. The cheek itself is cooked very slowly in a salted chicken stock and then finished in clarified butter. The intramuscular fat of the cheek and a small amount of fat left surrounding the cheek combined with the slow cooking creates an unbelievably soft, rich texture. There's too much fat between the meat and the skin in the pig cheek to form a natural crackling so, to create the effect, I developed the maltose crackling. Maltose is a liquid sugar derived from malted grains. It has the unique ability to shatter; in contrast to cane sugar, which would become chewy like toffee. Maltose is much less sweet than cane sugar so it makes the perfect faux crackling.

SLOW-COOKED PIG CHEEK, PRUNES, CAULIFLOWER CREAM, MALTOSE CRACKLING, PERFUMED WITH PRUNE KERNEL OIL

SERVES / 8

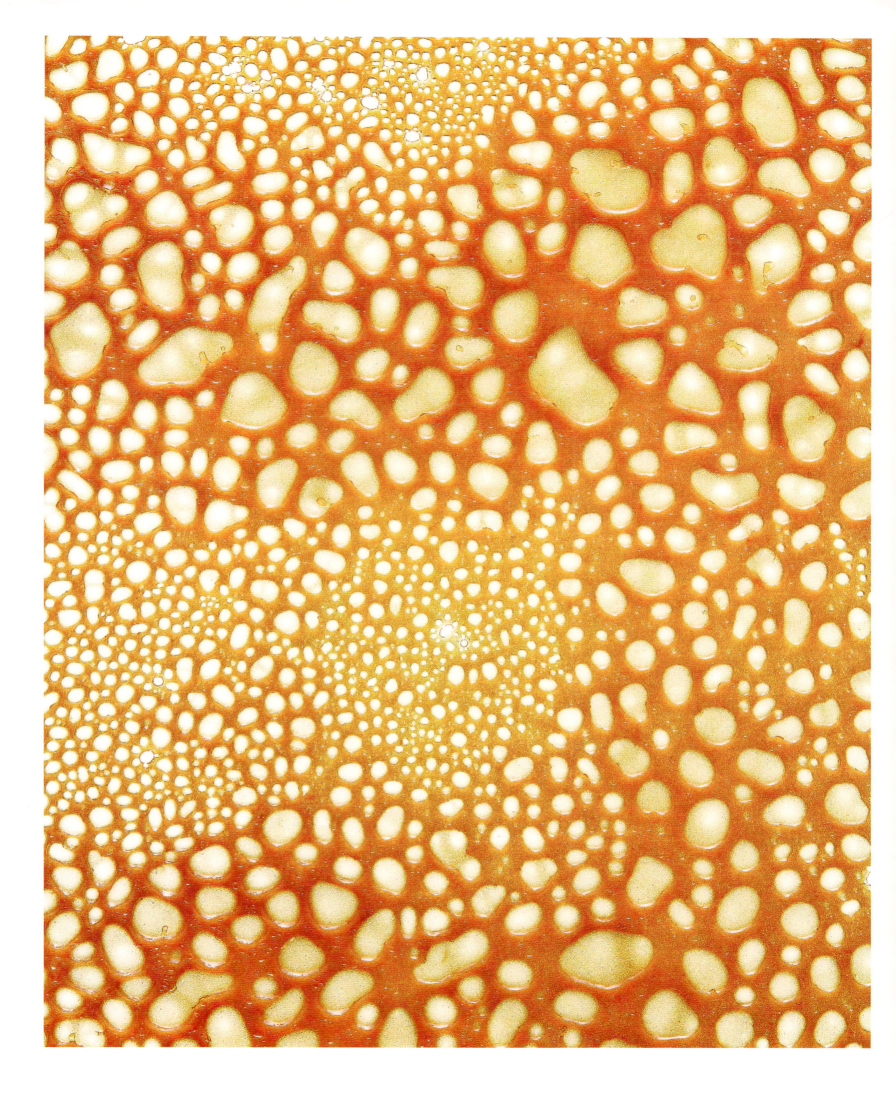

01

PIG CHEEK

8 WHOLE PIG CHEEKS
400 ML (14 FL OZ) CHICKEN STOCK
   (SEE BASIC RECIPES)
40 G (1½ OZ) SEA SALT
400 G (14 OZ) CLARIFIED BUTTER
   (SEE BASIC RECIPES)

In a large pot of salted boiling water, blanch each pig cheek—one at a time—for 1 minute each. Refresh in iced water. Roughly trim each pig cheek, leaving skin and fat around the cheek meat section. Place the cheeks into a large cryovac bag with the chicken stock and sea salt. Seal and steam in a combi-oven at 85°C (185°F) for 6 hours.

Remove from the steamer and refresh the bag in iced water until the cheeks are cold. Remove the cheeks from the bag and fully trim all of the skin and most of the fat away from the meat, leaving just a thin layer of fat around the meat. Trim the cheek to a 5 x 10 cm (2 x 4 inch) rectangle. Place the cheeks in a new cryovac bag with the clarified butter. Seal and refrigerate until required.

02

MALTOSE CRACKLING

250 ML (9 FL OZ) LIQUID MALTOSE

Line a large baking tray with a silicone baking mat. Pour the liquid maltose onto the mat, place in a 220°C (425°F/Gas 7) oven and allow the maltose to rapidly bubble for 8–10 minutes or until it has achieved a deep golden colour.

Remove from the oven and allow to cool completely. Once the maltose is cold and hard, break it into small pieces and put it into a food processor. Process to a fine powder. Cut a 10 x 15 cm (4 x 6 inch) rectangular hole from an acetate sheet to form a template. You will need to have about a 10 cm (4 inch) border of acetate around the cut-out. Lay the template on a baking tray lined with a silicone baking mat. Put the maltose powder into a medium–fine sieve and sift the powder into the template to a thickness of roughly 1 mm (½2 inch). Carefully lift the template and repeat: you will need a minimum of 8 rectangles, and you may need to make extra to allow for breakages. Remelt the maltose in a 180°C (350°F/Gas 4) oven for 5–6 minutes until it lightly bubbles. Allow the sheets to cool and store in an airtight container between layers of silicone paper, with silica gel to ensure they don't stick together.

03

PRUNES

28 UNPITTED PRUNES
100 ML (3½ FL OZ) PEDRO XIMENEZ NOBLE
   SOUR VINEGAR
100 ML (3½ FL OZ) PEDRO XIMENEZ SHERRY

Place the prunes in a bowl and pour over 300 ml (10½ fl oz) cold water, cover and refrigerate overnight. Tip the prunes and soaking liquid into a large saucepan and shake gently until they settle into a single layer, then add the vinegar and sherry. Bring to a simmer and cook over low heat for 20 minutes, making sure the prunes are always covered by the liquid. Top up with cold water if necessary.

Remove the pan from the heat and set aside to cool. Drain the prunes and reserve the liquid.

Slip the stones from the prunes and discard. Return the pitted prunes to the cooking liquid and set aside until ready to reheat.

04

CAULIFLOWER CREAM

100 G (3½ OZ) UNSALTED BUTTER
2 ESCHALLOTS, FINELY DICED
1 GARLIC CLOVE, FINELY DICED
1 INNER WHITE CELERY STALK,
   FINELY DICED
300 G (10½ OZ) CAULIFLOWER FLORETS
625 ML (21½ FL OZ) CHICKEN STOCK
   (SEE BASIC RECIPES), OR ENOUGH TO
   COVER BY 2 CM (¾ INCH)

In a medium saucepan, melt 50 g (1¾ oz) of the unsalted butter. Add the eschallots, garlic and celery and sweat until translucent. Add the cauliflower florets and the chicken stock. Simmer on high heat until most of the liquid has been evaporated. Be careful not to allow the vegetables to colour when the liquid gets low. While the cauliflower is hot, put the solids and syrupy juices into an upright blender. Blend on high with the remaining unsalted butter until smooth. Pass through a fine drum sieve. Cover and refrigerate until required.

05

TO FINISH

100 ML (3½ FL OZ) PURE CREAM (35% FAT),
   WHIPPED

Reheat the cheeks in the bag in a steamer or combi-oven at 85°C (185°F) for 15 minutes or until hot all the way through. Drain the cheeks well and keep warm.

Gently reheat the cauliflower cream, then fold through the whipped cream and season to taste.

Reheat the prunes.

Line a baking tray with silicone paper and place the warmed cheeks on it, leaving enough space between each cheek to top each cheek with a maltose rectangle. Put the cheeks into a 200°C (400°F/Gas 6) oven for about 3–4 minutes to allow the maltose to melt over them.

06

TO PLATE

PRUNE KERNEL OIL

Place 2 prunes in the centre of each warmed serving bowl. Top with half a tablespoon of cauliflower cream then top with a pig cheek. Dress each pig cheek with a teaspoon of prune kernel oil. Serve.

Cherries, nougat and chocolate. The combination is something you just want to eat, delicious and straightforward.

CHOCOLATE, CHERRIES, NOUGAT

PREPARATION / 1 DAY
SERVES / 8

01

CHOCOLATE & CHERRY SORBET

500 ML (17 FL OZ) STRAINED UNSWEETENED
  CHERRY JUICE
160 G (5¾ OZ) CASTER (SUPERFINE) SUGAR
20 G (¾ OZ) LIQUID GLUCOSE
325 ML (11 FL OZ) WATER
20 G (¾ OZ) VALRHONA COCOA POWDER
15 G (½ OZ) AMEDEI CHUAO (EXTRA DARK
  CHOCOLATE 70%), FINELY CHOPPED

Place the cherry juice in a small saucepan and
reduce by half over medium heat. Combine
the reduced cherry juice with the remaining
ingredients in a clean saucepan. Bring to
the boil, whisking constantly. Remove from
heat. Put the mixture in a blender and blend
well. Pour through a fine sieve. Allow to cool
completely, then churn in an ice-cream
machine. Freeze until required. Makes about
500 g (1 lb 2 oz).

02

SOFT CHOCOLATE GANACHE

50 G (1¾ OZ) VALRHONA MANJARI
  64% CHOCOLATE
50 G (1¾ OZ) AMEDEI CHUAO (EXTRA DARK
  CHOCOLATE 70%)
125 ML (4 FL OZ) PURE CREAM (35% FAT)
25 G (1 OZ) UNSALTED BUTTER, DICED,
  AT ROOM TEMPERATURE

Finely chop the chocolate and combine in a
heatproof bowl. Bring the cream to just below
boiling point and pour over the chocolate,
stirring until the chocolate has melted and
the mixture is smooth. Cool the chocolate until
it reaches 30°C (86°F) and whisk in the butter
until well incorporated, smooth and glossy.
This ganache is used at room temperature
and will need to be made 2 hours prior to
plating the dessert to allow it to cool down
to room temperature.

03

CARAMELISED ALMONDS

100 G (3½ OZ) CASTER (SUPERFINE) SUGAR
50 G (1¾ OZ) BLANCHED ALMOND KERNELS,
  WELL ROASTED

Put the caster sugar in a saucepan with
enough water to just wet and dissolve the
sugar. Cook over medium–high heat until it
reaches an even golden caramel. Remove from
heat. Add the roasted almonds then remove
each almond individually with a fork and place
on a tray lined with a silicone baking mat.
Allow almonds to cool completely. Store in
an airtight container until required.

04

DRIED CHERRY, NOUGAT &
CARAMELISED ALMOND MIXTURE

50 G (1¾ OZ) DRIED SOUR CHERRIES,
  ROUGHLY CHOPPED
50 G (1¾ OZ) CARAMELISED ALMONDS
  (SEE ABOVE), ROUGHLY CHOPPED
50 G (1¾ OZ) NOUGAT (SEE BASIC RECIPES),
  ROUGHLY CHOPPED

Combine the cherries, almonds and nougat.
Weigh 50 g (1¾ oz) of this combined mixture
and set aside in an airtight container for
the chocolate bark recipe below. Store the
remaining 100 g (3½ oz) in a separate airtight
container until required.

05

DRIED CHERRY, NOUGAT
& CARAMELISED ALMOND
CHOCOLATE BARK

100 G (3½ OZ) VALRHONA MANJARI
  64% CHOCOLATE
50 G (1¾ OZ) DRIED CHERRY, NOUGAT
  AND CARAMELISED ALMOND MIXTURE
  (SEE ABOVE)

Line a tray with silicone paper. Melt the
chocolate over a water bath and allow to
cool slightly. Add the dried cherry, nougat
and caramelised almond mixture. Quickly
mix and spread out on the lined tray into as
thin a layer as possible. Refrigerate the bark
until required.

06

COMPRESSED CHERRIES

50 G (1¾ OZ) CASTER (SUPERFINE) SUGAR
200 ML (7 FL OZ) FRESHLY SQUEEZED BING
  CHERRY JUICE, FROM APPROXIMATELY
  400 G (14 OZ) FRESH BING CHERRIES
16 LARGE WHOLE FRESH BING CHERRIES

Combine the sugar and cherry juice and stir
until the sugar is dissolved. Cut the cherries in
half around the stone, then twist to separate
the two halves and carefully remove the stone
with the point of a small, sharp knife.

Put the cherry halves in a cryovac bag
with the sweetened cherry juice. Compress
and seal the bag in a vacuum machine. Put the
cherries into the refrigerator and keep the bag
sealed for at least 4 hours to allow the cherries
to macerate.

07

TO FINISH

Remove the cherries from the cryovac bag
and carefully slice them into thin discs.
Put the cherry discs back into the juice
until required.

Remove the dried cherry, nougat and
caramelised almond chocolate bark from the
refrigerator and use a sharp knife to cut it into
thin strips.

08

TO PLATE

½ QUANTITY VANILLA CUSTARD CREAM
  (SEE BASIC RECIPES)

Place half a teaspoon of room-temperature
chocolate ganache in the centre of each
serving plate and spread out with the back
of a spoon. Place 2 teaspoons of the vanilla
custard cream on the ganache. Place a few
strips of the chocolate bark on top of the
cream. Top with a couple of teaspoons of
the reserved cherry, nougat and caramelised
almond mixture. Add a few discs of the
compressed cherries. Layer with more
room-temperature chocolate ganache,
chocolate bark and cherry, nougat and
caramelised almond mixture. Finish with
a few more compressed cherry discs and
a scoop of the chocolate cherry sorbet. Serve.

GRASS TREE & WALLABY TAIL

AUSTRALIA'S INDIGENOUS FLORA AND FAUNA IS UNIQUE. THE QUESTION IS, WHY HAVE WE, AS CHEFS, RESISTED MAKING USE OF IT FOR SO LONG?

MURRAY COD / MACCULLOCHELLA PEELII
HARVEST / YEAR ROUND

Josh told us how Wardandi people had always divided the year into six distinct seasons and how the seasons were identified by the natural cycle of animals and plants.

Indigenous bush food has not been on Australian chefs' radar until recently. In general it has been a very underappreciated resource for non-Indigenous Australians since European settlement. There are many reasons for this; primarily, I think, there has been a dismissive cultural cringe attached to bush foods. Many chefs, myself included, had found the strong, intense and sometimes harsh flavours of bush food not really compatible with the idea of European cuisine. For the most part, bush food is foraged in diverse and remote parts of the country, from where it is only practical to ship this food dried or frozen. This doesn't show the ingredients in their best light.

There have been pioneers in the native food industry. People such as horticulturalist Peter Hardwick in the 1970s began investigating native plant species that were suitable for commercial cropping: fruit species such as riberries and *Davidsonia* and leaf species such as lemon myrtle and Dorrigo pepper. In the 1980s, chef Jean-Paul Bruneteau and Jenny Dowling opened Rowntrees restaurant in Sydney, specialising in native produce. Then Vic Cherikoff started up a distribution company marketing and supplying native Australian ingredients to the restaurant industry. In the 1990s, brother and sister Raymond and Jennice Kersh championed Australian native bush food at their restaurant Edna's Table. Aside from these people and a few other pioneers, most Australian chefs tended to dismiss bush tucker as 'kitsch' and 'tourist-oriented'.

My eyes were opened to the possibilities of Australia's unique flora when I attended the first Margaret River Gourmet Escape. I was taken on a tour by an Aboriginal leader named Josh Whiteland from Wardandi country in Western Australia near Margaret River. He explained to a group of chefs—including Alex Atala, René Redzepi and David Chang—about the local native food sources of his region. He told us how Wardandi people had always divided the year into six distinct seasons and how the seasons were identified by the natural cycle of animals and plants. A given season occurs when a certain fish is spawning or when a particular tree is in flower.

This experience illustrated to me how much I didn't know about native Australian edible flora. Since that episode I have been determined to explore which native plants are available and to see if I can source them in their fresh form. Through this exploration I found Mike and Gayle Quarmby, who have done extensive work in this field.

Mike and Gayle now supply a number of chefs in Sydney and Melbourne with fresh, seasonal native Australian produce; such as lemon aspen, which is much more subtle and delicious in its fresh form than when it was previously available dried or frozen. Fresh muntries, which taste and look like miniature apples the size of a marble, are now picked and distributed seasonally between January and March. Native coastal greens are grown by Mike and Gayle at their farm in the Coorong area of South Australia and feature on a dish with Murray cod. Murray cod itself is a fish indigenous to our fresh waterway the Murray River, which runs through New South Wales, Victoria and South Australia.

Our native food includes other indigenous fish and fauna. In many ways it makes a lot of sense to eat meat such as kangaroo and wallaby rather than grazing animals. Wallaby tail features on my menu. I cook it slowly in salted butter and it has an extraordinary flavour and texture. Australia's indigenous flora and fauna is unique. It's not the whole story of the development of an Australian cuisine but it should be part of it.

HAM HOCK BROTH
3 WHOLE HAM HOCKS
250 G (9 OZ) MAPLE WOOD CHIPS
50 ML (1¾ FL OZ) GRAPESEED OIL
50 G (1¾ OZ) GARLIC, SLICED
100 G (3½ OZ) ESCHALLOTS, SLICED
100 G (3½ OZ) INNER WHITE CELERY
   STALKS, SLICED
100 G (3½ OZ) JAMON, SLICED
2 FRESH BAY LEAVES
2 LITRES (70 FL OZ) CHICKEN STOCK
   (SEE BASIC RECIPES)
1 TEASPOON XANTANA (FERMENTED
   CORNSTARCH)

Split the ham hocks in half lengthways with a cleaver. Set up a cold smoking apparatus and cold smoke the ham hocks over the maple wood chips for 1 hour.

Put the grapeseed oil into a large heavy-based stockpot and gently sweat the garlic, eschallot and celery. Add the jamon, smoked ham hocks, bay leaves and chicken stock. Bring to the boil, skim, reduce the heat to very low and simmer for 2 hours. Remove from the heat and allow to infuse for a further 1 hour.

Strain through a fine sieve. You should have approximately 1 litre (35 fl oz) of stock remaining. Put the stock in a clean saucepan and bring to a simmer.

Transfer 100 ml (3½ fl oz) of the stock into a small bowl. Sprinkle the xantana over the top and whisk well until smooth. Pour this back into the hot stock, whisking over heat until well combined. Increase the heat and bring to a hard boil for 5 minutes or until slightly thickened. Pass through a fine sieve and refrigerate until required.

INDIGENOUS MOLLUSCS, HAM HOCK BROTH, GRASS TREE

SERVES / 8

02

GRASS TREE HEART

60 CM (24 INCH) TALL GRASS TREE
1 LITRE (35 FL OZ) STILL MINERAL WATER
½ LEMON, JUICE

Cut the grass tree in half lengthways using a pruning saw. The part you need is the section of white new fronds that are about to emerge from the tree. Remove this section using a sharp knife. Trim away any pale green colour, ensuring only the tender white section is used. Soak the fronds in the combined mineral water and lemon juice to stop discolouration. Set aside until required.

03

TO FINISH

500 G (1 LB 2 OZ) STRAWBERRY CLAMS
500 G (1 LB 2 OZ) PIPIS
500 G (1 LB 2 OZ) PERIWINKLES
500 G (1 LB 2 OZ) TULIP SHELL MOLLUSCS

Steam the strawberry clams and the pipis separately until the shells just open. Cool and remove the meat. Use a sharp knife to remove the gut sacs from both the pipis and clams. Set aside in the refrigerator until required. Steam the periwinkles and tulip shell molluscs for 30 minutes at full steam. Cool and remove the meat from the shell with a wooden skewer. Clean and remove the gut sacs, leaving only the flesh of each. Cut each mollusc in half lengthways. Refrigerate until required.

04

TO PLATE

50 G (1¾ OZ) UNSALTED BUTTER
SEA SALT

Heat 500 ml (17 fl oz) of the thickened ham hock broth in a large wok or wide-rimmed saucepan. Add all of the cleaned and reserved molluscs and the unsalted butter. Stir well for approximately 1 minute until the molluscs are just heated through. Check the seasoning of the broth and adjust with sea salt if necessary. Drain the grass tree fronds and add them to the broth. Continue to cook for a further 30 seconds. Divide the molluscs, broth and grass tree fronds between eight warm serving bowls to serve.

Josh Whitehead cut a grass tree in half and explained how this is a food source for the Wardandi people: grass trees are particularly plentiful in the Margaret River region. I had no idea that this rough, hard and blackened grass tree was in any way edible. Once the grass tree is cut open, the inside where the new fronds are developing is actually tender and edible. I found it similar to the heart of the palm tree. Unfortunately, this ingredient won't be on my menu at Quay as grass trees take up to 50 years to mature and it is illegal to harvest them from the bush unless you are an Indigenous Australian. The only alternative for me would be to buy them from a nursery: at more than $100 per tree, it is not a practical ingredient, but it does demonstrate the diverse possibilities of the Australian bush.

01

NATIVE COASTAL GREENS & LEMON ASPEN

100 G (3½ OZ) BARILLA (COORONG
   SPINACH)
150 G (5½ OZ) KARKALLA (SEA SUCCULENT)
100 G (3½ OZ) MUNYEROO (NATIVE
   PURSLANE)
50 G (1¾ OZ) SEA PARSLEY (SEA CELERY)
32 FRESH LEMON ASPEN FRUITS

Pick through the native coastal greens,
keeping only the small tips and leaves: discard
any larger leaves and stems. Wash well, drain
and set aside until required.

   Pick and remove any stems from the lemon
aspen fruit and set aside until required.

02

SEAWEED DRESSING

1 SMALL ESCHALLOT, FINELY DICED
SEA SALT FLAKES
2 SHEETS OF SWEET KOREAN
   TOASTED NORI
100 ML (3½ FL OZ) GRAPESEED OIL
1 TEASPOON LEMON JUICE

Put the eschallot in a mortar with a good
pinch of sea salt flakes and crush with a pestle
until a paste is formed.

   Roughly chop the nori, add to the mortar
with a small amount of the oil and combine
until a rough paste is formed.

   Drizzle in the remaining oil and lemon
juice and combine well.

03

MARRON

8 MARRON, 250 G (9 OZ) EACH

Place the live marron in plenty of iced water
and leave for a minimum of 15 minutes to
help humanely dispatch them. Bring a large
saucepan of salted water to the boil. Blanch
the marron for 1 minute then return to the
iced water. This will help in extracting the
meat from the shell. Use a large kitchen knife
to cut the head from the marron. Use kitchen
scissors to cut along both sides of the softer
underside shell. Peel the underside back and
then use your fingers to carefully pull the tail
meat from the shell, keeping the skin intact.
Remove the fine film of skin from the belly
of the marron then score one cut down the
centre of the belly, being careful not to cut
all the way through, then open out the flesh.
Set aside in the refrigerator until required.

04

TO FINISH

8 PIECES OF BINCHOTAN (WHITE)
   CHARCOAL
50 ML (1¾ FL OZ) GRAPESEED OIL
SEA SALT FLAKES
100 G (3½ OZ) CLARIFIED BUTTER
   (SEE BASIC RECIPES), MELTED

Heat the binchotan charcoal directly over a gas
burner until glowing red and allow the outside
to turn white. Put the hot charcoal into a small
Japanese-style barbecue (hibachi). Place a
wire rack over the barbecue and allow half an
hour for the heat to really build.

Brush the marron liberally with the
grapeseed oil and season well with the sea
salt flakes. Put the marron on the grill, skin
side down. Allow the heat to slightly roast the
skin for 1–2 minutes. Turn the marron over
and finish cooking for 2–3 minutes. Remove
marron from the grill, brush with melted
clarified butter and allow to rest for 1 minute.

   Meanwhile, blanch the coastal greens in
salted boiling water for 30 seconds. Brush with
melted butter and season with sea salt flakes.

   Gently warm the lemon aspen fruit in a
small saucepan with a small amount of the
melted clarified butter and sea salt.

05

TO PLATE

Place a marron in the centre of each warmed
serving plate. Dab a few dots of the seaweed
dressing around the marron. Garnish marron
with the warmed lemon aspen and coastal
greens and serve.

CHARCOAL-GRILLED MARRON, NATIVE COASTAL GREENS & LEMON ASPEN

SERVES / 8

01

WALLABY TAIL

50 G (1¾ OZ) SEA SALT
1 KG (2 LB 4 OZ) CLARIFIED BUTTER
  (SEE BASIC RECIPES), MELTED
3 KG (6 LB 12 OZ) WALLABY TAILS
200 ML (7 FL OZ) REDUCED VEAL GLAZE
  (SEE BASIC RECIPES)

Grind the sea salt to a fine powder and add to the clarified butter. Cut each wallaby tail into 4 sections. Put the wallaby tail and salted clarified butter into a large cryovac bag and seal. Steam the wallaby tail at 85°C (185°F) for 8 hours.

When the wallaby is cooked, remove from the steamer and allow to cool at room temperature. When cool enough to handle, open the bag and remove the tail. Transfer 200 ml (7 fl oz) of the salted butter into a clean saucepan with the veal glaze. Melt together over a gentle heat and set aside until required.

Pick the meat from the wallaby tail bones, ensuring the meat is free from sinew and cartilage. Put the meat into the saucepan containing the veal glaze and butter mixture. Set aside until required.

02

TO FINISH

400 G (14 OZ) BABY GOLDEN ORACH
  (MOUNTAIN SPINACH)
100 G (3½ OZ) UNSALTED BUTTER
SEA SALT

Pick and wash the golden orach leaves. Put the unsalted butter in a shallow frying pan and melt over gentle heat. Add the golden orach and gently wilt. Season with sea salt and drain on a clean tea towel (dish towel).

Gently reheat the wallaby tail over a low flame.

03

TO PLATE

64 WILD GARLIC FLOWERS

Place 3 tablespoons of the glazed wallaby meat in the centre of each warmed serving bowl. Top with wilted golden orach leaves. Garnish with wild garlic flowers. Serve.

WALLABY TAIL SLOWLY COOKED IN SALTED BUTTER, WILTED GOLDEN ORACH, WILD GARLIC

SERVES / 8

GAYLE & MIKE QUARMBY

INDIGENOUS PRODUCE SUPPLIERS
REEDY CREEK / SOUTH AUSTRALIA

Mike and Gayle's mission with Outback Pride is to replicate Rex's model of significant mentorship; to develop an industry that people could access without leaving their traditional lands.

In 2011 I moved house, and growing in the new backyard was a lilly pilly tree. Within a couple of months the bright pink fruits started to form. I knew lilly pillies were a type of native fruit but before this I had only ever tasted them frozen. The fresh fruit was so much more dynamic and alive with flavour and they sparked an idea for a new dessert at Quay. The challenge was to find someone who could, on a regular basis, harvest the fresh fruit on a commercial scale and send it to me at Quay within a couple of days. This requirement proved very difficult to fulfil. Most people who made lilly pilly jam and conserves did so with fruit from their own trees. It seemed no one was able to supply this native fruit fresh on a large scale until I found the Outback Pride website. The website listed a vast array of native fruits, herbs and spices, so I rang the phone number and spoke to Mike Quarmby.

I asked Mike the simple question, 'Can I get hold of fresh lilly pillies?' Mike's response was, 'Well, I can't see why not.' He told me he had lilly pilly trees growing on his own property at Reedy Creek in South Australia but they wouldn't be available until May and no one had ever asked for them fresh before. He then went on to ask me what variety I would like. I had no idea that different varieties existed; as it turns out, there are several varieties of edible lilly pillies and riberries available. A couple of months later Mike and Gayle came up to visit me in Sydney to show me what they produced. The range was remarkable, fruits and herbs that I had never heard of before but they were all dried or frozen, of course. I asked whether I could get hold of this produce fresh. This was the start of a relationship which kicked off a new direction for Mike and Gayle's business.

The Quarmbys had set up Outback Pride in 2001 as a response to the tragic loss of their son Daniel. Both Mike and Gayle were looking for something to help them heal through helping others. Gayle's father had told her, 'During hard and tragic times the best thing to do is to choose to stand up.' He had urged her to 'find a pathway to healing, a pathway that was directed towards the open sharing of skills to help others'.

Gayle's father, Rex Battarbee, was a landscape painter and had many outback friends of the western Arrernte people. Rex taught Albert Namatjira and his kin to paint with watercolours and helped promote the Aboriginal art industry. So Mike and Gayle decided to return to Gayle's childhood home in Alice Springs, in central outback Australia, where she'd grown up playing with children of the desert and learning about traditional foods from the elders.

Gayle was shocked when she realised that the plight of outback communities had worsened since her youth. As Mike's background was in commercial horticulture, they proactively followed Gayle's father's efforts and advice and helped establish community market gardens growing native food plants. Over time, this program expanded to include more than 25 remote outback communities. Mike's extensive knowledge of plant propagation has saved some indigenous food plants, such as the passion berry—a rare variety of bush tomato—from the brink of extinction.

So Mike and Gayle decided to return to Gayle's childhood home in Alice Springs, in central outback Australia, where she'd grown up playing with children of the desert and learning about traditional foods from the elders.

Gayle was shocked when she realised that the plight of outback communities had worsened since her youth. As Mike's background was in commercial horticulture, they proactively followed Gayle's father's efforts and advice and helped establish community market gardens growing native food plants. Over time, this program expanded to include more than 25 remote outback communities. Mike's extensive knowledge of plant propagation has saved some indigenous food plants, such as the passion berry—a rare variety of bush tomato—from the brink of extinction.

Mike and Gayle's mission with Outback Pride is to replicate Rex's model of significant mentorship; to develop an industry that people could access without leaving their traditional lands. Mike and Gayle purchase the produce from the communities and have developed a large range of outback and traditional food products, spice mixes, relishes and an array of frozen and dried traditional fruits for the food service industry.

My challenge to Mike and Gayle—to provide some of this indigenous produce to the restaurant industry, fresh rather than preserved so people could truly appreciate its unique qualities—met with an immediate response. More fruit trees, such as lilly pilly, lemon aspen and muntries, were planted on their property at Reedy Creek and Mike also started cultivating an array of fresh greens such as karkalla, barilla, sea parsley and saltbush so that the produce could be freshly picked and transported to city restaurants within 24 hours of harvesting. Mike and Gayle now supply fresh native produce to more than 100 restaurants all over the country.

LEFT: Samphire growing in sandy soil.

BELOW LEFT: The greyish-green leaves of saltbush.

RIGHT: Lemon aspen.

01

GREEN APPLE SYRUP

3 KG (6 LB 12 OZ) GRANNY SMITH APPLES
1 SMALL ESCHALLOT
SEA SALT
100 ML (3½ FL OZ) EXTRA VIRGIN OLIVE OIL

Peel the apples and coarsely grate them into a bowl. Tip the grated apple into a sieve lined with muslin (cheesecloth) and squeeze out all the juice into a clean bowl. This should yield 1 litre (35 fl oz) of juice. If you have access to a rotary evaporator put the juice in the machine's flask and reduce to 150 ml (5 fl oz). Alternatively, reduce the apple juice in a stainless steel saucepan on a rapid simmer. Cool completely.

Finely dice the eschallot and place in a bowl with a pinch of salt, the cooled apple reduction and the olive oil and whisk until well combined. Set aside until required.

02

FROZEN CRÈME FRAÎCHE

400 G (14 OZ) CRÈME FRAÎCHE
SEA SALT
1 LITRE LIQUID NITROGEN

Whisk the crème fraîche with a pinch of salt until soft peaks form. Wearing appropriate protective eyewear and gloves, pour the liquid nitrogen into an insulated bowl or a small styrofoam container (see glossary for more safety information). Working in small batches, carefully drop half teaspoons of the crème fraîche into the liquid nitrogen until you have made 40 roughly shaped crème fraîche nuggets. After approximately 30 seconds in the liquid nitrogen the crème fraîche will have frozen. Remove with a slotted spoon into a sealed container and place in the freezer until required.

03

TO FINISH

120 PISTACHIO NUTS
64 SILVER SORREL LEAVES
   (OR BUCKLER-LEAF SORREL)
40 ALASKA VARIEGATED
   NASTURTIUM LEAVES
32 APPLE MINT LEAVES
24 ALASKA VARIEGATED NASTURTIUM
   FLOWER BUDS
56 SAMPHIRE STEMS
40 BARILLA (COORONG SPINACH) SPRIGS
200 FRESH MUNTRIES
32 WHOLE WHITE MICROCUCUMBERS,
   EACH 1–2 CM (⅜–¾ INCH) LONG

Shell the fresh pistachio nuts. Pick, wash and dry all the herbs, shoots and buds. Pick the samphire and barilla so you are only using the top 3 cm (1¼ inches) of each shoot. Wash and dry the muntries. Lightly rinse and dry the microcucumbers.

04

TO PLATE

Combine the muntries, pistachio nuts and microcucumbers and toss gently in a large bowl. Pour the green apple syrup over and gently mix to coat. Use a slotted spoon to divide the mixture evenly between serving bowls. Place 5 frozen crème fraîche nuggets on top of each serving. Scatter the samphire, barilla, herbs and buds evenly over each bowl. Serve.

FRESH MUNTRIES & PISTACHIO NUTS, CRÈME FRAÎCHE, SILVER SORREL, NASTURTIUMS

SERVES / 8

Murray cod is an Australian native freshwater fish of exceptional quality with thick and juicy white flesh. In this recipe I have paired it with deep umami-rich flavours. I make the oyster crackling by first cold smoking the rock oysters, dehydrating them and then frying them in hot oil. They have a wonderful flavour and texture which, combined with kombu, anchovy juice and butter, creates an intense dressing for the Murray cod. Cumbungi, native Australian bulrush, is an underused vegetable of great texture and interest.

STEAMED MURRAY COD, CUMBUNGI, SMOKED OYSTER CRACKLING, ANCHOVY & ROASTED SEAWEED BUTTER

SERVES / 8

01

DRY SMOKED OYSTER CRACKLING

24 SYDNEY ROCK OYSTERS (OR OTHER
   ROCK OYSTERS)
500 G (1 LB 2 OZ) MAPLE WOOD CHIPS
1 LITRE (35 FL OZ) GRAPESEED OIL,
   FOR DEEP-FRYING

Set up a cold smoking apparatus. Shuck
the oysters and place the oyster flesh on
a perforated tray to fit the smoker. Cold
smoke the oysters for 1½ hours. Cut the
oysters in half lengthways, put them on a
baking tray lined with silicone paper and
dry them in a 50°C (120°F) oven, turning
occasionally, for about 5 hours until the
oysters become like leather.

   Set aside 24 of the oyster halves for the
anchovy and roasted seaweed butter: see
recipe below.

   Heat the grapeseed oil to 170°C (325°F)
and deep-fry the remaining oyster halves until
slightly puffed and crisp. Drain, cool and store
in an airtight container until required.

02

ANCHOVY & ROASTED SEAWEED BUTTER

2 SHEETS OF COMPRESSED,
   LAYERED KOMBU
100 ML (3½ FL OZ) GRAPESEED OIL
24 SMOKED AND DRIED OYSTER HALVES,
   RESERVED FROM ABOVE
150 G (5½ OZ) UNSALTED BUTTER
1 TEASPOON LEMON JUICE
10 ML (⅜ FL OZ) FERMENTED ANCHOVY
   BRINE

Fry the sheets of kombu in the grapeseed oil in
a large frying pan over medium–high heat until
golden brown. Drain well. Cool and crumble
with your hands until you have fine even flakes.

   Roughly chop the reserved oyster halves.
Keep all ingredients at hand until you are
ready to finish the dish.

03

CUMBUNGI

4 REEDS OF CUMBUNGI (BULRUSH)

Peel away the first several layers of cumbungi,
exposing the soft inner core. Slice the inner
core into 2 mm (¹⁄₁₆ inch) thick discs. Reserve
the slices in cold water until required.

04

MURRAY COD

1.5 KG (3 LB 5 OZ) WHOLE MURRAY COD
   (OR FIRM WHITE-FLESHED FISH)
SEA SALT FLAKES
100 G (3½ OZ) CLARIFIED BUTTER
   (SEE BASIC RECIPES), MELTED

Scale and gut the Murray cod. Season both
inside and out with sea salt flakes.

   Brush the fish liberally with clarified butter.
Wrap the fish in an envelope of silicone paper.
Place in a fish kettle and steam over rapidly
simmering water for 15–20 minutes or until
just cooked through.

05

TO FINISH

100 G (3½ OZ) CLARIFIED BUTTER
   (SEE BASIC RECIPES), MELTED
SEA SALT FLAKES

Remove the fish from the steamer and allow
to rest for 5 minutes. Meanwhile, make the
anchovy and roasted seaweed butter sauce by
melting the reserved unsalted butter gently
and adding the chopped roasted kombu
crumbs and chopped oysters with the lemon
juice and fermented anchovy brine. Mix well.
Taste and adjust seasoning with more
anchovy brine if needed.

   Blanch the cumbungi in boiling salted
water for 30 seconds, brush with the clarified
butter and season with sea salt flakes.

06

TO PLATE

Peel back the skin from the Murray cod and
carefully remove 4 even portions from each
side of the fish, being careful to leave the
bones behind. Place a portion in the centre
of each warmed serving plate. Quickly flash
the oyster crackling in a 200°C (400°F/Gas 6)
oven on a flat tray for 30 seconds. Dress the
fish with a generous spoonful of the anchovy
and roasted seaweed butter. Garnish with the
oyster crackling and cumbungi.

Through my research into native Australian flora I have come across a unique berry that is endemic to Tasmania. The snowberry grows wild in alpine regions of southern Tasmania and is at its peak in the month of March. At this stage no one grows the snowberry commercially and it can only be harvested from private land. I contacted Kris Shaffer, who has spent 20 years researching, passionately cultivating and advising on indigenous Tasmanian flora, to help me forage for this unique berry. I'm investigating the possibility of having this berry grown on a larger scale so that it can be discovered by more Australian chefs.

SNOWBERRIES

PREPARATION / 1 DAY
SERVES / 8

01

SNOWBERRIES
500 ML (17 FL OZ) WATER
250 G (9 OZ) CASTER (SUPERFINE) SUGAR
1 VANILLA BEAN, SPLIT, SEEDS SCRAPED
160 FRESH SNOWBERRIES

Combine the water with the sugar and vanilla bean in a small saucepan, stirring over high heat until the sugar is dissolved. Bring to the boil then remove from the heat.

Pass through a fine sieve into a bowl and chill completely.

Put the snowberries and syrup into a large cryovac bag and seal at medium vacuum. Allow to macerate in the bag in the refrigerator for 24 hours before using.

02

MILK ICE CREAM
150 G (5½ OZ) CASTER (SUPERFINE) SUGAR
100 G (3½ OZ) EGG YOLKS
1 LITRE (35 FL OZ) FULL-CREAM JERSEY
  MILK
50 G (1¾ OZ) TRIMOLINE (INVERTED
  SUGAR SYRUP)
100 ML (3½ FL OZ) PURE JERSEY CREAM
  (35–40% FAT)

Combine the caster sugar and egg yolks in a large bowl and whisk well until pale and creamy. Gently heat the milk and trimoline in a small saucepan until it reaches 85°C (185°F). Pour the hot milk over the egg yolk mixture, whisking continuously. Transfer the mixture to a double boiler and stir constantly until the mixture returns to 85°C. Pour this mixture directly into an upright blender and blend on high for 5 minutes. Strain the mixture through a fine sieve into a glass container. Whisk in the jersey cream until well combined. Refrigerate for 24 hours to age the mixture before churning in an ice-cream machine 1 hour before serving.

03

FROZEN VANILLA MOUSSE
1¾ SHEETS OF TITANIUM-STRENGTH
  GELATINE
250 ML (9 FL OZ) FULL-CREAM JERSEY MILK
175 G (6 OZ) CASTER (SUPERFINE) SUGAR
1 VANILLA BEAN, SEEDS ONLY
70 G (2½ OZ) EGGWHITE
175 ML (5½ FL OZ) PURE CREAM (35% FAT)
75 G (2¾ OZ) DOUBLE CREAM
  (45–50% FAT)
1 LITRE LIQUID NITROGEN

Soak the gelatine sheets in cold water. Put the milk, 50 g (1¾ oz) of the caster sugar and the vanilla bean seeds in a saucepan and bring to a simmer. Squeeze out the gelatine and add to the hot milk mixture, whisking until dissolved. Pour the mixture through a fine sieve into a clean bowl. Set the bowl over ice and whisk periodically until the milk is just looking like it wants to set.

In the meantime make an Italian meringue. Heat the remaining caster sugar with just enough water to wet it and dissolve the sugar. Stir over high heat just until the sugar crystals have completely dissolved, then bring the sugar to 118°C (244°F) softball stage. Whisk the eggwhites in an electric mixer at high speed until soft peaks are formed. With the motor still running, slowly pour on the hot sugar syrup. The eggwhites will dramatically increase in volume. Once all the sugar syrup has been added, turn the speed to medium and keep the machine whisking for a further 5 minutes.

Combine the thin and thick cream and whisk to soft peaks.

In a clean bowl, combine the Italian meringue, just-setting milk and gelatine mixture, and the cream mixture. Fold together until well incorporated. Refrigerate for a minimum of 4 hours to fully set.

Put the set milk mousse into a piping bag with a 2 cm (¾ inch) round nozzle. Wearing appropriate protective eyewear and gloves, pour the liquid nitrogen into an insulated bowl or a small styrofoam container (see glossary for more safety information). Pipe the milk mousse into the liquid nitrogen and allow to remain in the liquid nitrogen until completely frozen and the liquid nitrogen has evaporated. If using a styrofoam container, transfer the frozen milk mousse to a metal bowl. Using the end of a rolling pin, gently break it up into small pieces. Put the frozen mousse into an airtight container and freeze until required.

04

MERINGUE
150 G (5½ OZ) EGGWHITE
150 G (5½ OZ) CASTER (SUPERFINE) SUGAR
150 G (5½ OZ) ICING (CONFECTIONERS')
  SUGAR

Put the eggwhites into the bowl of an electric mixer with the whisk attachment. Turn the motor on high and gradually add the caster sugar as the mixture continually whisks to firm peak stage.

Remove the whipped eggwhites from the machine and sift the icing sugar over the top. Fold the icing sugar through with a spatula until well incorporated. Lightly spray two large silicone baking mats with vegetable oil. Place 2 rounded tablespoons of the meringue mixture onto each mat and, with a large spatula, spread the meringue out to an even 2 mm (⅟₁₆ inch) thickness. Put the meringue into a 90°C (195°F/Gas ¼–½) oven and dry out for approximately 1 hour. Cool completely, break into 5 cm (2 inch) shapes and store with silica gel in an airtight container.

05

TO FINISH
1 QUANTITY MILK BISCUIT
  (SEE BASIC RECIPES)

Break the milk biscuit into rough 5 cm (2 inch) shapes.

06

TO PLATE
1 QUANTITY VANILLA CUSTARD CREAM
  (SEE BASIC RECIPES)

Place 1 tablespoon of vanilla custard cream in the centre of each chilled serving bowl. Gently spread out with the back of the spoon. Place 1 tablespoon of frozen vanilla mousse pieces over the cream then place a couple of the meringue and milk biscuit pieces into the cream.

Drain the snowberries from the syrup and spoon a generous tablespoonful over each dessert. Top with another half-tablespoon of frozen vanilla milk mousse pieces and, at the last moment, place a quenelle of milk ice cream to one side of the dessert. Serve.

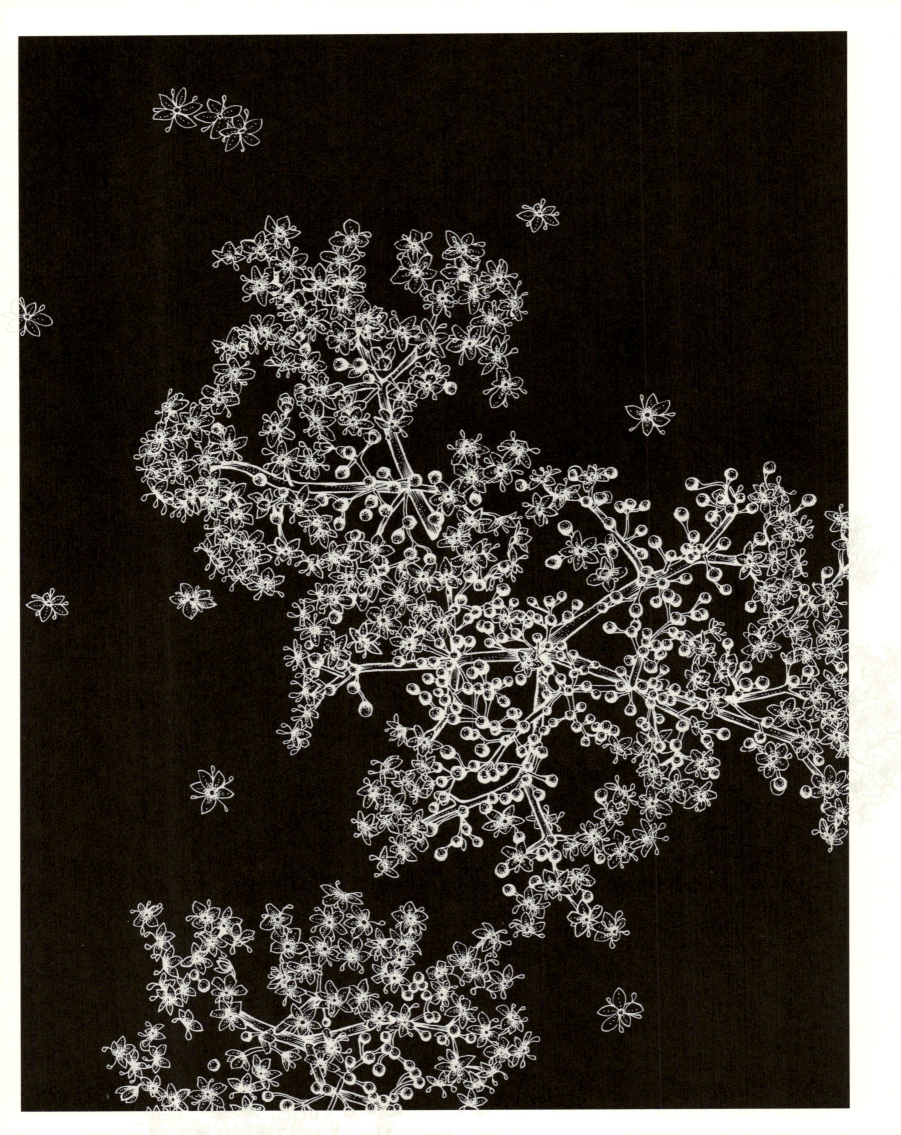

SEARCH FOR PURITY

ORGANUM IS THE MAGIC THAT HAPPENS WHEN ELEMENTS ARE COMBINED, LEADING TO A SENSE OF SOMETHING NEW, SOMETHING PURE.

ELDERFLOWER / SAMBUCUS NIGRA
HARVEST / LATE SPRING

One element informs the next element: there is layering and the aim is to achieve balance and purity. The experience of eating a perfect dish can place you right in the moment.

What I mean by purity is a sense of balance and harmony within a dish. When all the elements come together perfectly, when the selection of ingredients and the nature of those ingredients are fully expressed through considered technique. When these ingredients work together to create something new. When flavours are intense and clear but are also balanced and in harmony with each other. When textures combine to create sensory pleasure. The idea of Organum is the magic that happens when elements are combined, leading to a sense of something new, something pure.

Original creation can only come from deep and considered thought. To me, a new dish is something so special, it is a gift. Originality is not created in a vacuum, but it comes from knowledge and your own life experiences.

I recently had the chance to talk with a Japanese Buddhist monk and what resonated with me is that one of the aims of Buddhism is to live in the moment and truly experience the present, appreciating the whole and each of its parts at the same time. He gave the example of a Japanese Zen garden not having a centre, not having a main focal point; but every part of the garden is as important as any other and one part informs and relates to the next part.

In this sense it's like the structure of a perfect dish. One element informs the next element: there is layering and the aim is to achieve balance and purity. The experience of eating a perfect dish can place you right in the moment.

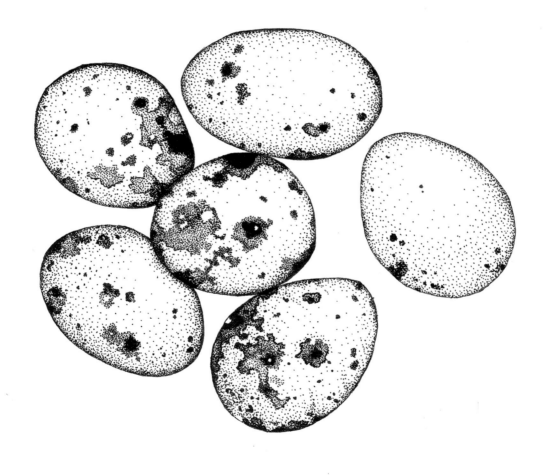

01
SPANNER CRABS
2 LIVE SPANNER CRABS, 700 G
  (1 LB 9 OZ) EACH
SEA SALT

Submerge the crabs in a large tub of iced water for 1 hour to help humanely dispatch them. Bring a large saucepan of salted water to the boil.

Add the crabs to the saucepan and boil for 8 minutes. Remove the crabs to a tray, transfer to the refrigerator and allow to chill for 1 hour.

Crack and remove as much white leg and body meat from the crabs as possible. Avoid any brown meat. Shred the crab meat with your fingers and place in a bowl. Refrigerate until required.

02
WHITE CORN JUICE
10 WHITE SWEET CORNCOBS

Use a sharp knife to remove the kernels from the corncobs and juice in an electric juicer. Pass through a fine sieve and reserve in the refrigerator until required.

03
HEART OF PALM
1 WHOLE PALM HEART
GRAPESEED OIL, TO DRESS
SEA SALT

Prepare the palm heart by peeling off the layers until you have only the central core left. Slice the central core of the palm heart into 1 mm (1/32 inch) thick discs. Set aside until required. Just before serving, lightly dress the palm heart slices with grapeseed oil and season with sea salt.

04
TO FINISH
25 G (1 OZ) UNSALTED BUTTER

In a large saucepan, heat the white corn juice over low to medium heat, stirring constantly. Once the juice has reached simmering point it will thicken slightly. Whisk in the butter until melted and mixed through.

Add the crab meat to the corn juice and bring just to simmering point. Remove from the heat.

05
TO PLATE

Pour a ladleful of crab meat and corn juice in the centre of each warmed serving bowl. Place a small mound of palm heart on top of each. Serve.

This dish embodies my idea of purity in many ways. It has a simplicity that is very elegant and flavours that work harmoniously together. The flavour of young heart of palm has always reminded me of delicate white corn. White corn juice, which thickens naturally when heated and works beautifully as a simple broth, is married with freshly cooked spanner crab. The mouth feel of this dish—its textures and flavours—creates an idea of something very pure.

HEART OF PALM, SPANNER CRAB, WHITE CORN JUICE

SERVES / 8

TAKUAN

1 DAIKON (WHITE RADISH), WITH
   GREENS ATTACHED
FINE SEA SALT
100 G (3½ OZ) FRESH RICE BRAN
20 ML (¾ FL OZ) GOOD-QUALITY
   AGED SOY SAUCE
20 ML (¾ FL OZ) BROWN RICE VINEGAR
20 ML (¾ FL OZ) HIGH-QUALITY MIRIN
   (RICE WINE)
10 G (⅜ OZ) YOUNG GINGER, VERY
   THINLY SLICED

Wash the daikon but do not peel it. Tie a string around the greens of the daikon radish and hang in a well-ventilated sheltered area; for example, from the rafters of a covered balcony. The idea is to naturally dry the daikon for 10 days, ideally in spring with a temperature range of approximately 10–22°C (50–72°F). After 10 days the daikon should be very flexible and feel lighter. Make sure there are no signs of mould or insect infestation. Remove the green top from the daikon and discard. Peel off the skin with a sharp knife. Cut the daikon into 10 cm (4 inch) sections along its length. Weigh the daikon and calculate the required salt quantity at 4% of the weight of the daikon.

Put the salt and rice bran into a large bowl with the soy sauce, brown rice vinegar, mirin and ginger and mix well. Add the daikon pieces and massage the rice bran mixture into the daikon all over.

Place the daikon and rice bran mixture into a large cryovac bag. Seal with a vacuum machine on a medium setting.

Store the bag of daikon and pickling mixture in a cool, dark, dry place; ideally, a cellar environment or a cupboard in a cool corner of the kitchen. This pickle is traditionally pickled for around 6 months in Japan but for my purposes the pickle is perfect to use after about 10 weeks.

02

KINOME OIL

50 FRESH KINOME SPRIGS
200 ML (7 FL OZ) GRAPESEED OIL

Put the kinome and grapeseed oil into a blender and process for 1 minute on high. Pour the mixture into a cryovac bag and seal on a vacuum machine or use a clean, airtight jar. Allow the oil to infuse, in the refrigerator, for 1 week. Before using the oil you will need to strain the mixture through a muslin-lined sieve and discard the solids.

LIGHTLY FERMENTED
SHIITAKE MUSHROOMS

8 MEDIUM-SIZE FRESH SHIITAKE
   MUSHROOMS
2 GENEROUS PINCHES FINE SEA SALT
100 ML (3½ FL OZ) GRAPESEED OIL

Remove the stalks from the shiitake mushrooms and peel away the skins. Use a sharp knife to slice the shiitake horizontally across the cap, into several thin slices; ideally, no more than 2 mm (1/16 inch) thick. Spread the freshly sliced shiitake mushrooms out on a large tray. Evenly sprinkle the sea salt over the mushroom slices. Pour the grapeseed oil over and turn to ensure the slices are well coated. Put into a cryovac bag and seal using a vacuum machine on medium pressure. Keep the mushrooms at room temperature in the cryovac bag for 8–12 hours. This will intensify the flavour of the shiitake mushrooms.

Shaved tulip shell molluscs—hand-harvested just two kilometres off the coast of Sydney— have a really wonderful texture similar to abalone. Takuan pickles are a very special pickle developed in Japan: the daikon radishes are sun-dried for up to two weeks before being pickled in salt and rice bran.

04
ALMOND & CITRON LEAF KUZU

500 ML (17 FL OZ) WATER
10 CM (4 INCH) PIECE DRIED KOMBU
50 G (1¾ OZ) KATSUOBUSHI
   (OR SHAVED BONITO)
50 ML (1¾ FL OZ) JAPANESE WHITE
   SOY SAUCE
25 ML (1 FL OZ) MIRIN (RICE WINE)
150 G (5½ OZ) FRESHLY BLANCHED
   RAW ALMONDS, SKIN REMOVED
4 CITRON LEAVES, OR 4 KAFFIR
   LIME LEAVES
1 TABLESPOON KUZU STARCH

To make dashi, put the water and kombu into a large saucepan and bring to 90°C (195°F). Remove from the heat, immediately add the katsuobushi and allow to infuse for 1 hour. Add the soy sauce and mirin to season. Strain the dashi and discard the solids.

Roast the blanched almonds in a medium oven until very lightly toasted. Warm the dashi in a small saucepan. Put the dashi and almonds into a blender and process for 2 minutes on high. Crush the citron leaves in your hand and add to the blender. Blitz for 5 seconds. Remove the mixture from the blender and allow to infuse in a bowl for 20 minutes.

Pass the mixture through a fine muslin-lined sieve, applying a small amount of pressure to assist the extraction. Discard the solids. Put the liquid into a fresh saucepan. Whisk in the kuzu starch until smooth, then put the saucepan over medium heat as you constantly whisk. The mixture will rapidly thicken. Turn the heat to low and continue to whisk, cooking out the starch flavour, for a minimum of 5 minutes. Put the thickened mixture into a small plastic container, cover and refrigerate. This mixture needs to be made a minimum of 6 hours before assembling the finished recipe, and can be made up to 3 days in advance.

05
TULIP SHELL MOLLUSC

16 TULIP SHELL MOLLUSCS (SEA SNAILS
   OR PERIWINKLES CAN BE USED
   IF UNAVAILABLE)

Put the live tulip shell molluscs into a large bowl of iced water for 1 hour to help humanely dispatch them. Put the molluscs into a steamer on high steam for 20 minutes. Remove from the steamer and chill the molluscs in a large bowl of iced water. Remove the meat from the shells using a bamboo skewer. Trim away all of the intestines, leaving only the meat. Cut the molluscs into paper-thin slices. Store in an airtight container in the refrigerator until required.

06
TO FINISH

32 GAI LAN (CHINESE BROCCOLI) FLOWERS
SEA SALT

Remove the petals from the gai lan flowers, wash and dry. Open the takuan container and remove one piece of daikon. Wipe away any loose bran then lightly rinse to remove any residual bran. Dry the pickle with a clean tea towel (dish towel). Thinly slice the pickle into 1 mm (1/32 inch) slices. Set aside until required.

Open the shiitake mushroom bag, remove from the bag and lightly squeeze the mushrooms to extract any excess juice. Put the mushrooms in a clean bowl. Add the sliced tulip shell molluscs and takuan pickles. Dress this mixture with two tablespoons kinome oil and lightly season with sea salt. Mix well.

07
TO PLATE

Place 2 half tablespoons of the kuzu mixture, slightly apart, on each serving plate. Top with an even amount of the mollusc, shiitake and pickle mixture. Garnish with gai lan petals and serve.

SHAVED TULIP SHELL MOLLUSC, TAKUAN PICKLES, KINOME

PREPARATION / 12 WEEKS
SERVES / 8

JUDE McBAIN

ALMOND GROWER
WILLUNGA / SOUTH AUSTRALIA

This story highlights the benefits of forming direct relationships with growers and producers. I would have never discovered the textural intricacies and growing stages of almonds if I had not pursued a working relationship with Jude.

Several years ago, on holiday in France, I tried green almonds for the first time: these late-spring, fuzzy, green-shelled almonds were being sold in the markets. Cracking them open, I discovered a young almond that was fresh and milky yet crisp. It was quite different from the fully developed hard almonds that are usually roasted.

When I returned home I made it my mission to find a supplier of these wonderful green almonds. This proved difficult as most of the almonds grown in Australia tended to be produced on a large scale with mechanical harvesting. These farms weren't interested in harvesting the almonds while still green. I asked Jane Casey, my chestnut supplier, if she knew anyone who grew almonds on a small enough scale that they might be willing to pick them green.

She put me in touch with Jude McBain from Blue Cottage Almonds in South Australia. I asked Jude if she would be interested in supplying green almonds to me. She said she was willing to give it a go although it was not something she had done before. It meant hand picking the almonds and posting them to

me via Australia Post. Regular consignments of almonds have been arriving in the Quay kitchen every November and this relationship has been going on now for many years.

Jude and Ian McBain bought their four hectare (10 acre) almond orchard at the top of Almond Grove Road near Willunga, South Australia, in 1993. Moving to the country and buying the orchard was a tree change for these two town dwellers. Although both Jude and Ian had farming family backgrounds, Jude admits they fell in love with the romance of the idea. Reality soon struck when they realised they had purchased an orchard full of paper shell almond trees that were on their last legs. Harvests started to diminish year by year despite their best efforts to turn things around.

The hard decision was finally reached that they would have to replant their whole orchard. After a lot of research, rather than replanting American paper shell varieties, which were the fashion in the seventies and eighties, they would stick with the old European brownskin hard shell almonds. Many of these had been planted in the district for more than 100 years, had adapted to

local conditions and been bred into genuine Willunga varieties. This proved to be a good decision, as Jude decided to market and sell her almonds at the newly formed Willunga Farmers Market. Because Jude's almonds had local history and not many people grew these varieties, she had a great local story and an authentic product to sell.

Jude recalls my original enquiry for green almonds as being 'a bit out there'. The first batch she sent me were so young they had not formed an actual nut but were a thin shell encasing a jellylike substance that was slightly bitter. As it turned out we needed to wait another month before the almonds would form the classic green almond milky crispness. I now buy almonds from Jude at three distinct stages: the classic green crisp almond; the fully developed hard almond; and I have also found a use for those slightly bitter jelly almonds. After slightly blanching the jelly almonds in boiling water for 10 seconds, the jelly sets and becomes as sweet as a grape. These almonds feature in my local crayfish sashimi dish.

TOP RIGHT: Green almonds.
BELOW: Almond grove, Willunga, South Australia.
LEFT AND BELOW RIGHT: Dried almonds, waiting to be shelled.

Local crayfish caught only an hour up the coast from Sydney has a beautiful blue-green shell and firm sweet flesh. We buy these crayfish live and keep them in our tank at the restaurant. They are humanely dispatched, by firstly plunging them into a bucket of iced water for an hour, then spiking and briefly blanching them. The flesh is in pristine sashimi condition when sliced and paired with citrus, elderflowers, crème fraîche and very young green almonds that are still in their soft jelly stage. This is a highly seasonal dish of mid-spring when the almonds and elderflowers first appear. There is something special about a dish that can only exist for a few weeks of the year.

SASHIMI OF LOCAL CRAYFISH, GRAPEFRUIT, GREEN ALMONDS, CRÈME FRAÎCHE, BERGAMOT MARMALADE, ELDERFLOWERS

SERVES / 8

01
CRAYFISH SASHIMI
1 KG (2 LB 4 OZ) LOCAL CRAYFISH

Plunge the live crayfish into a large bucket of heavily iced water for 15 minutes. This will help to humanely dispatch it. After 15 minutes, place the tip of a large sharp knife between the eyes and spike the crayfish. Transfer the crayfish to a large saucepan or stockpot of boiling salted water. Blanch for exactly 1 minute then return the crayfish to the iced water to cool.

Remove the tail from the crayfish head with a sharp heavy knife. Discard the head or use it to make stock for another recipe. Use a pair of scissors to cut away the underside of the crayfish tail shell and carefully remove the meat. Allow the crayfish tail meat to rest, covered, in the refrigerator for 12 hours. This will make it easier to thinly slice. When ready, using a sharp sashimi knife, slice the crayfish into 4 mm (3/16 inch) thick slices. Refrigerate until required.

02
GRAPEFRUIT
3 YELLOW GRAPEFRUIT
500 ML LIQUID NITROGEN

Segment the grapefruit and place the segments in a stainless steel bowl. Wearing appropriate protective eyewear and gloves, pour the liquid nitrogen over the grapefruit segments and allow them to fully freeze: the liquid nitrogen will evaporate. (See glossary for more safety information.) Break up the hard grapefruit segments with the end of a rolling pin to produce frozen individual grapefruit cells. Put the frozen cells into an airtight container and freeze until required.

03
LEMON CRÈME FRAÎCHE
1½ TEASPOONS LEMON JUICE
150 G (5½ OZ) CRÈME FRAÎCHE

Whisk the lemon juice into the crème fraîche, pour into an airtight container and refrigerate until required.

04
GREEN MANGO PICKLE
1 FIRM GREEN MANGO
150 ML (5 FL OZ) WHITE VERJUS

Peel the green mango and cut into paper-thin slices using a Japanese mandolin. Place the slices and verjus into a cryovac bag and seal on a vacuum machine. Refrigerate for a minimum of 1 hour before using and for no longer than a few days.

05
GREEN ALMONDS
56 GREEN ALMONDS, AT THE JELLY STAGE IN EARLY SPRING

Carefully slit open the almond shells with a sharp knife, without piercing the kernel. Place the almonds directly into cold water as you are shelling. Bring a saucepan of water to the boil and blanch the almonds for 15 seconds then refresh in iced water. These almonds should be blanched no more than 1 hour before serving or they will discolour.

06
TO FINISH
100 ML (3½ FL OZ) WHITE SOY SAUCE
100 ML (3½ FL OZ) GRAPESEED OIL
50 G (1¾ OZ) BERGAMOT JAM (SEE BASIC RECIPES)

Spread the crayfish meat out in a single layer on a tray lined with silicone paper. Mix the white soy sauce and grapeseed oil together well. Brush the mixture over the top of each slice.

Put the bergamot jam into a piping bag.

07
TO PLATE
8 CLUSTERS OF FRESH ELDERFLOWERS

Place half a tablespoon of the lemon crème fraîche in the centre of each serving plate and spread it out with the back of the spoon. Place 3 slices of the green mango pickle on top of the crème fraîche. Cover with 2 tablespoons of frozen grapefruit cells. Pipe 3–4 dots of bergamot jam on top. Lay an equal number of crayfish slices on each plate. Garnish with the green almonds and, at the last minute, destem the elderflowers and sprinkle them evenly over each plate. Serve.

Kakai pumpkins are an anomaly of nature. They have been developed from Austrian naked-seed pumpkins traditionally used for the production of Styrian pumpkin seed oil. The seeds, which have no hull, have a delicious flavour and texture when they are picked fresh from the pumpkins. In this recipe they provide the textural element that contrasts with the delicate crayfish and mud crab velvet.

CRUSTACEAN VELVET, FRESH KAKAI PUMPKIN SEEDS, PUMPKIN & CRUSTACEAN JUICE

SERVES / 8

01

CRAYFISH MOUSSELINE

600 G (1 LB 5 OZ) LIVE TASMANIAN
  CRAYFISH
1 EGGWHITE
FINE SEA SALT
160 ML (5¼ FL OZ) PURE CREAM (35% FAT)

Plunge the crayfish into a large bucket of
heavily iced water for 15 minutes. This will
help to humanely dispatch it. After 15 minutes,
place the tip of a large sharp knife between
the eyes and spike the crayfish. Transfer
the crayfish to a large saucepan or stockpot
of boiling salted water. Blanch for exactly
1 minute then return the crayfish to the iced
water to cool for 10 minutes.

Remove the legs and feelers and reserve
in a bowl in the refrigerator. Remove the tail
from the head with a sharp heavy knife. Use a
pair of scissors to cut away the underside of
the crayfish tail shell and carefully remove the
meat. Discard the head and tail shell or freeze
for another use.

Trim the tail meat of any tougher skin and
rough edges and reserve this trim with the
legs and feelers. Remove the digestive tract
and discard. Slice the cleaned, trimmed tail
meat into rough 2 cm (¾ inch) thick slices.
Chill in the refrigerator for 1 hour.

You should have around 200 g (7 oz) of
raw crayfish flesh. Set up a food processor
and process the crayfish flesh on high speed
for 20 seconds. Add the eggwhite and a
good pinch of salt and process for a further
30 seconds. Stop and scrape down the sides
of the food processor bowl. With the motor
running, slowly pour in the cream in a thin
stream. The mousseline should become
thick and glossy by the time all the cream
is incorporated. Transfer from the food
processor into a small stainless steel bowl,
cover and refrigerate until required.

02

MUD CRAB

500 G (1 LB 2 OZ) MUD CRAB
SEA SALT

Plunge the mud crab into a large bucket of
heavily iced water for 15 minutes. This will
help to humanely dispatch it. After 15 minutes,
place the tip of a large sharp knife between
the eyes and spike the mud crab.

Put the crab directly into boiling salted
water, reduce to a simmer and cook for
approximately 8 minutes. Transfer the crab
onto a steel tray and refrigerate for 2 hours.
Once the crab is chilled, remove the large front
claws and set aside. Remove all of the legs
from the mud crab and put aside in a separate
bowl. Crack the main shell open and remove
the body meat. Discard any of the brown
mustard. Crack the two main front claws and
remove the meat: add it to the body meat
and finely shred all the meat with your fingers.
Cover and refrigerate until required. You
will need approximately 100 g (3½ oz) of
this meat.

03

PUMPKIN & CRUSTACEAN JUICE

1 LARGE OR 2 SMALL KAKAI PUMPKINS,
    4 KG (9 LB) TOTAL WEIGHT
STILL MINERAL WATER (OPTIONAL)
RESERVED CRAYFISH AND MUD CRAB LEGS
50 G (1¾ OZ) UNSALTED BUTTER
¼ FENNEL BULB, DICED
2 ESCHALLOTS, DICED
1 GARLIC CLOVE, DICED
2 THYME SPRIGS
100 ML (3½ FL OZ) UNOAKED CHARDONNAY
SEA SALT
½ TEASPOON XANTANA (FERMENTED
    CORNSTARCH)

Peel the kakai pumpkins and discard the peelings. Split the pumpkins in half and remove all of the seeds. Soak the seeds in cold water and remove as much flesh as you can from the seeds, using your hands. Reserve all the pumpkin seeds in fresh cold water and refrigerate. Using an electric juicer, juice the pumpkin flesh. Pour the juice through a fine sieve lined with muslin (cheesecloth) into a bowl. Measure the juice: you should have at least 1 litre (35 fl oz) of liquid. If you don't have this much you will need to top up the juice with fresh still mineral water to make 1 litre (35 fl oz) total.

Remove the crayfish and mud crab legs from the refrigerator and, using the back of a heavy knife or a small mallet, bruise and crack all of the shells to expose the flesh.

Melt the butter in a large saucepan. Add the fennel, eschallots, garlic, thyme and cracked crustacean legs. Gently sweat, being very careful not to add any colour. Deglaze the pan with the wine, stir well then increase the heat to evaporate the wine. Once the wine has virtually disappeared, add the strained pumpkin juice. Simmer over very low heat for 40 minutes then remove from the heat and allow to stand for a further 40 minutes. Carefully strain the liquid through a fine sieve double-lined with muslin into a bowl. Be careful not to apply any pressure to the solids, but allow the liquid to naturally filter through. Discard the solids. Reheat the liquid to simmering point. Taste and adjust the seasoning with sea salt.

Transfer 100 ml (3½ fl oz) of the liquid into a small bowl. Sprinkle the xantana over the top and and whisk well until smooth. Pour this back into the hot liquid, whisking over heat until well combined. Simmer on low heat for 3–4 minutes. Strain the liquid through a clean muslin-lined sieve and set aside the pumpkin and crustacean juice in the refrigerator until required.

04

TO FINISH

1.5 LITRES (52 FL OZ) GRAPESEED OIL
2 EGGWHITES
SEA SALT
2 TEASPOONS UNSALTED BUTTER

Put the grapeseed oil in a large, wide, shallow saucepan. You will need a minimum depth of 10 cm (4 inches) of oil. Warm the oil to 80°C (175°F) and maintain this temperature. Put the mousseline into a clean stainless steel bowl. Remove the reserved mud crab meat from the refrigerator and use your hands to squeeze out as much moisture as possible. Add the meat to the mousseline and stir through well.

Whisk the eggwhites in a clean bowl to form medium stiff peaks. Immediately place 1 large heaped tablespoon of eggwhite onto the mousseline and whisk through vigorously. Then quickly place the remaining eggwhite on top and lightly fold through with a spoon to create the velvet mixture. Using a large kitchen spoon, create heaped ovals of the velvet mixture approximately 8 cm (3¼ inches) long and 6 cm (2½ inches) wide. Slide 8 of these spoonfuls directly into the warm oil and poach for 2 minutes on each side or until cooked through. They should be light but slightly springy to the touch.

Put all of the reserved pumpkin seeds into a small saucepan with 150 ml (5 fl oz) of the reserved pumpkin and crustacean juice. Bring to simmering point and season with sea salt. Add the unsalted butter and stir through.

Reheat the remaining pumpkin and crustacean juice in a separate saucepan to simmering point.

05

TO PLATE

Using a slotted spoon carefully remove each crustacean velvet and place one directly into the centre of each warmed serving bowl. Spoon a generous heaped tablespoon of kakai pumpkin seeds over each velvet. Put the warm crustacean and pumpkin juice into a warm teapot. Serve the velvets to your guests and pour the juices over them at the table.

This is one of my most sensual and pure plays on texture. The yielding, fragrant masterstock chicken against the smoky, silky eggplant cream, contrasted with salted daikon and slippery sashimi sea scallops, has great interplay. For me, the perfume of this dish is what makes it so elegant: the ginger-infused milk curd and the intoxicating aroma of the Korean cold-pressed virgin black sesame oil.

FRAGRANT POACHED
CHICKEN, SALTED DAIKON,
SMOKED EGGPLANT CREAM,
SASHIMI SEA SCALLOPS,
GINGER-SCENTED MILK CURD,
VIRGIN BLACK SESAME

SERVES / 8

01

FRAGRANT POACHED CHICKEN

3 LITRES (105 FL OZ) CHICKEN STOCK
   (SEE BASIC RECIPES)
300 ML (10½ FL OZ) DARK SOY SAUCE
300 ML (10½ FL OZ) SHAOXING RICE WINE
   (CHINESE RICE WINE)
300 G (10½ OZ) YELLOW ROCK SUGAR
7 STAR ANISE
4 PIECES CASSIA BARK, 10 CM (4 INCHES)
   LONG
1 BUNCH ASIAN SPRING ONIONS
   (WHITE PART ONLY)
50 G (1¾ OZ) GINGER, THINLY SLICED
30 G (1 OZ) GARLIC, SLICED
1 ORANGE, PEEL ZESTED
1.6 KG (3 LB 8 OZ) FREE-RANGE CHICKEN

Put all of the ingredients except the chicken into a 7 litre (245 fl oz) stockpot with a tight-fitting lid, bring to the boil and simmer on high for 10 minutes without the lid. Strain the liquid into another stockpot, discarding the solids. Bring the liquid back to a full boil then put the whole chicken—breast side down—into the pot. Immediately put the lid on the pot and turn off the heat. Remove from the heat and allow to stand for exactly 1 hour. Remove the chicken from the liquid and place on a draining tray. Refrigerate for at least 45 minutes or until required.

   Note: with this cooking method the chicken flesh will appear slightly pink, but it will be cooked through. The flesh should give between your fingers: if it doesn't, you will need to cook it a little longer.

02

SMOKED OIL

500 ML (17 FL OZ) EXTRA VIRGIN OLIVE OIL
1 SMALL GARLIC CLOVE
100 G (3½ OZ) WHOLE SMOKED EEL, CUT
   INTO 1 CM (⅜ INCH) THICK PIECES
25 G (1 OZ) FLAKED BONITO

Put all ingredients into a cryovac bag and seal. Cook in a water circulator at 50°C (120°F) for 30 minutes. Allow the oil to cool for 10 minutes. Open the bag and strain the ingredients through an oil filter bag or layered muslin (cheesecloth). Discard the solids and reserve the oil.

03

SMOKED EGGPLANT CREAM

500 ML (17 FL OZ) SMOKED OIL
¼ LEMON, JUICE
1 GARLIC CLOVE, FINELY SLICED
2 SMALL, FIRM, SUPER-FRESH EGGPLANTS
   (AUBERGINES)
SEA SALT

Put the smoked oil, lemon juice and garlic into a large cryovac bag. Sit the bag inside a container with the ends folded over to allow easy access to the oil. Peel the eggplants one at a time and immediately dice into 2 cm (¾ inch) square cubes. Put the eggplant cubes straight into the oil before they have a chance to oxidise. Repeat until all the eggplant has been used. When choosing the eggplant, freshness is imperative so that the seeds are very small and have not turned black inside the eggplant. If you cannot find super-fresh eggplants avoid using the more seeded parts of the eggplants. In this case you may need three or more eggplants. All these steps are important to keep the eggplant white.

   When the eggplant is submerged in the oil, seal the bag then steam in a water circulator at 95°C (195°F) for 40 minutes until the eggplant is soft. Strain the eggplant away from the oil and process the eggplant in a blender. You may need to add a little of the cooking oil to obtain a smooth consistency. Pass through a fine drum sieve. Season and allow to cool.

04

EGGWHITE PEARLS

4 EGGWHITES
1 LITRE (35 FL OZ) GRAPESEED OIL

Strain the eggwhites through a medium sieve and discard any material that does not come through the sieve with gentle pressure. Heat the grapeseed oil in a large heavy-based saucepan to 50°C (120°F). Put the strained eggwhite into a medium-size hypodermic syringe with a 0.5 mm (25 gauge) needle. In one slow but direct motion squeeze the eggwhite through the syringe into the hot oil. The eggwhite will form very small pearls. Allow to set for 1 minute then, using a rubber spatula, release the pearls from the bottom of the pan in a smooth motion. Allow another 30 seconds of setting, then strain the oil and the eggwhites through a fine sieve. Place the eggwhite pearls on a tray lined with silicone paper. Reserve the oil and repeat the process until you have about 1 tablespoon of pearls (enough for 8 flowers).

05

SCALLOP PEARL FLOWERS
1 SEA SCALLOP
1 TABLESPOON WHITE SOY SAUCE
1 TABLESPOON CRÈME FRAÎCHE
½ DAIKON

Finely dice the sea scallops to 3 mm (⅛ inch). Dress the scallops in the white soy sauce and place on paper towel to dry.

Whip the crème fraîche to firm peaks. Lay some plastic wrap on the bench and cut it into 10 cm (4 inch) squares. Place a plastic wrap square over a shot glass then put a small dot (⅛ teaspoon) of crème fraîche in the centre. Next put ⅛ teaspoon of diced scallop on top. Gathering the plastic wrap corners together, squeeze the scallops and crème fraîche to form a tight ball. Twist the plastic tightly and place each ball in the refrigerator to set for 30 minutes (or 5 minutes in a blast freezer). Repeat the process until you have 8 balls. Using the same method with plastic wrap and shot glasses, place ½ teaspoon of eggwhite pearls in the centre of each piece of plastic. Spread out the eggwhite pearls to form a single layer roughly the size of an Australian 50-cent piece (about 3 cm or 1¼ inch diameter). Carefully unwrap the scallop and crème fraîche balls and place a ball in the middle of the eggwhite pearls. Gather up the corners of the plastic to form a pearl. Allow these pearls to set in the refrigerator until required.

Fold some sturdy aluminium foil into a long, V-shaped rest and sit it fold down in some rice to keep it steady, with the wider part of the V upright. This will act as a rack to hold your scallop pearl flowers in shape. Use a 2 cm (¾ inch) diameter round cutter to stamp out a cylinder from the daikon. Use a Japanese mandolin to slice the cylinders into 1 mm (¹⁄₃₂ inch) thin discs. You need 56 discs (7 discs for each of 8 flowers). Blanch these discs in boiling water for 10 seconds and refresh in iced water. Drain and pat the discs dry. Overlap 7 discs in a circular pattern—they will gradually form a point—making a small cone shape. Place these cones in the foil rest and set aside in the refrigerator until required.

06

FRAGRANT OIL
100 ML (3½ FL OZ) EXTRA VIRGIN KOREAN
   BLACK SESAME OIL
50 ML (1¾ FL OZ) EXTRA VIRGIN KOREAN
   WHITE SESAME OIL
½ TEASPOON JASMINE TEA
15 G (½ OZ) GINGER, THINLY SLICED
15 G (½ OZ) LONG GREEN SPRING ONIONS,
   WHITE PART ONLY, THINLY SLICED

Put all of the ingredients into a cryovac bag. Heat in a water circulator to 40°C (105°F) for 30 minutes. Allow to cool. Strain and discard the solids.

07

GINGER MILK CURDS
45 G (1½ OZ) GINGER, THINLY SLICED
500 ML (17 FL OZ) MILK
SEA SALT
25 ML (1 FL OZ) VEGETABLE RENNET
25 ML (1 FL OZ) STILL MINERAL WATER

Put the ginger and milk in a saucepan and bring to 70°C (160°F) then remove from the heat. Allow to infuse for 30 minutes then strain and discard the solids. Season with salt.

Just before serving, make the ginger curds two at a time in eight ramekins with a capacity of 50 ml (1¾ fl oz) each. Warm 100 ml (3½ fl oz) of the ginger-infused milk to 35°C (95°F). Mix the vegetable rennet and mineral water together. Put 2 ml (¹⁄₁₆ fl oz) of the rennet mixture into a syringe, swirl the milk around in the saucepan and shoot the rennet into the warm milk. Working very quickly, fill two ramekins. Repeat this process three more times until all eight ramekins are filled. Allow to set, which will take about 2 minutes.

08

TO FINISH
SEA SALT
10 LARGE SEA SCALLOPS, FINELY SLICED
   INTO 1 MM (¹⁄₃₂ INCH) THIN DISCS
50 ML (1¾ FL OZ) WHITE SOY SAUCE
12 SALTED DAIKON TWISTS
   (SEE BASIC RECIPES)

Remove the chicken breast meat from the frame and shred the meat with your fingers. In a bowl, dress the chicken liberally with the fragrant oil and season with salt.

Dress the sliced scallops with the white soy sauce and a little of the fragrant oil. Dress the daikon twists with the fragrant oil.

09

TO PLATE
30 PEA FLOWERS
48 WASABI FLOWERS

Place a generous spoonful of smoked eggplant cream in the centre of each plate. Spread out with the back of the spoon. Start layering the chicken breast, sea scallops and daikon twists. Make a space for the scallop pearl flower. Place the flower petal cone in first, then unwrap the scallop pearl and place the pearl in the centre of the cone the right way up. Using a dessertspoon, scoop half of the ginger milk curd carefully onto the salad. Dress with a little more fragrant oil then scatter the pea flower petals and wasabi flowers over the top. Serve.

FROZEN AGED FETA SHARDS
500 G (1 LB 2 OZ) TRADITIONALLY AGED
 GREEK FETA
1 LITRE LIQUID NITROGEN

Place the block of aged feta in the freezer for 2 hours or until firm enough to shave. Wearing appropriate protective eyewear and gloves, pour the liquid nitrogen into an insulated bowl or a small styrofoam container (see glossary for more safety information).

Remove the frozen feta and use a Japanese mandolin to shave 4–5 slices, as thinly as possible, into the bowl of liquid nitrogen. Allow the liquid nitrogen to further freeze the cheese for 30 seconds. Remove with a slotted spoon, put in an airtight container and store in the freezer. Repeat until all the feta has been used.

02

OLIVE SOURDOUGH CRUMBS
100 G (3½ OZ) PITTED LIGURIAN OLIVES
250 ML (9 FL OZ) OLIVE OIL
2 SLICES SOURDOUGH BREAD, 2 CM
 (¾ INCH) THICK, CRUSTS REMOVED

Put the pitted olives and 50 ml (1¾ fl oz) of olive oil in the bowl of a small food processor and blend well. Pour the paste onto a small tray and soak the sourdough slices, pressing down into the mixture on both sides of the bread to soak up all the oil.

Dehydrate the oil-soaked bread in an 80°C (175°F/Gas ¼–½) oven or dehydrator for approximately 6 hours or until the bread is dry and crisp. When dry, crumble the bread into rough 5 mm (¼ inch) pieces. Heat the remaining oil in a large non-stick frying pan over medium–high heat and fry the crumbs until crisp. Drain well, cool and store in an airtight container until required.

LEMON CRÈME FRAÎCHE
50 G (1¾ OZ) CRÈME FRAÎCHE
1 TEASPOON LEMON JUICE

Combine the crème fraîche and lemon juice well, cover and refrigerate until required.

CELERY HEART, AGED FETA, RARE HERBS & FLOWERS

SERVES / 8

LEMON JUICE VINAIGRETTE

½ ESCHALLOT, FINELY DICED
PINCH SEA SALT
2 TEASPOONS LEMON JUICE
¼ TEASPOON DIJON MUSTARD
2 TABLESPOONS EXTRA VIRGIN OLIVE OIL

Mix the eschallot, salt and lemon juice. Allow the eschallot to soften for about 5 minutes. Add the mustard and mix well. Whisk in the olive oil until well incorporated and set aside until required.

05

TO FINISH

64 PEA FLOWERS
32 ICE PLANT BUDS
64 SMALL NASTURTIUM LEAVES
64 SMALL BUCKLER-LEAF SORREL SPRIGS
32 SALAD BURNET SPRIGS
40 TINY CELERY FLOWER SPRIGS
80 WHITE EDIBLE LINARIA FLOWERS
40 CURLY CRESS SPRIGS
16 SMALL SWEET CICELY SPRIGS
2 TABLESPOONS TINY SICILIAN CAPERS
   IN OIL
2 CELERY HEARTS, WELL TRIMMED

Separate the pea flower petals and discard the stems. Wash all herbs and flowers in cold water and allow to dry in a single layer on a clean tea towel (dish towel).

Drain the capers well.

Use a Japanese mandolin to finely shave the celery hearts into a large bowl. Immediately dress the shaved celery hearts with the lemon vinaigrette.

06

TO PLATE

Place a teaspoon of the lemon crème fraîche in the centre of each serving plate and gently spread out with the back of the spoon. Place a small handful of the dressed, shaved celery heart on top of the crème fraîche. Place 8–10 olive crumbs on each pile of celery with 8–10 capers. Add a couple of slices of the shaved frozen feta on top with a small pinch of the combined herbs and flowers. Add another small handful of the celery heart, more frozen feta and a handful of herbs and flowers. Serve.

This salad utilises many of the rarer herbs and flowers that June Henman and I have researched over the years. Combined with shaved celery heart, barrel-aged feta, Sicilian capers and olive sourdough crumbs, this dish is a light and aromatic way to start a meal. It embodies simplicity, complexity and the beauty of nature.

JUNE HENMAN

HERB & FLOWER RESEARCHER
INGLESIDE / NEW SOUTH WALES

'Peter's enthusiasm and support for the path I was on was inspirational and an affirmation of what I was trying to achieve. When Peter first talked to me about growing delicate edible flowers for him, that prompted a new direction for the farm and another delight.'

June's story as a herb enthusiast began many years ago when she was a young woman visiting the isle of Crete. She watched local village women gather wild herbs and leaves from the mountainside to use in their salads and cooking. Little did she realise that a seed had been planted for her future direction. June had been working for many years in documentary television for the BBC in London and later as a freelance researcher and associate producer in Sydney; but in 1989 a career change took place.

June was convinced there should be more to a salad than iceberg lettuce. She used her research skills to discover a wealth of information about the ancient medicinal and culinary uses of herbs. She decided to follow her dream and rented two greenhouses in the Warriewood valley in the north of Sydney. Here she started to grow rare, hard-to-find herbs and baby lettuce leaves. Her aim was to create a true mesclun mix that she could supply to local restaurants. Two greenhouses soon became six and the Salad Farm was born.

I first met June in 2007 and was so impressed with her salad mixes that I began buying them for Quay. It didn't take long before I was asking June if she could grow specific herbs and edible flowers for me. June recalls: 'I remember well my first meeting with Peter Gilmore. I carted into Quay my books and catalogues and we spent many hours poring over and discussing what was possible for me to supply him with. Peter's enthusiasm and support for the path I was on was inspirational and an affirmation of what I was trying to achieve. When Peter first talked to me about growing delicate edible flowers for him, that prompted a new direction for the farm and another delight.

'Whenever he phoned I knew I had another mountain to climb to source a herb or leaf he had come across on his travels.'

June's Salad Farm grew to include custom-made salad mixes, baby herb mixes and edible flowers. She was supplying chefs all over Sydney. In 2010 June decided it was time to sell the farm and retire. I remember June doing this very reluctantly. By 2012 the farm was owned by Tony Mann and Paul Bottell of Export Fresh and renamed Petite Bouche. They decided to invest in the farm and increase the scale and output. June soon found herself rehired as a consultant to continue to research and develop an even greater range of rare and unusual herbs and edible flowers.

June Henman is an incredibly passionate person to work with and a true trailblazer on the Sydney food scene. It is such a pleasure to be able to continue working with her and the new owners of Petite Bouche.

ORGANUM / SEARCH FOR PURITY

Mangosteens and feijoas are two of the most exotically fragrant fruits on the planet. Both have, in my opinion, the perfect acid-sweet balance. The mangosteens I use are grown in tropical North Queensland and the feijoas, a native of South America, tend to be grown in the cooler regions of Australia and New Zealand. This dessert perfectly represents the idea of simplicity and purity.

MANGOSTEEN, FEIJOA, COCONUT

SERVES / 8

01

FEIJOA ICE CREAM

13 FEIJOAS
220 G (7¾ OZ) CASTER (SUPERFINE) SUGAR
130 G (4½ OZ) EGG YOLKS
180 ML (6 FL OZ) PURE CREAM (35% FAT)

Peel and seed the feijoas and juice with an electric juicer. Pass the juice through a fine sieve. Measure 600 ml (21 fl oz) juice and save any leftover for another use.

Combine half the juice with the sugar and egg yolks in a large stainless steel bowl. Reserve the remaining juice in the refrigerator until required.

Whisking continuously, cook the juice, sugar and egg mixture over a double boiler until it reaches 85°C (185°F). Cool over ice. Once completely cold, whisk in the cream and the chilled reserved feijoa juice. Churn in an ice-cream machine and freeze until required. Makes approximately 1 litre (35 fl oz).

02

COCONUT CREAM

100 ML (3½ FL OZ) MILK
100 ML (3½ FL OZ) PURE CREAM (35% FAT)
50 G (1¾ OZ) CASTER (SUPERFINE) SUGAR
100 G (3½ OZ) COCONUT CREAM POWDER
80 G (2¾ OZ) DOUBLE CREAM (45–50% FAT)

Combine the milk, cream (35% fat) and sugar in a saucepan over medium–high heat, stirring until the sugar dissolves. Bring to the boil. Put the coconut cream powder into a heatproof bowl and pour the boiling milk and cream mixture over, whisking well as you pour in the liquid. Put it in the refrigerator to cool completely.

Put the cooled coconut cream mixture into a bowl with the double cream and whisk together with a hand whisk until firm peaks form. Store in the refrigerator until required.

03

MANGOSTEEN TEARS

24 MANGOSTEENS
2 LITRES LIQUID NITROGEN

Peel the mangosteens. Wearing appropriate protective eyewear and gloves, pour 1 litre of the liquid nitrogen into an insulated bowl or a small styrofoam container (see glossary for more safety information). Add 4 whole mangosteens at a time to the liquid nitrogen for 30 seconds. Remove with a slotted spoon to a sealed container and place in the freezer. Process all the mangosteens this way then leave in the freezer for 3 hours.

After 3 hours set up the remaining liquid nitrogen following the safety protocols above. Using a fine microplane, grate the frozen mangosteens, one at a time, into the liquid nitrogen. Avoid grating the large segment that contains the seed. After you have grated 3 of the mangosteens, stop and stir the gratings with a fine slotted spoon then remove to a sealed container and place in the freezer. Continue until all the mangosteens are processed.

04

TO FINISH

16 MANGOSTEENS

Peel the mangosteens and break into segments. Discard the large segment of each mangosteen that contains the seed.

Remove the coconut cream from the refrigerator and whisk again until soft peaks form.

05

TO PLATE

Place a tablespoon of freshly whisked coconut cream in the bottom of each serving bowl. Spread this out with the back of the spoon to form a 10 cm (4 inch) diameter disc. Use a tablespoon to shape a large quenelle of feijoa ice cream and place it in the centre of the coconut cream. Press the ice cream down with the back of the spoon to flatten slightly. Scatter with an even amount of the fresh mangosteen segments. Top with another half tablespoon of coconut cream and flatten it out over the mangosteens with the back of the spoon. Place 2 large tablespoons of frozen mangosteen tears over each dessert and gently spread out over the surface with the back of the spoon to form a flat even surface. Serve.

PETER GILMORE

EXECUTIVE CHEF
SYDNEY / NEW SOUTH WALES

'Firstly I would like to thank my family: my strongest supporter and best friend, my wife Kath; my two beautiful sons, Isaac and Joe; my mum and dad, Dawn and John and my sister Nicole, all of whom unconditionally love and support me.'

There are three people with whom I worked very closely to produce this book, and I consider them friends. I would like to deeply thank Jane Lawson, Reuben Crossman and Brett Stevens.

Jane Lawson is a talented cook and author in her own right. Jane worked with me on formatting my recipes and the text for this book.

Reuben Crossman was the designer of my first book, *Quay*, and shared my vision for *Organum* from the outset. Reuben is a perfectionist and his skill for creative direction and design is exceptional. He has captured the emotion and feeling I wanted to convey in *Organum* perfectly.

Brett Stevens's astonishing photography for this book was technically challenging and beautifully realised. The collaborative process of working closely with these three talented individuals was truly rewarding.

This book would not exist without the faith and support of the management team at Murdoch Books. Their belief in the project and the trust they have shown me has made it possible.

Special thanks to Adriana Picker for her beautiful botanical illustrations.

I would like to thank the many producers, farmers and suppliers I have worked with over the years. In particular I would like to thank:

Tim and Elizabeth Johnstone
Wayne Hulme and David Allen
Mike and Gayle Quarmby
Anthony Puharich and David Blackmore
Stephen and Karen Welsh
Paul and Idylle Lee
Josef and Antonia Gretschmann
Jude McBain
June Henman

for their time, effort and contribution to this book.

I would like to acknowledge and thank Leon and John Fink for their belief and support over the years. At the time of writing this book I have enjoyed a collaborative working relationship with Leon and John as Executive Chef at Quay for 13 years. During this time I have been very proud of our achievements. Among the highlights are the five consecutive years Quay has been listed in the S. Pellegrino World Top 50 Restaurants and the twelve consecutive years Quay has held three hats and three stars in the *Sydney Morning Herald Good Food Guide* and *Australian Gourmet Traveller* respectively. Leon and John's strong love and enthusiasm for the restaurant industry has been unwavering. Their belief in the art of the restaurant and their continued patronage of fine dining in Sydney is something to be respected and I am truly grateful for the opportunities it has given me.

I would like to thank all of the team at Quay, past and present. A wonderful group of dedicated professionals working as a team is what it takes to make a restaurant work at this level.

Special thanks to Quay's General Manager, Kylie Ball: her support and professionalism has kept us all on track at Quay over the years.

I would like to thank Robert Cockerill (on the left) and Sam Aisbett, my two right-hand men in the kitchen. Sam and Rob have both been with me for years and are the most loyal, passionate and talented chefs I could ever hope to work with.

BASIC SUGAR SYRUP

500 G (1 LB 2 OZ) CASTER (SUPERFINE)
   SUGAR
500 ML (17 FL OZ) WATER

Combine the sugar and water in a large
saucepan over high heat, stirring until the
sugar has dissolved. Bring to the boil then
immediately remove from the heat. Cool and
store in an airtight container in the refrigerator
until required. Yields about 1 litre (35 fl oz).

BERGAMOT JAM

4 LEMONS
4 ORANGES
1 BERGAMOT ORANGE OR 1 DROP OF
   BERGAMOT FOOD-GRADE ESSENTIAL OIL
150 G (5½ OZ) CASTER (SUPERFINE) SUGAR

Zest all the citrus fruit and finely dice the zest.
Remove any white pith from the fruit then
segment the flesh over a bowl, reserving all
the juice. Triple blanch the combined zest
in boiling water. Put the blanched zest into
a large saucepan with the flesh, juice, sugar
and 100 ml (3½ fl oz) cold water. Heat over
medium heat, stirring periodically until the
jam begins to thicken. Continue cooking
over low heat for a further 10 minutes and
be careful it does not burn. Cover and
refrigerate until required.

BRIOCHE

6 EGGS
500 G (1 LB 2 OZ) PLAIN (ALL-PURPOSE)
   FLOUR
15 G (½ OZ) SALT
70 ML (2¼ FL OZ) MILK
30 G (1 OZ) CASTER (SUPERFINE) SUGAR
15 G (½ OZ) FRESH YEAST
350 G (12 OZ) UNSALTED BUTTER,
   SOFTENED
OLIVE OIL SPRAY

Crack the eggs into a bowl and set aside.
Put the flour and salt in an electric mixer
fitted with a dough hook and combine on low
speed. Warm the milk and sugar in a saucepan
until it reaches body temperature. Remove
from the heat and mix in the crumbled fresh
yeast, then pour the mixture onto the eggs
and whisk together.

Pour the egg and yeast mixture into the
flour and mix on low speed for 20 minutes.
After 20 minutes, add the butter 15 g (½ oz)
at a time, every 2 minutes until the butter
has been used up.

Spray a 23 x 15 x 9 cm (9 x 6 x 3½ inch)
loaf (bar) tin with spray oil then lightly flour,
tipping out the excess. Put the dough in the
tin and refrigerate for 12 hours to cold prove.

Remove the tin to a bench in a warm area
of the kitchen and prove at room temperature
for 8 hours.

Bake at 170°C (325°F/Gas 3) for
15 minutes. Do not open the door, but turn the
temperature down to 150°C (300°F/Gas 2) and
cook for a further 25 minutes. Remove from
the oven to cool on a wire rack for 10 minutes
in the tin then remove from the tin and allow
to cool completely for a few hours.

If you are making this for the brioche
porridge on page 102, it is best to make it
the day before.

BASIC
RECIPES

CHICKEN STOCK

5 KG (11 LB 4 OZ) CHICKEN BONES (FRAMES
    AND WINGS)
2 LARGE BROWN ONIONS, CHOPPED
3 CARROTS, CHOPPED
3 INNER WHITE CELERY STALKS, CHOPPED
100 ML (3½ FL OZ) GRAPESEED OIL

Wash the chicken bones under cold running
water to remove any excess blood, then drain
and put aside. Sweat the vegetables in a large
stockpot in the grapeseed oil. Add the chicken
bones and lightly sauté, being careful not to
add too much colour. Add 8 litres (270 fl oz)
of cold water and bring to the boil. As soon
as it boils, turn down the heat to achieve
a very gentle simmer (the stock should be
just ticking over). Skim the stock with a ladle
and continue to simmer for 4 hours. After 4
hours, skim the stock again with a ladle. Strain
the stock carefully through a chinois or fine
strainer. Allow the stock to cool completely and
refrigerate until required. This recipe should
yield 5 litres (175 fl oz) of chicken stock.

CLARIFIED BUTTER

2 KG (4 LB 8 OZ) UNSALTED BUTTER

Use a large stockpot with a capacity of
15 litres (525 fl oz). A stockpot is needed,
as the butter will foam and you do not want
it to spill over. Put the butter in the pot over
medium–high heat. As the butter melts it will
begin to foam. Allow this to happen but monitor
the heat, as you do not want the butter to
caramelise (as for brown butter). The foaming
and melting will take about 10 minutes. Reduce
the heat to low and when the foaming subsides
use a ladle to skim off any scum from the
surface. Heat on low for a further 5–10 minutes,
then turn the heat off and allow to sit for a few
minutes. Once the surface is completely clear of
impurities, ladle out the clear butter into a clean
container. Be careful not to disturb the milk
solids that will remain on the bottom of the pot.
Once all the clear butter is ladled out, you can
discard the milky solids in the base of the pot.
You should now have at least 1 litre (35 fl oz) of
clarified butter.

Clarified butter is good to use for sautéing
meat and vegetables. It will not burn as easily
as unclarified butter because the milk solids
have been removed.

CULTURED CREAM

15 ML (½ FL OZ) MILTON ANTIBACTERIAL
    STERILISING LIQUID, OR SIMILAR
1 LITRE (35 FL OZ) PURE JERSEY CREAM
    (35–40% FAT)
¼ TEASPOON CHEESE CULTURE (MM100)

Using the sterilising liquid, follow the
manufacturer's instructions to sterilise a
saucepan, whisk, stainless steel spoons,
a tray and a 1 litre (35 fl oz) plastic or glass
container with a lid in which to ferment the
cream. Drain the sterilised utensils on the
sterilised tray. It is important to sterilise this
way, not only for food safely reasons, but
because a particular environment is required
for the cheese culture to survive and obtain
the right flavour.

Heat the cream to 90°C (195°F) in a
saucepan then cool to 25°C (77°F). Add the
cheese culture and whisk to combine well.
Pour the cream mixture into the sterilised
plastic or glass container and cover with the
lid. Put the container into a styrofoam box
insulated with clean tea towels (dish towels).
Put the lid on top of the box and place in a
warm area of the kitchen with a temperature
of at least 20°C (68°F) and not exceeding
26°C (79°F). Leave the cream to ferment for
72 hours and check after this time. It should
smell sweet but slightly sour. Refrigerate the
cream until required.

CULTURED BUTTER

1 QUANTITY OF CULTURED CREAM
    (SEE ABOVE)

Pour the cultured cream into an electric mixer
with a whisk attachment. Cover with a clean
tea towel (dish towel) to catch any splatter
and turn the speed to high. Beat until the
cream splits into liquid and solid. Once the
cream has split, remove the solids (butter)
to a clean bowl. You can reserve the liquid
(buttermilk) for another use if you desire.

Wearing plastic gloves, wash the butter
under cold running water, manipulating
and squeezing continually for 5 minutes.
This process helps to remove excess liquid.
Return the butter to the bowl. Cover until
required. Refrigerate if not using within
a couple of hours.

MILK BISCUIT

1 LITRE (35 FL OZ) MILK
100 G (3½ OZ) LIQUID GLUCOSE

Heat the milk and glucose to 85°C (185°F).
Froth with a stick blender. Using a slotted
spoon, scoop off the froth—making sure you
drain any run-off—and place the froth on a
tray lined with silicone paper. Dry in an 80°C
(175°F/Gas ¼–½) oven for 30–40 minutes or
until dry and brittle.

Store in an airtight container until required.

MILK SKIN

1 LITRE (35 FL OZ) MILK

Pour the milk into a half gastronorm tray or a
small roasting pan. Heat the tray of milk over
two gas burners until the milk comes to a high
simmer. Turn off the heat and allow the milk
to cool: as it does, a skin will form over the top.
Cut a sheet of silicone paper to fit the size of
the tray and place the silicone paper directly
onto the milk. The skin should stick to the
silicone paper. Carefully lift off the paper and
dry the milk skin, on the paper, under heat
lamps or in a 100°C (200°F/Gas ½) oven for
about 10–15 minutes.

You should be able to repeat this step
three times with the same milk.

Once the milk skin has fully dried, remove
the skin from the paper and place in an
airtight container. Set aside until required.

NOUGAT

90 G (3¼ OZ) COCOA BUTTER
60 G (2¼ OZ) EGGWHITES
170 G (6 OZ) CASTER (SUPERFINE) SUGAR
100 G (3½ OZ) LIQUID GLUCOSE
1 VANILLA BEAN, SEEDS ONLY
460 G (1 LB) HONEY
240 G (8¾ OZ) ROASTED ALMONDS

Melt the cocoa butter and keep warm. Put the eggwhites in an electric mixer with the whisk attachment. Put the sugar, glucose and vanilla seeds in a small saucepan and add just enough water to make a paste. Set aside until required.

Put the honey in a second small pan and bring towards 160°C (320°F) over high heat. When it reaches 158°C (316°F) turn the electric mixer on to high speed. Pour the hot honey in a steady stream onto the eggwhites and whisk on high until the mixture is well combined. Continue to whisk on high speed for 1 minute then reduce to medium speed and continue to whisk while you heat the sugar.

Meanwhile, put the saucepan with the sugar mixture over high heat and stir just until the sugar has dissolved. Bring to 160°C (320°F) then, returning the electric mixer to high speed, pour the hot sugar onto the meringue in a steady stream. Turn the mixer down to medium speed and beat for a further 3 minutes.

Add the warm cocoa butter and continue to beat for approximately 2 minutes. The mixture will split then re-emulsify.

Turn the mixer speed to low and add the almonds. Allow to mix for 20 seconds then turn off the beaters. Spread the nougat evenly over a tray lined with a large sheet of silicone paper, to a 5 cm (2 inch) thickness.

Top with another sheet of silicone paper and smooth over with your hands.

Put the tray in the freezer for about 2 hours until the nougat is set. Remove and store in an airtight container for up to a week.

This recipe will make more than you need but you can use the remaining nougat in other recipes or simply enjoy it on its own.

OYSTER CREAM

12 UNSHUCKED SYDNEY ROCK OYSTERS
10 G (⅜ OZ) FENNEL, DICED
10 G (⅜ OZ) INNER WHITE CELERY STALK, DICED
10 G (⅜ OZ) BULB SPRING ONION, DICED
10 ML (⅜ FL OZ) GRAPESEED OIL
500 ML (17 FL OZ) MILK
5 G (⅗₁₆ OZ) AGAR AGAR

Shuck the oysters, reserving the meat and juice. Sweat the fennel, celery and spring onion in a small saucepan with the grapeseed oil, being careful not to add any colour to the vegetables. Add the milk and bring close to boiling point, then remove the pan from the heat and add the oyster meat. Allow everything to infuse for 20 minutes while cooling. Strain the milk and discard the solids.

Pour the milk through a fine sieve into a saucepan. Return the pan to the heat and, while whisking, add the agar agar. Reheat the milk to 90°C (195°F), continuing to whisk to activate the agar agar, and cook for 1 minute. Remove the pan from the heat and allow to cool. Add the oyster juice, stir well and pass the mixture through a sieve lined with a double layer of muslin (cheesecloth). Refrigerate the milk until fully set. Put the mixture in a small saucepan and reheat while mixing well with a stick blender. Refrigerate again until needed.

RICE LACE

25 G (1 OZ) GLUTINOUS RICE FLOUR
450 ML (16 FL OZ) WATER

Mix the glutinous rice flour and water together with a whisk until well incorporated. Heat a non-stick frying pan over medium heat, add 1 tablespoon of rice mixture to the hot pan and shake vigorously. Allow the water to evaporate over the heat: a lacy pattern should form over the surface of the pan. Allow the bottom to completely dry before you turn over with a spatula. Flip over and dry the other side completely. Try not to let the rice lace colour: it should be as white as possible. When completely dry remove to a cooling rack. Note that in between batches, you need to vigorously stir the mix as the flour settles to the bottom. Once the lace is completely cool, store in an airtight container, for up to 2 days.

SALTED DAIKON TWISTS

½ DAIKON
SEA SALT

Cut the daikon into 10 cm lengths. Using a Japanese mandolin, thinly slice the daikon into 1.5 mm (¹⁄₁₆ inch) thin strips. Julienne these strips, and lightly salt the daikon julienne. Allow the daikon to wilt for 15 minutes, then discard the liquid. Gently wash the salt away from the daikon and pat dry. Gather some of the strands into a bundle about 1 cm (⅜ inch) thick and twist the strands together until it resembles a braid. Repeat the process until you have 12 twists, then set aside until required.

SOY MILK CREAM

300 ML (10½ FL OZ) MILK
300 ML (10½ FL OZ) FRESH SOY MILK
5 G (⅗₁₆ OZ) AGAR AGAR
FINE SEA SALT

Combine the milk and soy milk in a small saucepan and bring close to boiling point, then remove from the heat.

Whisk in the agar agar. Return to the heat and reheat the milk to 90°C (195°F), while continuing to whisk to activate the agar agar. Remove from the heat and allow the milk to set. Once set, put the soy milk cream into a blender and blend until smooth. Season to taste with sea salt. Refrigerate until needed and reheat just before you are ready to serve.

VANILLA CUSTARD BASE

400 ML (14 FL OZ) PURE CREAM (35% FAT)
2 VANILLA BEANS, SPLIT, SEEDS SCRAPED
3 EGG YOLKS
1 WHOLE EGG
80 G (2¾ OZ) CASTER (SUPERFINE) SUGAR

Preheat the oven to 160 °C (315°F/Gas 2–3). Put the cream and vanilla beans in a medium saucepan. Heat together until the cream just begins to boil, then remove the pan from the heat. Whisk the egg yolks, whole egg and sugar together in a stainless steel bowl. While whisking the eggs, slowly pour on the hot vanilla cream. Mix well and then remove the vanilla beans.

Strain the mixture into four 175 ml (5½ fl oz) ceramic ramekins, then place the ramekins in a baking tray of water to form a bain-marie. Put the baking tray in the oven and cook the custard as you would a crème brûlée, for about 30–35 minutes, or until the custard is just set. Remove the custards from the bain-marie and place in the refrigerator for 5–6 hours, or until they are fully chilled and set. Remove the skin from the top before using. This recipe makes 400 g (14 oz).

VANILLA CUSTARD CREAM

200 G (7 OZ) CHILLED VANILLA
   CUSTARD BASE
100 ML (3½ FL OZ) PURE CREAM (35% FAT)
100 G (3½ OZ) DOUBLE CREAM
   (45–50% FAT)

Put the chilled vanilla custard with the combined creams in a bowl and whisk until soft peaks form. Cover and refrigerate until required.

VEAL STOCK

10 KG (22 LB) VEAL BONES (KNUCKLES
   AND SHINS)
4 PIG'S TROTTERS, SPLIT IN HALF
750 ML BOTTLE GOOD-QUALITY RED WINE
5 BROWN ONIONS, CHOPPED
4 CARROTS, CHOPPED
50 ML (1¾ FL OZ) GRAPESEED OIL
10 RIPE TOMATOES, CUT IN HALF

Wash the veal bones and pig's trotters under cold running water, then drain well. Place the bones and trotters in a heavy-based baking tray and roast in the oven at 200°C (400°F/Gas 6) until nicely browned. When the bones are browned, remove them from the tray and put them in a large stockpot. Take the tray that the bones were browned in and place it on the stovetop. Remove any rendered fat, then heat the tray over medium heat and add the red wine. Use a wooden spoon to scrape the bottom of the tray to release any caramelisation left from the bones. Reduce the wine until 200 ml (7 fl oz) remains, then pour the wine into the stockpot with the bones.

In a large frying pan, sauté the onion and carrot in the grapeseed oil until well coloured. Deglaze the pan with 500 ml (17 fl oz) of water, stir well and add the contents to the stockpot. Add another 14.5 litres (490 fl oz) of water to the pot, bring the stock close to boiling point, then turn the heat down so the stock is barely simmering. Add the tomato halves and slowly simmer for 8 hours, skimming the stock occasionally with a ladle to remove any excess fat. Strain the stock through a fine conical strainer, being careful not to disturb the bones too much. Do not remove the bones before straining, as this will make the stock cloudy. Allow the stock to cool, then refrigerate until required. Any excess fat will solidify on top of the stock and is easily removed before use. This recipe should yield about 8 litres (280 fl oz) of veal stock.

VEAL GLAZE

1 BROWN ONION, CHOPPED
1 CARROT, CHOPPED
50 ML (1¾ FL OZ) GRAPESEED OIL
500 G (1 LB 2 OZ) VEAL OR BEEF TRIMMINGS
4 GARLIC CLOVES, BRUISED WITH THE
   BACK OF A KNIFE
500 ML (17 FL OZ) GOOD-QUALITY
   RED WINE
8 LITRES (280 FL OZ) VEAL STOCK
6 RIPE TOMATOES, CUT IN HALF
2 THYME SPRIGS

In a large stockpot, sauté the onion and carrot in the grapeseed oil until lightly browned. Add the veal or beef trimmings and continue to sauté until the meat is well browned. Add the garlic and red wine. Reduce the wine until there is only 100 ml (3½ fl oz) of the liquid left, then add the stock, tomatoes and thyme. Reduce the stock on a medium simmer until it has halved in quantity. Strain through a fine conical strainer lined with muslin (cheesecloth). You should now have a demi-glaze (half-reduced stock).

To make a glaze, return the demi-glaze to a clean stockpot and reduce over high heat until you have the required viscosity for glazing and saucing meats. Generally, from 4 litres (140 fl oz) of demi-glaze, you will need to reduce it to somewhere between 800 ml (28 fl oz) and 500 ml (17 fl oz) to achieve a glaze. The further you reduce, the heavier the glaze.

ABOUT THE RECIPES

Although these recipes are detailed they are direct from the Quay kitchen and unmodified for domestic use, so if you are cooking from this book in a home kitchen you may find cooking times vary depending on the oven or cooktop you are using. Commercial equipment is generally a little more powerful.

We have used 20 ml (4 teaspoon) tablespoon measures.

We use 65 g (extra large) eggs.

Some recipes make a larger quantity than is required for serving: this is because it is impossible to make a smaller volume of certain components and it also maintains consistency of texture for others.

EDIBLE FLOWERS

Make sure you follow the advice on the types of edible flowers used and only substitute flowers that are edible, organically grown and have not been sprayed with pesticides.

Special note: day lilies (*Hemerocallis* sp.) are generally edible; however, some varieties may not be, so please check carefully which variety you are using and do not substitute any other type of lily for day lilies. Most other lilies are not edible and could be poisonous.

GLOSSARY

GLOSSARY

10-year-aged Korean soy sauce / available from Table 181 *www.table181australia.com*

agretti / a succulent seaside herb originating in Italy. Seeds are available online.

amaranth (Chinese spinach) / available from good Asian speciality food grocers.

ammonium bicarbonate / available from speciality baking suppliers and some continental delicatessens.

angasi (flat) oyster / native to Tasmania and Southern Victoria, similar to a European belon (flat) oyster.

Australian native currants / picked in the wild in Tasmania. Substitute redcurrants if they are not available.

barilla (Coorong spinach) / *Tetragonia impexicoma* is a native Australian spinach available from Outback Pride *www.outbackpride.com.au*

binchotan (white) charcoal / high-quality charcoal made from Japanese oak, available from Chef's Armoury *www.chefsarmoury.com*

black sesame oil, virgin / a product of Korea, available from Table 181 *www.table181australia.com*

cold smoker / we use a purpose-built cold smoker made by Tom Cooper Kold Smoker *www.kold.com.au*

cryovac / a system of heat-resistant plastic bags with vacuum sealing for poaching in liquid or steaming. For home cooks, if you develop a relationship with your local butcher you may be able to purchase cryovac bags from them and once you have filled the bags you can return and ask them to heat seal them for you prior to cooking.

cumbungi / Australian native bulrush (*Typha* sp.) available from Outback Pride *www.outbackpride.com.au*

day lily / see note at left about edible flowers.

espuma gun / a gas-charged whipped cream gun available from good kitchen supplies stores.

fermented anchovy brine / we use Colatura di Alici di Cetara, available from gourmet food suppliers and selected delicatessens.

gai lan (Chinese broccoli) / both stems and flowers can be used; only the flowers are used in this book. Available from Asian grocers.

Gastrovac / a machine that cooks food in liquid under vacuum pressure. Because liquids under vacuum boil at a much lower temperature, using the Gastrovac you can cook a piece of protein at an actual temperature of, say, just 60°C (140°F) even while the liquid is actually boiling around the protein. This results in the liquid penetrating and tenderising the meat without overcooking the protein with temperature. I have found this works particularly well with lean prime cuts of protein.

ice plant / (salty ice plant) an edible succulent. Seeds are available online.

isomalt / a type of sugar–alcohol polymer used in this book to make a clear, hard, colourless toffee.

jagallo nero / a type of curly, loose-leaf kale originally from Italy. Seeds are available online.

karkalla (sea succulent) / *Dishphyma crassifolia* sub. *calvellatum* is native to coastal southern Australia and available from Outback Pride *www.outbackpride.com.au*

kinome / the young leaves of the sansho (Japanese pepper) bush, seasonally available from good Japanese grocery stores.

koji / *Aspergillus oryzae*. For more detail see page 134. Available from Gem Cultures Inc *www.gemcultures.com*

Korean black miso / available from Table 181 *www.table181australia.com*

kuzu / a natural starch used for thickening, also known as kudzu or Japanese arrowroot. Available from Japanese specialist grocers.

lemon aspen / *Achronychia oblongifolia* is a white or yellow berry-sized Australian native fruit available from Outback Pride *www.outbackpride.com.au*

lilly pilly / *Syzygium paniculatum* is a berry-sized native Australian fruit available from Outback Pride *www.outbackpride.com.au*

liquid nitrogen / a liquid form of nitrogen gas with a temperature of –196°C (–321°F) is used to instantly freeze various ingredients in this book. Available from specialist gas suppliers. Always follow the proper safety procedure when working with liquid nitrogen: wear appropriate protective eyewear and gloves and always pour nitrogen into an insulated bowl or small styrofoam container. Avoid splashing liquid nitrogen on your body and take particular care with your eyes. Never consume liquid nitrogen directly. Allow food that has been frozen in liquid nitrogen some time for the gas to completely evaporate before consuming.

marron / an Australian native freshwater crayfish, which could be substituted with a local freshwater crayfish or langoustine (scampi).

minutina / also known as herba stella or buck's horn plantain, *Plantago coronopus* is a succulent herb. Seeds are available online.

muntries / *Kunzea pomifera* is a native Australian berry-sized fruit. See recipe on page 217. Available from Outback Pride *www.outbackpride.com.au*

munyeroo / *Portulaca oleracea* is native Australian purslane, available from Outback Pride *www.outbackpride.com.au*

Murray cod / a native Australian freshwater fish found in the Murray River. A good substitute would be a thick, white-fleshed fish similar to cod.

pipi / *Donax deltoides* is a native Australian clam which can be substituted with vongole or similar.

rockweed / a seaweed unique to southern Korea. Available from Table 181 *www.table181australia.com*

sea parsley (sea celery) / *Apium prostratum* is a native Australian coastal parsley, available from Outback Pride *www.outbackpride.com.au*

Shimonita negi / this type of negi (green onion) originated in the Japanese town of Shimonita and is reputed to take one year to grow to full size; it is sometimes referred to as the one-year onion. Seeds are available online.

starch sheets / potato starch sheets are used in this book for the crisp topping on the jersey cream recipe on page 111. Available from Table 181 *www.table181australia.com*

strawberry clam / *Hippopus hippopus* is a medium-sized clam found in Australian waters, also known as the bear paw clam.

trimoline (inverted sugar syrup) / available from good bakery or pastry supply stores.

trumpeter / a large saltwater fish of the Latridae family, generally caught in Tasmanian waters. It can be substituted with turbot or brill.

tulip shell molluscs / New South Wales local shellfish similar to a periwinkle or sea snail.

vegetable rennet / used for setting milk in cheesemaking. Available from CheeseLinks *www.cheeselinks.com.au*

wheat starch flour / available in good Asian grocery stores.

white soy sauce / shiro shoyu is a clear, light golden-coloured soy that is actually a byproduct of the traditional Japanese shoyu (soy sauce) making process. It is used in this book to briefly marinate fish without leaving the dark soy stain. Available from specialist Japanese grocers.

xantana (fermented cornstarch) / a type of xanthan gum used for thickening, it is available from gourmet supply stores.

yin yang beans / also known as calypso bean or orca bean, this is a black-and-white dried bean with the opposite coloured spot on each section resembling the yin yang symbol. Available online.

21

25

26

34

37

38

41

51

55

62

66

71

75

80

87

93

94

101

105

110

121

129

139

142

150

161

168

171

180

186

192

197

205

206

209

216

220

225

231

234

240

244

253

256

265

INDEX

A

abalone
    Roasted greenlip abalone, heirloom
        cucumbers, barletta onions, seaweed
        72–3
    Squab & abalone, spring garlic custard,
        rare cultivated herbs, umami consommé
        157, 162–3
agretti 276
    South Australian octopus & agretti 50
Allen, Dave 57
almonds
    Almond & citron leaf kuzu 233
    Almond cake 42
    almond growing 237–9
    Almond ice cream 42
    Caramelised almonds 196
    Citrus & almonds 40–3
green almonds 237, 239
    Pulled almond tuiles 43
    Spring almonds 141
amaranth (Chinese spinach) 276
    Fried amaranth leaf 140
ammonium bicarbonate 276
Anchovy & roasted seaweed butter 221
Angasi oysters 276
    Cold smoked Angasi oysters, aromatic
        cultured cream, salty ice buds 32
apples: Green apple syrup 217
Aromatic cultured cream 32
Aromatic oil 36
Asian cuisines 118
Australian cuisine 118
Australian native currants 276

B

barilla (Coorong spinach) 276
Battarbee, Rex 210, 213
Bay & juniper infused butter 96
beans
    Whole-bean miso 188
    yin yang beans 277
beef
    Poached Blackmore Wagyu, roasted whole-
        bean miso, caramelised Angasi oysters,
        lactic acid fermented scorzonera 186–9
    Raw smoked Blackmore Wagyu, fresh dory
        roe, horseradish juice soured cream,
        milk skin 91–2
beetroot: Slow-roasted chioggia & albino
    beetroot, violets, truffles, native currants
    22–3
Bergamot jam 272
binchotan charcoal 276
Bitter chocolate black pudding 88
Black miso mixture 123
Black pudding & morel cream 182
Blackmore, David 177
Bone marrow 27
    Rendered smoked bone marrow 182
Braised quail, brioche porridge, roasted
    chestnut cream, truffle, chestnut floss
    102–3
brine, fermented anchovy 277
Brioche 272
    Brioche porridge 103
    Steamed brioche 100
broccoli
    gai lan (Chinese broccoli) 277
    Roasted one-year onion, white sprouting
        broccoli, jagallo nero, minutina, smoked
        bone marrow 27, 31
broth
    Ham hock broth 202
    Light shiitake, wakame & anchovy broth 72
    Smoked pork rib broth 136
Brown butter 39
Buckwheat, roasted 151
Buddhism 228
Bull's Blood leaves 23
bush food 199–200
butter
    Clarified 273
    Cultured 273

C

caramel
    Caramelised almonds 196
    Caramelised starch sheets 113
    Salted caramel whip 113
Cauliflower cream 193
Celery heart, aged feta, rare herbs & flowers 254–5
Charcoal-grilled marron, native coastal greens & lemon aspen 207
cherries
    Chocolate & cherry sorbet 196
    Chocolate, cherries, nougat 194–6
chestnuts
    Chestnut floss 103
    Roasted chestnut & mushroom cream 89
    Roasted chestnut cream 102
chicken
    Chicken cooked in cream, steamed brioche, green walnuts, vin jaune emulsion 99–100
    Chicken stock 273
    Fragrant poached chicken, salted daikon, smoked eggplant cream, sashimi sea scallops, ginger-scented milk curd, virgin black sesame 248–51
chilli
    Fermented chilli paste 67
    Hermit crab, fermented chilli & bean blossoms 64–7
    Summer tomatoes, golden aromatic broth 36
chocolate
    Bitter chocolate black pudding 88
    Chocolate & cherry sorbet 196
    Chocolate, cherries, nougat 194–6
    Soft chocolate ganache 196
citrus
    Almond & citron leaf kuzu 233
    Citrus & almonds 40–3
    see also lemon
Clarified butter 273
Clear tomato juice 36
Coconut cream 264
Cold smoked Angasi oysters, aromatic cultured cream, salty ice buds 32
cold smoker 276
corn: White corn juice 230
crab
    Heart of palm, spanner crab, white corn juice 230
    Hermit crab, fermented chilli & bean blossoms 64–7

crayfish
    Crayfish consommé 63
    Crayfish mousseline 246
    Sashimi of local crayfish, grapefruit, green almonds, crème fraîche, bergamot marmalade, elderflowers 241–2
    Tasmanian crayfish, wilted day lilies 63
creams
    Aromatic cultured cream 32
    Black pudding & morel cream 182
    Cauliflower cream 193
    Coconut cream 264
    Cultured cream 273
    Garlic cream 54
    Horseradish juice soured cream 92
    Lemon crème fraîche 42, 242
    Oyster cream 274
    Roasted chestnut & mushroom cream 89
    Roasted chestnut cream 102
    Smoked eggplant cream 250
    Soy milk cream 274
Crocker, Jules 60
Crustacean velvet, fresh kakai pumpkin seeds, pumpkin & crustacean juice 245–7
cryovac 276
Cultured butter 273
Cultured butter with eschallots & garlic 20
Cultured cream 273
cumbungi 276
Custard cream mixture 112

D

desserts
    Chocolate, cherries, nougat 194–6
    Citrus & almonds 40–3
    Feijoa ice cream 264
    Fresh muntries & pistachio nuts, crème fraîche, silver sorrel, nasturtiums 217
    Frozen vanilla mousse 224
    Jersey cream, prune, salted caramel, milk & sugar crystals 111–13
    Mangosteen, feijoa, coconut 263–4
    Milk ice cream 224
    Snowberries 222–4
dory roe
    Dory roe with lemon zest 78, 172
    Fresh dory roe 92

dressings
    Anchovy & roasted seaweed butter 221
    Bay & juniper infused butter 96
    Brown butter 39
    Cultured butter with eschallots & garlic 20
    Lemon juice vinaigrette 255
    Seaweed dressing 207
    White soy & seaweed dressing 96
Dried XO garnish 126
dry-ageing 154, 178
Duck poached in green plum masterstock, umeboshi, spring almonds, amaranth 140–1

E

edible flowers 18, 258, 276
eel
    Eggwhite & smoked eel pearl flower 78
    Tapioca cooked in eel stock 79
egg yolks, Salted 172
eggplant
    Mushroom, miso & eggplant paste 166
    Smoked eggplant cream 250
    Steamed eggplant 167
    Textural mushrooms, eggplant, miso 164–7
Eggwhite & smoked eel pearl flower 78
Eggwhite pearls 250
espuma gun 277
Evening primrose flowers, dried 173

F

Feijoa ice cream 264
fermentation 154
fermented anchovy brine 277
Fermented chilli paste 67
Fermented Swiss brown mushrooms 166
Fermented white lentil leaves 68
feta: Frozen aged feta chards 254
Field mushroom gills 88
flavour 10, 153, 153–4
flowers, edible 18, 258, 276
Forbidden rice mixture 122
Fragrant oil 251
Fragrant poached chicken, salted daikon, smoked eggplant cream, sashimi sea scallops, ginger-scented milk curd, virgin black sesame 248–51
Fresh muntries & pistachio nuts, crème fraîche, silver sorrel, nasturtiums 217
Frozen vanilla mousse 224

G

gai lan (Chinese broccoli) 277
Garden peas, cultured butter, sea salt, crisp
    pea blossoms 20–1
Garlic cream 54
Garlic oil 67
Gastrovac 277
Ginger milk curds 251
goose
    Goose masterstock 122
    My roast goose, forbidden rice, black miso,
        soy milk cream, hatsuka radish, wasabi
        flowers 122–3
grass trees 203
Green almonds 237, 239, 242
Green apple syrup 217
Green mango pickle 242
Green rice 148
Gretschmann, Josef & Antonia 107

H

Ham hock broth 202
Hardwick, Peter 200
harmony 9, 10, 228
Heart of palm, spanner crab, white corn juice
    230
heirloom vegetables 18, 28
Henman, June 255, 258–9
herbs 258
Hermit crab, fermented chilli & bean blossoms
    64–7
Horseradish juice soured cream 92
Hulme, Wayne 57, 60

I

ikijime 53, 57
Ikijime Tasmanian squid, squid ink custard,
    pink turnips, society garlic flowers 53–4
Indigenous molluscs, ham hock broth,
    grass tree 202–3
isomalt 277

J

jagallo negro 277
Jersey cream, prune, salted caramel, milk
    & sugar crystals 111–13
Jersey milk bavarois 113
Jerusalem artichoke leaves 96
Johnstone, Tim & Elizabeth 18, 28
Joto Fresh Fish 57, 60

K

kakai pumpkins 245
karkalla (sea succulent) 277
kinome 277
Kinome oil 232
koji
    Koji 134, 277
    Pork belly, milk curd, roasted koji, sesame,
        kombu, smoked pork rib broth 136–7
kombu, Roasted layered 137
Korean black miso 277
Korean ingredients 145
Korean soy sauce, 10-year-aged 276
kuzu 277

L

Lactic acid fermented scorzonera 185
Lee, Paul & Idylle 145
lemon aspen 200, 215, 277
    Native coastal greens & lemon aspen 207
Lemon crème fraîche 42, 242, 254
Lemon curd 42
Lemon juice vinaigrette 255
lentils: Fermented white lentil leaves 68
Light shiitake, wakame & anchovy broth 72
lilly pilly 210, 277
liquid nitrogen 277

M

McBain, Jude & Ian 236–7
maltose 190
Maltose crackling 193
Maltose powder 189
Mangosteen, feijoa, coconut 263–4
Mangosteen tears 264
marron 277
    Charcoal-grilled marron, native coastal
        greens & lemon aspen 207
Meringue 43, 224
Milk biscuit 273
Milk ice cream 224
Milk skin 273
minutina 277
molluscs
    Indigenous molluscs, ham hock broth,
        grass tree 202–3
    Shaved tulip shell mollusc, takuan pickles,
        kinome 232–3
Mud crab 246
mullet roe 154

muntries 200, 277
    Fresh muntries & pistachio nuts, crème fraîche, silver sorrel, nasturtiums 217
munyeroo 277
Murray cod 198, 200, 218, 277
    Steamed Murray cod, cumbungi, smoked oyster crackling, anchovy & roasted seaweed butter 218–21
mushrooms
    Black pudding & morel cream 182
    Dried shiitake skins 148, 182
    Fermented Swiss brown mushrooms 166
    Field mushroom gills 88
    Large field mushroom gills 167
    Light shiitake, wakame & anchovy broth 72
    Mushroom, miso & eggplant paste 166
    Roasted chestnut & mushroom cream 89
    Shiitake mushroom powder 88, 167
    Smoked & confit pig jowl, shiitake, shaved sea scallop, Jerusalem artichoke leaves, juniper, bay 84, 95–6
    Textural mushrooms, eggplant, miso 164–7
    Walnut floss, bitter chocolate black pudding, fungi 84, 86–9
My roast goose, forbidden rice, black miso, soy milk cream, hatsuka radish, wasabi flowers 122–3

N
Native coastal greens & lemon aspen 207
Nougat 274

O
octopus: South Australian octopus & agretti 50
Olive sourdough crumbs 254
onions
    Roasted one-year onion, white sprouting broccoli, jagallo nero, minutina, smoked bone marrow 27
    Shimonita negi 277
organic dairy farming 107
Organum 9, 10
Outback Pride 210, 213
oysters
    Cold smoked Angasi oysters, aromatic cultured cream, salty ice buds 32
    Dry smoked oyster crackling 221
    Oyster cream 274

P
Pasture-raised veal, rendered smoked bone marrow, bitter chocolate black pudding, grey ghost mushrooms 181–2
peas
    Garden peas, cultured butter, sea salt, crisp pea blossoms 20–1
    pea flowers 18
pickles
    Green mango pickle 242
    Takuan pickles 232
pipis 277
Poached Blackmore Wagyu, roasted whole-bean miso, caramelised Angasi oysters, lactic acid fermented scorzonera 186–9
Poached trumpeter, potato cream, salted mullet roe, fermented white lentil leaves 68–9
Pomegranate molasses crumbs 22
pork
    Pork belly, milk curd, roasted koji, sesame, kombu, smoked pork rib broth 136–7
    Slow-cooked pig cheek, prunes, cauliflower cream, maltose crackling, perfumed with prune kernel oil 154, 190–3
    Smoked & confit pig jowl, shiitake, shaved sea scallop, Jerusalem artichoke leaves, juniper, bay 84, 95–6
    Smoked pork rib broth 136
    Smoky pork cheek 148
Potato purée 69
Prune juice syrup 112
Puharich, Anthony 178
Puharich, Victor 178
Pulled butter toffee 112
pumpkin
    Crustacean velvet, fresh kakai pumpkin seeds, pumpkin & crustacean juice 245–7
    Young kakai pumpkin, brown butter 39
purity 10, 228, 230

Q
quail: Braised quail, brioche porridge, roasted chestnut cream, truffle, chestnut floss 102–3
Quarmby, Mike & Gayle 200, 210–13, 214

R
Raw smoked Blackmore Wagyu, fresh dory roe, horseradish juice soured cream, milk skin 91–2
recipes 276
reduction 154
Redzepi, René 28
Rendered smoked bone marrow 182
rice
    Forbidden rice mixture 122
    Green rice 148
    Koji 134
    Rice lace 274
Roasted greenlip abalone, heirloom cucumbers, barletta onions, seaweed 72–3
Roasted one-year onion, white sprouting broccoli, jagallo nero, minutina, smoked bone marrow 27
rockweed 277

S
salads
    Celery heart, aged feta, rare herbs & flowers 254–5
    Slow-roasted chioggia & albino beetroot, violets, truffles, native currants 22–3
salt-curing 154
saltbush 214
Salted caramel whip 113
Salted daikon twists 274
Salted egg yolks 172
Salted mullet roe 68
salty ice plant 18, 31, 277
samphire 214
Sashimi of local crayfish, grapefruit, green almonds, crème fraîche, bergamot marmalade, elderflowers 241–2
Sashimi seafood preparation 79
scallops
    Scallop pearl flowers 251
    Smoked & confit pig jowl, shiitake, shaved sea scallop, Jerusalem artichoke leaves, juniper, bay 84, 95–6
scorzonera 186
    Lactic acid fermented 185
sculptural composition 84
sea parsley/celery 277
Sea urchin custard 173

S *(continued)*

seafood 46, 57, 60
    Charcoal-grilled marron, native coastal
        greens & lemon aspen 207
    Cold smoked Angasi oysters, aromatic
        cultured cream, salty ice buds 32
    Crayfish mousseline 246
    Crustacean velvet, fresh kakai pumpkin
        seeds, pumpkin & crustacean juice
        245–7
    Dory roe with lemon zest 78, 172
    Dry smoked oyster crackling 221
    Eggwhite & smoked eel pearl flower 78
    Fresh dory roe 92
    Heart of palm, spanner crab, white corn
        juice 230
    Hermit crab, fermented chilli & bean
        blossoms 64–7
    Ikijime Tasmanian squid, squid ink custard,
        pink turnips, society garlic flowers 53–4
    Indigenous molluscs, ham hock broth,
        grass tree 202–3
    Oyster cream 274
    Roasted greenlip abalone, heirloom
        cucumbers, barletta onions, seaweed
        72–3
    Sashimi of local crayfish, grapefruit,
        green almonds, crème fraîche, bergamot
        marmalade, elderflowers 241–2
    Sashimi seafood preparation 79
    Scallop pearl flowers 251
    Sea urchin custard 173
    Shaved tulip shell mollusc, takuan pickles,
        kinome 232–3
    Smoked & confit pig jowl, shiitake, shaved
        sea scallop, Jerusalem artichoke leaves,
        juniper, bay 84, 95–6
    South Australian octopus & agretti 50
    Squab & abalone, spring garlic custard, rare
        cultivated herbs, umami consommé 157,
        162–3
    Tasmanian crayfish, wilted day lilies 63
    The reef 76–9
    Wild sea prawns, cured mullet roe, salted
        egg yolk, sea urchin custard, dried
        evening primrose 170–3
    XO sea 125–7
seaweed
    Anchovy & roasted seaweed butter 221
    Seaweed & sesame seed mixture 148
    Seaweed dressing 207
    White soy & seaweed dressing 96

sesame oil, virgin black 145, 276
sesame seeds 145
    Seaweed & sesame seed mixture 148
Shaffer, Kris 223
Shaved tulip shell mollusc, takuan pickles,
    kinome 232–3
Shiitake mushroom powder 88, 167
Shiitake mushrooms, lightly fermented 232
Shimonita negi 277
Slow-cooked pig cheek, prunes, cauliflower
    cream, maltose crackling, perfumed with
    prune kernel oil 154, 190–3
Slow-roasted chioggia & albino beetroot,
    violets, truffles, native currants 22–3
smell, sense of 154
Smoked & confit pig jowl, shiitake, shaved sea
    scallop, Jerusalem artichoke leaves, juniper,
    bay 84, 95–6
Smoked eggplant cream 250
Smoked oil 250
Smoked pork rib broth 136
Smoky pork cheek 148
Snowberries 222–4
South Australian octopus & agretti 50
soy
    Soy milk cream 274
    White soy & seaweed dressing 96
    white soy sauce 277
Spring almonds 141
Spring garlic custard 163
Squab & abalone, spring garlic custard, rare
    cultivated herbs, umami consommé 157,
    162–3
squid: Ikijime Tasmanian squid, squid ink
    custard, pink turnips, society garlic flowers
    53–4
starch sheets 277
Steamed Murray cod, cumbungi, smoked
    oyster crackling, anchovy & roasted
    seaweed butter 218–21
stock
    Chicken stock 273
    Veal stock 275
Stonepot organic green rice & buckwheat,
    roasted seaweed, shiitake skin, pig cheek
    146–51
strawberry clams 277
Sugar crystals 43
Sugar syrup, basic 272
Summer tomatoes, golden aromatic broth 36
sun-drying 154

T

Takuan pickles 232
Tapioca cooked in eel stock 79
Tasmanian crayfish, wilted day lilies 63
test garden 18
Textural mushrooms, eggplant, miso 164–7
texture 10, 84
The reef 76–9
tomatoes
    Clear tomato juice 36
    Semi-dried tomatoes 36
    Summer tomatoes, golden aromatic broth 36
trimoline (inverted sugar syrup) 277
trumpeter 277
    Poached trumpeter, potato cream, salted
        mullet roe, fermented white lentil leaves
        68–9
tulip shell molluscs 277
turnips: Ikijime Tasmanian squid, squid ink
    custard, pink turnips, society garlic flowers
    53–4

U

Umami consommé 154, 157–8
umami (fifth taste) 157
umami-rich foods 154
Umeboshi purée 140

V

vanilla
    Frozen vanilla mousse 224
    Vanilla custard base 275
    Vanilla custard cream 275
veal
    Pasture-raised veal, rendered smoked bone
        marrow, bitter chocolate black pudding,
        grey ghost mushrooms 181–2
    Veal glaze 275
    Veal stock 275
vegetable rennet 277
vegetables, lactic acid fermented 185
Vic's Premium Quality Meat 177, 178
Victor Churchill 178
Vin jaune emulsion 100
visual appeal 84

W

Wagyu beef 177
    Poached Blackmore Wagyu, roasted whole-
        bean miso, caramelised Angasi oysters,
        lactic acid fermented scorzonera 186–9
    Raw smoked Blackmore Wagyu, fresh dory
        roe, horseradish juice soured cream,
        milk skin 91–2
wallaby tail 200
    Wallaby tail slowly cooked in salted butter,
        wilted golden orach, wild garlic 208
walnuts
    Chicken cooked in cream, steamed brioche,
        green walnuts, vin jaune emulsion
        99–100
    Walnut floss, bitter chocolate black
        pudding, fungi 84, 86–9
wasabi 130, 132, 133
wasabi flowers 130, 133
Welsh, Stephen & Karen 130
wheat starch flour 277
White corn juice 230
White soy & seaweed dressing 96
white soy sauce 277
Whiteland, Josh 200, 203
Whole-bean miso 188
Wild sea prawns, cured mullet roe, salted egg
    yolk, sea urchin custard, dried evening
    primrose 170–3

X

xantana (fermented cornstarch) 277
XO sauce 124, 127
XO sea 125–7
XO sea stock 126

Y

yin yang beans 277
Young kakai pumpkin, brown butter 39